Faces

Volume Five

Faces of Suicide
Volume Five

A fifth collection of stories from the heart, compiled by members of the Parents of Suicides - Friends and Families of Suicides Internet Community.

The Parents of Suicides - Friends and Families of Suicides Internet Community began on October 9, 1998. Our mission is to offer understanding, support, information, connections and hope to anyone whose life has been affected by suicide loss. This was the first English-speaking community in the world to provide grief support after suicide loss through the Internet. It is completely managed and tended to by volunteers, members of the groups who help in memory of someone whose life remains in their hearts.

~~~~~~~~~~

Copyright

Copyright: November 2018. All rights reserved. No part of any story within this book may be reproduced by any means without written permission from the author. Requests for permission to share should be sent to Karyl Chastain Beal at **karylbeal@bellsouth.net** or **cfofswga@cs.com**, and then they will be passed on to the authors.

~~~~~~

Table of Contents

Stories

Landon D. Adams 12

Benjamin Hal Armstrong 17

Peter Allen Asencio, Jr. 22

Taylor Asher Bruell 28

Tyler James Bushmiller 38

Cindy Marie Carroll 48

Sheryl Champagne 55

Kaitlyn Kimberly Cook 65

Leah Renae Cox 82

William Charles Dehmer 87

Dennis James Ewing 95

Deborah Ann Martinie Hardin 102

Kevin Alexis Hiciano 111

Carter Michael Howard 115

Matthew Tyler Hudson 128

Dewey Vantroy Johnson 134

John Trenton Kirby 140

Ryland Joseph Louis Kresse 149

Ethan T. Meetz 157

Lisa Elaine Mewbourne 162

Dennis Lee New 178

Scott Anthony Parise, Jr. 184

Erick Plunkett 191

Shawn Preston Rego 209

Donaway Shylow Rego 219

Dannielle Elaine Rogtke 225

Joe Dennis Scott 231

Scott Wilson Simpson 241

John Clayton Sims 249

Stephen Kenneth Sokolowski 255

Megan Kristine Vogt 267

Michael Gene Watson 274

Billy Lee Williams 280

Sean Adam Wiseman 289

Benjamin E. Joslin Yoshikawa 297

Photo Remembrance Gallery

Remembering Jeffrey Alan Amati 312

Remembering Tyler Alan Barton 312

Remembering Jason David Brandt 313

Remembering Christian Victoria Carrigan 313

Remembering Courtney Cherese Coin 314

Remembering Vincent Gamboa 314

Remembering Joshua David Goddard 315

Remembering Jessica Kassandra Haffer 315

Remembering Jeffrey Michael Hoffelder 316

Remembering Kenneth Thomas Hohman 316

Remembering Jeffrey Austin Kinder 317

Remembering Christine Marie Klein 317

Remembering Anthony Scott Martin 318

Remembering Jacob Leroy Masker 318

Remembering Dennis M. McCloskey 319

Remembering Matthew T. Laidlaw McIntosh 319

Remembering Sean A. Christopher McKitrick 320

Remembering Michael Joseph Melotto 320

Remembering Kathleen Ann Murray 321

Remembering Nicholas Tristan Novak 321

Remembering John Michael Pittman 322

Remembering Kyle Holden Rigby 322

Remembering Evan Andrew Ritter 323

Remembering Michael Anthony Rivas 323

Remembering Sgt. Ryan Patrick Schetter 324

Remembering Jason Brian Seek 324

Remembering David William Shelton.................................... 325

Remembering Jesse Anders Short-Gershman 325

Remembering Anthony James Shott 326

Remembering Andy Wayne Stirling 326

Remembering Lawrence Paul Ulrich..................................... 327

Remembering Marcus Tyler Walker....................................... 327

Remembering Jay Kelley Wall 328

Remembering Ciara Jolie Whitney... 328

Remembering Martha Elizabeth Williamson 329

Introduction

Faces of Suicide: Volume Five is a collection of stories about people who have taken their own lives written by family members or close friends who believe that their stories need to be told. There are 35 stories in this book.

~~~~~~

The Stories

Each story is unique, reflecting the complexities of suicide. All of the stories are real, written from the perspective of the authors based on their personal connections with the people remembered.

Some of the suicides may be total mysteries; what caused their self-inflicted deaths is baffling to people left behind. In other situations, people may have had struggles and challenges that they were unable to overcome. Their perception may have been clouded to the point that they didn't believe things would ever get better, so alone, they took that final step - removing any chance of resolution.

The people written about aren't statistics; they're real people who lived and are still loved. They aren't defined by the end of their lives. As you read the stories, please suspend judgment and read with compassion.

We hope that as you read their stories, your hearts will be moved. If something you read reminds you to be kinder and gentler, if a story motivates you to reach out to others, if the words of some of the story authors help you understand yourself or people around you better, then this book will have achieved a greater mission, that of helping to create a better, safer world.

~~~~~~

The Photo Remembrance Gallery

We've added a new section to the fifth volume of the Faces of Suicide books: a photo remembrance gallery. We are including 35 photos of people whose stories aren't in the book, submitted by parents and other loved ones.

As you look at their photos, check out their eyes and their smiles and see their personalities come through. And remember, they lived.

Appreciation

We offer sincere appreciation to each of our story authors. They willingly wrote stories about lives of people they love, even when the writing process required them to revive memories of situations which may have been unpleasant or painful. Then, after they wrote their stories, they had the courage to share those memories with the world in this book. The stories are truly gifts from their hearts.

~~~~~~

Editorial Team Members

This book was compiled, edited, prepared and published by an international team of dedicated volunteers who were committed to this special . Members of the *Faces of Suicide: Volume Five* team gave generously of their time and knowledge to prepare the stories and book for publication in memory of someone close to them who died by suicide.

Karyl Chastain Beal, Tennessee, mother of Arlyn Beal
Barb Estinson, Washington, mother of Donna Nichols
Claire Farmer, Georgia, mother of Corwin Farmer
Lisa Kofod. British Columbia, Canada, aunt of Johnathan August
Jean Ruthenbeck, Indiana, mother of Joe Ruthenbeck
Mare Sanford, Montana, mother of Jack Sanford
Nancy Toth, Pennsylvania, mother of Michael Toth

And a special thank you to our technical editors, without whom this book could not possibly have been published.

Technical Editors

Rosaleen McCabe, Dublin, Ireland, mother of Anthony Lawless
Anne Toner, Dublin, Ireland, friend of Anthony Lawless

The Cover Design

The cover design for Faces of Suicide: Volume five was created by Anne Toner of Dublin, Ireland.

Extra: Check out the following pages at the end of the book for more information:

How to join the POS – FFOS Internet Community
List of websites we maintain to reach out and educate
Other helpful resources

Landon D. Adams

16 March 1978 - 8 March 2008
Georgia

Landon D. Adams
by Debbie H. Mashburn (Mother)

My first son, Landon, was born on a cool spring day in March. Just kidding, there is no such thing as a cool day in middle Georgia. He was a sweet baby and the first grandchild in our family, so of course, he was spoiled. Lanny weighed 8 pounds, 11 ounces and the doctor joked about him riding a tricycle home from the hospital.

I had a long labor, ending in a C-section birth. Landon was in fetal distress. Did that affect him later in life? I guess we are always searching for a "why"?

When Landon was three years old his younger brother was born. They both grew up loving fishing, hunting, and everything outdoors. They were always close. They fought like all siblings do but always had each other's backs. When you saw one you saw the other. His brother was the daredevil in everything, but Landon had that safe fear built in, that kept him from doing really stupid things. They were a great balance for each other.

As Lanny got older, he developed a love for art and drawing at a young age that always stayed with him. Landon was very talented. He drew on everything, little slips of paper, candy wrappers, just everywhere.

Landon seemed to struggle in school with grades and seemingly with authority.

He was diagnosed with Attention Deficit Hyperactivity Disorder at an early age. Lanny was put on medication to control it. I sometimes wonder if that had some effect on him mentally, in his later years. They were so quick to medicate children to calm them down during that time frame.

Landon grew up continuing all his hobbies. Soon after high school, he fell in love, as young boys do. It was not too long before his first son came along. Lanny was so proud to be a dad. He went on to have a total of four children, two boys, and two girls.

Unfortunately, they were all four by different mothers. This caused great distress in Lanny's life, both financially and when trying to spend time with his children. Of course, this weighed heavily on him constantly.

Landon had many girlfriends, always the same type and background, always troubled, sometimes by drugs. I mean nothing against them, no one is better than anyone else, it was just the circumstances they ended up in. I can see now that Lanny was trying to save them all, to help them, to fix them all. Sadly, he, nor any of us, realized that he was the most broken of them all. He did not have the ability to fix anyone else.

Lanny laid flooring, carpet, tile, and wood, as his trade. He was a perfectionist, so he was very good at what he did. He and his brother tried to start their own business at one point, but they were unable to handle the business end, so went back to laying flooring together for another company once again. They were working together when we lost Lanny.

Landon had a wonderful laugh, a belly laugh that everyone knew and loved. Thank goodness I can still hear it to this day and it helps get me through his loss. He loved to dance and spend time with friends. He had so many friends, I wish Lanny had realized how many people loved him, but that was not the issue.

People that die by suicide do not really want to die and leave their loved ones to suffer. They are not thinking about any of that. They just want to end the pain. They lose hope, even if only for a few minutes, or seconds, and no one can live without hope.

One week before he was to turn 30 years old, on a typical Friday night, Landon called. We had a short conversation, during which we made plans to grill steaks on Saturday afternoon. We were providing the steaks and he was bringing the portobello mushrooms. I still cannot eat them to this day.

Landon and I talked and laughed about our week and as always as we hung up he said, "I love you, Momma", and I said, "I love you too, Baby". I went to bed believing everything was right with the world.

Then I was awakened by that call, the one every parent fears, at 3:30 a.m. It was my youngest son, telling me his dad had received a call that something was wrong with Lanny. I calmed him down and assured him that everything was probably fine. After all, I had just talked with Lanny earlier and we had plans for that afternoon. I told him I would find out what was going on and call him back.

So, I called our local 911 and had the operator connect me with the 911 in the county Landon lived in. When I told the lady that answered the phone who I was, she paused and told me she would get an officer to speak with me. My heart sank. It seemed like hours until someone came to the phone, though it was only seconds.

I knew something really was wrong. The detective came to the phone and told me he was so sorry to have to tell me on the phone, but my son was deceased, and it appeared it was by his own hand. A gunshot wound to the head. The detective kept on talking but I do not remember much of the rest of the conversation.

I just remember telling him I needed to go wake up my husband and tell him what had happened. Before I left the room I raised my hands up to the ceiling and said, "God, you are going to have to help me with this one "and He has walked every step with me since.

I woke up my husband and told him all that I knew. He thought I had just had a nightmare. He was right, but this one would never end.

They say hindsight is twenty twenty and I guess they are correct. Looking back over Landon's life, I can see so many signs I should have recognized. Though he was never treated for any mental illness, there were things I can see now.

But, I normalized them, I guess we all did. You know, life runs us instead of us running our lives sometimes, so we push things back and deal with what we understand, what we can control. The bottom line is,

Landon was a wonderful son, brother, and father. We all loved him so much and he was the last person you would ever expect to take his own life, but he did. There is no doubt, though I will never understand why. I have learned to just accept it as fact and live off the love and memories that remain. That is all we have now.

Suicide can happen to anyone, no matter what your circumstances in life are, no matter how or where you were raised, or how much you have or don't have. Suicide can happen. Always love the people in your life and let them know. Be there for them all and watch for signs. Be a good listener and let them know that they all matter!

About the Author
Debbie Mashburn, Landon's mother, is retired from civil service and works part-time preparing income taxes. She enjoys a personal relationship with our Lord, quilting, sewing, painting, crafting and spending time with family. Debbie has also become involved with the Tennessee Suicide Prevention Network, TSPN, participates in annual walks with the American Foundation of Suicide Prevention, AFSP and has led a Survivors of Suicide group. She never misses an opportunity to share Landon's story.

Benjamin Hal Armstrong

**1 September 1994 - 18 November 2015
Tennessee**

Benjamin Hal Armstrong
by Shawn Waddell (Mother)

Ben was born on Thursday, September 1, 1994, in Columbia, Tennessee. He brought joy, happiness, and laughter into the lives of all he met. As a baby, he was easy going and funny. He continued to grow into an outgoing young child and enjoyed being outdoors, camping, canoeing, swimming, fishing and riding his bike.

In 1999 and 2000, he became a big brother and loved showing his siblings the ropes of life. As a child, Ben loved to eat raw vegetables from the garden, so he would often not be hungry at dinnertime. Some of our happiest memories were times spent at the swimming pool and the beach.

Ben completed twelve years of education and graduated from Columbia Central High in 2014. School was difficult for Ben, as he struggled mightily with dyslexia. His high school graduation was a true success and hard earned.

After graduation, Ben never could seem to find his place. He worked a few odd-and-end jobs but just couldn't get a start at his adult life. Ben had struggled with depression for many years and never really dealt with the passing of his father in 2010. Counseling and medication were off and on over the years, more off than on.

Then, Ben was involved in a car crash in 2012 where his step-brother was killed. He and his girlfriend of two years weren't the best fit, as they argued endlessly but could never really free themselves of the other. Ben struggled with drug use as well. He was on probation, lost his drivers' license and was facing more charges, after being arrested in October of 2015.

In late October of 2015, Ben came to live with my husband and me after finally breaking up with his girlfriend. He had no job or way of paying for the apartment he was living in. The plan was to eventually go to work with my husband, as he works for himself.

My parents had recently moved from a house they had been in for forty years. They had accumulated a large amount of stuff. Ben was a great help to his grandparents in helping them move, organize, take stuff to landfill, etc. He would ride to work with me every day, help his grandparents around the house, and ride home with me later on.

During this time Ben found out that his girlfriend was pregnant. He was certain it was not his. They had been careless about birth control, but she had not gotten pregnant thus far. He also had a very big chance of being sterile as a result of surgery as an eight-year-old. This surgery should have been done before age one but the medical condition was diagnosed late and doctors told us he had a high chance of being sterile.

After Ben found out that his girlfriend was pregnant, he made an appointment to see if he was sterile, though he knew in his heart he was. He wanted to be a father and was prepared to raise the child as his. His girlfriend was not interested in that scenario.

The morning of the day Ben died, his girlfriend sent him an ultrasound picture. He texted me at work and asked me if it was okay for his grandfather to take him back to our house since he had no license or car. After a brief text conversation, I agreed, thinking he just wanted some time to think since he was overwhelmed.

We texted again around noon. Ben asked where he could find some paper to write his feelings down. This turned into his suicide note and a list of "pros and cons of being alive".

I asked my husband to check on Ben at lunch. He did and called me to say he was fine, had made some cookies, and was watching television. I relaxed some and went about my day.

I started trying to reach Ben by phone at 3:00 p.m. when I got off work. He wouldn't answer. I have a thirty-minute drive home but had a dental appointment that day. At 5:00 p.m. when I got out of the dentist I tried him again, no answer.

At this point, I had a feeling that my son was dead. For a second, I thought he may be in the shower and not answering, but the doom feeling only returned.

I got home at 5:30 p.m. and went straight inside and to Ben's room. The bed was unmade. There was a letter on the bed, but no Ben. I read the letter but for some reason was not terribly alarmed. I thought maybe he was just outside somewhere or had perhaps talked the ex-girlfriend into coming to pick him up.

The letter was all Ben's reasons for not wanting to live. He drew a line and then wrote, "Dear momma, I'm sorry for everything."

I called his girlfriend and asked her if Ben was with her. She said he wasn't. We talked about their last conversation earlier that day, the timing. She explained an argument they had on Facebook and blah, blah, blah.

I picked up a flashlight and started looking for Ben outside. He wasn't in the first few places I looked. Then I turned the corner to enter our small pole barn. Ben was there. He was hanging from an extension cord but in a seated position.

I screamed my head off, hung up the phone with his girlfriend and called my husband, who was minutes from home. I then called 911. I knew Ben was gone.

The night was chaos after that. Life has been like a strange, sad dream that has happened to someone else. This is not my life. I don't know when time will make this real to me. It's as if Ben found a job and apartment somewhere else and just doesn't call or need me anymore.

Depression got the best of Ben and prevented the love of his friends, his family, and any sense of comfort and confidence from reaching him. Depression lied to Ben, telling him he was worthless, a burden and undeserving of a great life.

In the note he left me, Ben wrote, "I truly don't see myself living a happy, successful life. I'll always be a burden, always be the fuck up."

Ben was wrong. Depression was wrong. The truth is this, Ben was an amazing person. He was the best thing to happen to my life. He was hilarious, caring, giving, and adventurous.

On a canoe trip with friends, Ben was the first person out of his own canoe, swimming to rescue others who were about to flip. Ben loved every kind of animal and could not say no to a stray. Ben was helpful to friends and family with all kinds of requests for help. He kindly checked on older family members, doing small chores for them, and he came home with funny stories. He hid his own pain the best he could until he could handle it no more.

Ben was loved beyond measure. He is deeply missed by all those who loved him. He had value and he was worthy. I wish Ben could have found a way to trust the voices of those who loved him.

About the Author
Shawn Waddell is Ben's mother. She lives in Franklin, Tennessee with her husband Joe and their dog, Beuford. She is a teacher.

Peter Allen Asencio, Jr.

4 May 1970 - 23 May 2006
Michigan

Peter Allen Asencio, Jr.
by LaDonna Deer (Mother)

Allen was born on May 4, 1970, in Beaumont Hospital, Royal Oak, Michigan. I had a very easy pregnancy, but the labor lasted for fourteen hours, with very hard contractions almost from the very beginning.

I didn't think this when I saw him in person, but when I saw his newborn picture taken at the hospital, I remember laughing to myself because I thought he looked like a little raisin. He weighed six pounds, nine ounces and was nineteen inches long.

I had already graduated from high school by the time Allen was born. We took him to his father's high school graduation a month after he was born. During our seven-year marriage, we had two other children. Theresa was born eleven months after Allen and Randy was born two-and-a-half years after Theresa. Their dad left when Allen was between six and seven years old and was not around much after that.

Allen started elementary school in Hazel Park, Michigan. Then we moved to Calumet City, Illinois. He finished elementary school after we moved to Beavercreek, Ohio.

Allen went into middle school when he lived with his dad in Fenton, Michigan. He was attending high school in Royal Oak, Michigan when he quit to get married and get a job. He got good grades all through school and made friends easily.

Allen was very serious about his role as big brother, always looking after his sister and little brother. Oh, he could fight with them, but no one else could. It still makes me smile when I remember one day not long after his dad left when Allen said to me with a very serious look, "Don't worry, Mom, I'll take care of all of us now." My little man.

Through his entire life, Allen was always taking care of people, family and strangers alike. I have five siblings; every one of them has told me at different times that they didn't only lose their nephew but also one of their best friends.

Allen went to live with his dad when he was thirteen. He started introducing himself to the outside world then as Pete. After that point in his life, my family and our close friends were the only people that knew him as Allen. Allen only stayed with his dad for three years and then went to live with my mom.

Allen struggled in relationships. He quit school during his senior year to marry his girlfriend, who was pregnant with his baby. Elizabeth was born in February 1988, but Allen and the baby's mother separated before her first birthday. They divorced not long after.

He was married two other times after that, but neither marriage lasted very long. He also had another daughter that I didn't know about until she was three or four years old. I didn't get to meet Taylor until the day of Allen's funeral; she was nine years old then.

Allen spent the majority of his adult life searching for two things: a father and a family of his own. When he moved in with my mom, he grew close to the older couple that lived next door to her.

He started calling them Pop and Mom. They obviously loved him. In many ways, they were a very good influence on him. After he died, during his viewing, the neighbor told me she felt like she had lost her son, and her husband was so distraught he couldn't even attend.

When Allen was in his twenties, he was diagnosed with bipolar disorder. Unfortunately, he was diagnosed at a time that I was probably in one of my worst episodes with the same illness. He didn't see himself to be anything like me, so he refused to accept the diagnosis and refused any kind of treatment. It was difficult to watch him cycle through the stages of bipolar disorder while refusing any kind of help.

Allen's daughter, Elizabeth, got pregnant and decided to get married in March of 2006. Allen and I worked closely together with her to help her plan the wedding. The day of Elizabeth's wedding was absolutely magical for all of us. Allen's huge smile never left his face the entire day. He told me at the end of the day that the only thing that could beat this was the birth of his grandchild.

Allen's last and longest lasting relationship was with a woman who had three young boys when they met. Allen helped her raise them as his own children. They had another son together, named Peter Allen III. (Little Peter was two-and-a-half years old when his father left us.)

Allen fought hard trying to save this relationship when problems started. He was an over-the-road truck driver and came off the road for a month to try to resolve their issues.

It appeared things had been worked out between Allen and his girlfriend. They invited me for dinner on the Sunday evening before he was scheduled to go back out on the road to work. He talked all evening about all the plans they had for their family. He had a positive outlook; he was optimistic about their future.

Allen walked with me out on to the porch when it was time for me to leave. We hugged each other and exchanged the words I love you. I drove home that night with a smile on my face and felt better about him than I had in a long time. I was happy that my son had finally found the happiness he had searched so long for.

Monday came and went. I was surprised that Allen didn't call to tell me where this new run was going to take him like he normally did. I decided to wait until Tuesday evening to call him.

When my phone rang at 6:38 p.m. on Tuesday, May 23, 2006, I had just finished dinner and was carrying my dishes to the sink Allen's girlfriend was on the phone; she told me that I needed to come to the house right away.

Assuming it was something with one of the kids that she was being dramatic about, I wasn't prepared for the words she said next. "Pete tried to kill himself."

I immediately hung up the phone and ran to the car.

I called her back and asked what had happened. She told me that they had had a big fight. As I drove to their house, I hung on to the word tried. I assumed that they had a fight and that he had done something stupid to get her attention.

As I got closer to their home, an ambulance zoomed past me. I pulled in front of the house and could see a lot of people standing in the yard, including two or three police officers. Everyone was there - except Allen.

An officer approached my car and asked who I was. I told him I was Allen's mother, and I asked if my son was in the ambulance that had just passed. He said yes. Another officer told me which hospital they were taking him to.

I drove to the hospital and asked to see Allen. I was told that the doctors were with him and that someone would get me soon. I don't know how many times I went again to ask to see my son. All my family and some friends finally arrived at the hospital. My brother and I headed to the desk to ask about Allen again, but this time I was going to insist they let me see him.

A doctor passed so I asked him if he could tell me anything about my son. When I gave him Allen's name, he told me to gather the family and follow him. We went into a small private room and sat down; someone closed the door.

The doctor sat across from me and said the words, "They worked on him in the ambulance and we've worked on him ever since he arrived here, but there's been no sign of life."

My response was, "What did you say?"

The doctor then said, "He's gone."

Those are the words that shattered my life and my heart.

I have to admit the why of Allen's suicide still makes no sense to me. He wasn't a quitter; he was a problem solver. Giving up was never an option for him before. It doesn't threaten to steal my sanity anymore, but I would still like to know why he gave up this time.

We didn't have the money to buy a plot and casket for Allen so we rented a casket and had the traditional viewing and funeral service for him. Following his funeral, though it broke my heart to do so, we had him cremated. When we received his cremains a week later, the funeral home took some out to give to Elizabeth and the remainder was placed in an urn. Allen's remains are buried in Plot B of my Mom's plot. (She passed away in 2002).

Elizabeth and her husband bought a model truck and trailer. They put the truck and trailer together and painted the truck light blue like the truck her dad had driven. They strapped the box holding her dad's cremains onto the trailer. Now, she keeps the urn displayed in a dominant place in her home.

Allen took his life twelve years ago. It's a miracle to me that I survived the first six months and am still here to tell Allen's story. I thank the grace of God, my other two children, my grandchildren, and the wonderful group called Parents of Suicides for my survival. I couldn't have done it without all of them.

I love Allen and miss him every single day. He left us at the age of thirty-six. It is an honor and a privilege to keep his memory alive by telling his story, and I'll do so until my last breath.

About the Author
Ladonna Deer is Allen's mother. She lives in Rochester Hills, Michigan. She lives for the moments she can spend with her kids and grandkids. She also enjoys reading and crocheting, walking and scrapbooking. She works full time.

Taylor Asher Bruell

7 March 2001 - 2 February 2016
Colorado

Taylor Asher Bruell
by Harry Bruell (Father)

To sum an entire life in a few pages is a difficult task, even when that life lasted less than fifteen years. Taya was brilliant, beautiful, creative and charismatic. I will rely heavily on Taya to tell her own story rather than try to describe her with more accolades. Here is what she wrote for an assignment in her high school English class two and a half years before she died, modeling a Langston Hughes poem with her own story:

Theme for Taya's Freshman English A
August 2013

The teacher said,
Go home and write a page tonight.
And let that page come out of you
Then it will be true.
Born in Bolivar, moved,
too young to be the new kid at school.
too old to say lived here all my life.
Twelve, an interesting age
Many things are happening
Many thoughts cross my head
A small preschool
Elementary school
a grade skipped
Middle school
There, too, a loss of a grade,
the young kid,
The child,
Why the heck should we listen to you?
Down, down down
High School
Freshman
Small kid
Weirdo
Yet I am not a child.

You say that you would not eat the food I eat,
Yet look how healthy and strong I am.
I know what is true for me, yet not for you
and in twenty years?
Times change
Soon you will feel the same.
Yet we are the same.
I am Jewish;
You are not.
Why should you not speak to me?
I like cats
I like to bike, to hike,
Many qualities you have.
We are separated
By a wall of glass
In a glass castle
Where no one is willing to lift a hammer.

Six months later, twelve-year-old Taya wrote this, just under two years before she died:

This is who I am
February 8, 2014

The color of the clouds. Fresh, clean, new color of my room since I was four. Makes me float on clouds. "This Land is Your Land, This Land is My Land," sung by my mother when I was little.
This is who I am.

My only true home, in the small town of Bolivar. Population one thousand. All my friends. Snow. Eaten from the glove of my small hand. Mixed with the soft feel of winter and the freedom of being outside in the snow.
This is who I am.

Purple, Blue, White, and Green. A striped arm pillow since I was small. Covered in tear stains and blood and memories. The scars of love. No longer circular, bent one way too much. Hello Pillow.
I couldn't read when I memorized my favorite book, the one with the dog on the cover, the touch of its smooth face.
This is who I am.

To the outside world Taya was a superstar. At age 14, she was a junior in high school (two grades ahead) and taking calculus at University of Colorado. Her high school selected her as one of three students to participate in a district-wide leadership program.

She co-founded the writing club, co-chaired the Environmental Task Force, and was featured on the PBS Newshour volunteering to teach seniors how to use computers. She had never received less than an A. She had a beloved best friend and a number of other friends. Her goal was to go to Johns Hopkins and become a surgeon and a writer.

But Taya wasn't happy and it was more than depression. She had a fear of abandonment that alternated between extremes of idealization and devaluation in her close relationships. She had an unstable sense of her own identity, often felt empty, had trouble controlling her anger and had dissociative feelings.

A year and a half before Taya died, she started an escalating pattern of self-harming behavior.

She wrote the following poem in May 2014, when she was 13, 20 months before she died.

there must be something
May 30, 2014

there must be something
in the way she cuts her hair
or the way
she swings her hips
as she walks.

*there must be something
in the way they stare at her
at her exposed back
the bruises just forming
recent.
there must be something
in the way she doesn't eat
her lunch
or the way
she never looks you
in the eye.
there must be something
in the way she looks
swinging
with rope round her neck.*

After Taya died, we found this description she wrote about how she often felt.

River
August 12, 2015

You don't know what it's like, to be bursting like a river inside, so much inside of you and nowhere for it to go. A sea of thoughts and emotions caught, trapped inside your body so your very skin starts to explode. Pores erupting because no one understands, no one cares. No way to escape or get out because it's all you, creating and filling and stretching your body with feelings. Every day is another straw on the already broken back - you're just waiting for it to fall apart and disintegrate. The waves rock inside and push and pull and there's no way to escape, no solace from this never ending nightmare. Everything hurts, just need to be alone and stay alone. Can't be around anybody who will kill yourself or your body or you, not you but what makes you you. Everybody and everything hurts like salt on a freshly cut wound. A rocket shooting off into space and then being stopped and turned around because it has no energy left. A spool of golden thread which keeps unraveling and unraveling until there's nothing left, just an empty roll of cardboard which is tossed away.

But what if it starts as that cardboard? Then what? Just tossed away immediately? Our society has protocol for the full spool of thread, but not the empty one. How can we define every being if there are no words to describe it? A river of thoughts with no words to speak them, a sea of emotions with no face to feel them.
I put on my face. But no one sees what's really inside.

Here is how Taya described her addiction to self-harm:

I thought I could get rid of the monster inside of me but I can't, it lurks and waits and pounces on me when I'm alone at three in the morning with a blade in my hand. We're all addicted to something that takes the pain away, that makes it better for the smallest amounts of time. My method just happens to be more noticeable than most. And I can't stop, I don't know if I'll ever be able to stop. What hurts the most is having to pretend that nothing hurts, that I'll always be fine. And every day I cut deeper, bleed more, and hate myself a little bit more. Everyone has scars that they don't want to talk about. Mine are just on my body as well as in my head. ... Everybody hates me. There's almost no time in my life when I feel alive. I'm alive, so alive when I can see my blood dripping. I'm so sick inside.

We didn't know everything that was going on, but we knew Taya was struggling. We took her to the psych emergency room two years earlier when she was attacking her older brother. We found an international therapist who was an expert for treating gifted children based in Canada and who worked with Taya remotely until her death.

Four months before she died we hospitalized Taya again after we found suicide notes on her bed. The hospital released her saying that she was not suicidal. We tried two local therapists to augment the remote therapist but Taya rejected them saying she wouldn't do any more talk therapy.

We then brought her to a psychiatrist who prescribed mood-stabilizing medication a few weeks before she died. Previously we had explored medical reasons for her behavior, had gotten an intensive hearing evaluation, had blood work taken and had consulted with an expert in residential psychiatric hospitals.

We know that she was fighting her demons and trying to understand what was happening to her when she wrote:

WS:1
December 29, 2015

I'm sorry.
I'm sorry that I don't understand anyone around me, least of all myself.
I'm sorry that what I say interferes with what you think, and that I even project my voice into the world.
I'm sorry that I can't feel your pain. I would share your burden if I could.
I'm sorry that sometimes I feel the need to express myself, to put out everything I feel into a few simple words merely for the sake of attempting to learn and to teach.
I'm sorry I'm not perfect, not anything that you wanted or hoped I would become. That I became this, this small little girl addicted to self destruction and the mysteries of perhaps.
I'm sorry I'm afraid. I'm afraid of who I might become - who I don't want to become. I'm afraid of what I do to other people around me. I'm afraid that one day, I might look back at myself and not know the girl that I see. That I will look back on myself and see a stranger, because that is what I have become.

Nothing made sense to us until a school counselor told us she thought Taya had a personality disorder. Jenny, our son and I independently looked at the criteria for the various personality disorders and we all immediately pinpointed Borderline Personality Disorder (BPD) as a clear description of Taya's behaviors. The writings, social media posts, blogs, and texts we found after she died only reinforced our belief that she had BPD.

Research shows that two to six percent of the general public suffer from BPD. It's an exceedingly difficult disease to treat and up to 10% of BPD sufferers die by suicide. Ninety percent of people with BPD attempt suicide and the average BPD sufferer has more than three lifetime attempts.

Taya was never officially diagnosed because the medical establishment, in the face of significant anecdotal evidence, doesn't recognize that BPD can exist before the age of 18. In our post-suicide journey, we have met many other parents in this horrible club who have lost children with BPD to suicide. BPD is a killer that is taking away thousands of young people every year and much of our mental health system is not activated to address BPD in children and adolescents.

Taya wrote this poem in the depths of her struggle with BPD

ghhfa
February 27, 2014

I am rolling through the water that never ends
attempting to stay afloat
someone comes by in a boat
and rescues the body next to me
the dead, cold body,
they look at me once
and never look back.
Their face was white with cold,
they had deep blue-green eyes,
eyes filled with pity, with hate
of helpless life forms like me.
They had blond hair,
grown out shoulder length,
with dark roots but still light enough,
to be blond. to be special.
Her favorite color is purple,
not deep, but light, lavender.
She is crafty, but not enough,
always someone better.

She has two cats and two dogs.
She is selfish, and evil inside.
I wonder how I know her.
I think because she's me.

In the last few weeks of Taya's life, we were panicked because we knew she was deteriorating but she wouldn't let us help her. We could see it in her eyes when they would "switch" and her beautiful soul was no longer shining back at us. Taya wrote this, two months before she died:

Let Me Tell You A Story
November 2015

So, there's this girl, right? And she's beautiful. I'm talking knockout, bombshell, blonde, skinny, confident. She looks perfect.
If but for her eyes. Because yes, they're blue, and wide set, and covered with nice shades. But they're scattered. The pupils are too wide, always, and seem to envelop more space than they do.
And they move; like startled prey, shoving everything else aside in their quest for safety. They never stop darting from whatever is chasing them, the invisible demons, which no one else sees.
Except for the stretches when they were perfectly still, and empty, although not lifeless by any means. Simply… gone from where they used to be. But these periods got longer and longer until suddenly the girl was perfectly still.

Taya's journey ended during a February snowstorm in 2016 when she turned the swing she and I had built in her room into a gallows. She wrote another set of suicide notes, sent a final text to her best friend, wrote "terminate" on the notepad on her phone, started her favorite song on her phone ("Fireflies" by Owl City), and stepped off of her stool at exactly midnight.

I found her hanging at 5:23 am the next morning when I went into her room to check on her and tell her that school had been canceled because of the snowstorm.

Though she wrote this poem a few years earlier, it may well have been what she was thinking in those few moments before she drifted off into unconsciousness, could no longer create the light, and closed her eyes forever.

Poem 3
August 26, 2013

Darkness. Shadows.
Closer. Coming Closer.
There is no light.
There is only the light which I create.
But I cannot.
Darkness is coming.
Eternal Darkness is soon.
Soon, I close these eyes forever.
It's coming closer.

Editor's note: *All writings by Taya were printed exactly as she wrote them.*

About the Author

Harry Bruell is Taya's father. After she died, Harry and his wife moved from Colorado to Santa Barbara, California, where Harry switched careers to lead a non-profit agency focused on supporting people with mental health diagnoses and/or disabilities in living the lives they choose. Harry has compiled a book of Taya's writings and is working on a book of how borderline personality disorder impacted her life.

Tyler James Bushmiller

2 February 1994 - 18 December 2012
Washington

Tyler James Bushmiller
by Doria Adams (Sister-in-Law)

Tyler was born on February 5, 1994, in Homer, Alaska. His mother was single, young who already had two kids. She was struggling to cope, so with encouragement from her mother, she gave him her baby for adoption when he was six months old, hoping it would be a better life for him.

Tyler was adopted by a couple from Boise, Idaho. His aunt and uncle lived in Boise and instantly fell in love with him. They later had two daughters that became like little sisters to Tyler. When Tyler was young, he spent much of his time with his cousins. He often talked them into being mischievous. His aunt and uncle shared a few of those memories with me.

Once, when his aunt and uncle weren't home, Tyler snuck the movie Jurassic Park into his cousin's house. Even though their parents had said they were too young to watch it, Tyler and the girls watched the movie anyway. Needless to say, they were scared for a long time.

Tyler was the friendliest person I knew. As a kid, even though he was told many times not to talk to strangers, he would often go up to random people and introduce himself. He'd then ask them their names. When they answered, he'd start telling them all about himself because - according to him - once he knew their name, they were his friends.

Tyler was someone who worried about how to make other people's lives better. He would give the shirt off his back to complete strangers if they needed it. Of course, they wouldn't be strangers for long because he would befriend them. He made friends everywhere he went. He was the first one to help people out or stand up for what was right. As cliché as it sounds, to know Tyler was to love Tyler.

Tyler was lanky with big feet. When he was a kid, he was klutzy and had many minor injuries. He was a big goofball; he loved to make people laugh.

When he was about eight years old, his parents decided to move to Washington. Being so far away from his aunt, uncle and cousins devastated Tyler. Although they would see each other from time to time, it wasn't the same. He told me that when he was with them, he felt accepted. He knew they loved him unconditionally.

While he lived in Washington, Tyler became very involved with his church youth group. He loved playing the guitar and often played during the church services. He was a talented poet and songwriter.

Eventually, Tyler grew out of his klutziness and participated in sports. He joined teams in cross-country, track and field and soccer. He won many ribbons and awards and even competed in State championships.

At the same time, he began struggling with feelings that made him feel as if he didn't belong or that he wasn't good enough. Like many teenagers, he rebelled. After he was put in juvenile detention, his parents decided to let him live on his own.

Despite his parents' decision, Tyler was able to get his Graduate Equivalency Diploma (GED) and to support himself financially. I know that it was a hard time for him. He even contemplated suicide, but he always did a great job of masking his pain.

Tyler worked at a Subway restaurant with my sister, who's twelve years younger than I am. Despite our age difference, she and I have a very close bond. She is my person, if you know what I mean.

At that time, we lived about six blocks from each other.
One day, my sister called to say she was bringing a co-worker over to my house. When she showed up with tattooed, lanky, 17-year-old Tyler, I didn't know what to think. My sister and Tyler eventually became a couple.

My sister and Tyler's relationship progressed pretty fast, so he soon moved in with her. They often came to the house I shared with my boyfriend, as we did theirs. Despite being years apart in age and having come from different worlds, he and I really connected. I guess you could say he had an old soul.

It wasn't long before my sister learned that she was pregnant. I was to know I would become an aunt. Of course, I'd be there for her. Because I cannot have kids, Tyler decided I was going to be a third parent. He even wanted me to take birthing classes with them.

We spent hours and hours talking about the baby. When we found out that the baby would be a boy, Tyler decided on the name Tyson because it literally means Tyler's son. His friends tried to tell him he was too young for so much responsibility, but he was happy. He wanted to be a dad. He worked hard to find a good job so he could support his new family.

Tyler got a temporary job, but he was a good worker, so his job soon became full-time. He and my sister decided to get married. I remember talking with Tyler at this time. He was so happy. He said he could see his future with his new little family and felt he was finding himself.

Tyler surprised my sister with the next addition to their family: a golden retriever puppy. He told my sister that their family now felt complete. They named her Daphne and treated her like their first child. Tyler had a heart of gold and an infectious personality.

Their wedding was very intimate. Just myself, my boyfriend, our dad, and one of Tyler's friends who officiated at the ceremony were there.

My sister's pregnancy was an exciting time. My boyfriend, sister, Tyler and I did everything together. Tyler and my boyfriend became friends. They thought they were grill-masters, so we had many barbecues. The only word I can think of to describe this time of life is perfect.

Then, Tyler began to have contact with his parents again. He wanted them to be part of his and his family's lives. They were happy for him and began to spend time with him and my sister.

Tyson was born at the end of August. It was one of the best and most joyful days of my life. I'll never forget how anxious and nervous the new father was. My sister's labor was long. Because of complications, the doctor decided that my sister would have a C section.

Only one person was allowed to be with her in the delivery room. Tyler told me, "This is the closest thing you will have to having a baby so you can go." I assured him I would be watching from the window and that would be fine.

After Tyson was born, the nurse wheeled him out to the nursery to measure him and weigh him. He had his little hand wrapped around Tyler's finger. Tyler was teary-eyed and kept looking at Tyson saying, "I'm your daddy." Then, he'd look at me and say, "This is my son." He was so proud.

Tyson wasn't an easy baby and required a lot of care. I would go to my sister's house pretty much daily to help with him. I will forever cherish those memories.

For Thanksgiving that year, Tyler and my sister were going to Tyler's parents' house for dinner. It was a big deal for Tyler because it had been a long time since he'd spent a holiday with them. My boyfriend was working and the rest of my family was doing their own thing, so I was just going to stay home alone.

Tyler wouldn't have that. He insisted I join them. I didn't want to intrude on such a special Thanksgiving for him, so I told him no, I was fine. He told me I was his family too. He refused to let me be alone, so I went. We had a good time. He showed us all of his trophies, his old room and videos of him as a baby. He was so adorable.

Tyler's family planned a get together in Oregon for Christmas. Tyler said his aunt and uncle and cousins were included. He kept telling me I could come. He wanted me to meet them. He was so excited to introduce his little family to them. He knew they would adore Tyson. He talked about it so much. He shared with me some memories of fun times he had had and how he couldn't wait to be with his cousins so they could tease each other like they always did.

On December 16th, I spent the whole day making Christmas candy with my sister. Tyler was there with one of his friends getting in our way and being goofy as usual. Little did I know it was the last occasion I would spend time with or even see Tyler.

The following day, Tyler, my sister, and Tyson were supposed to eat dinner at my house. Tyler didn't come; he said he was tired from work.

After dinner, my sister went home. She called me about 1:30 in the morning, which was unusual. I thought it must be an emergency. She was a little upset and told me that out of nowhere, Tyler started arguing with her. He was acting angry about something.

While I was on the phone, my boyfriend woke up. I told him what was going on, so he suggested we go over to their house, but I thought it was just a little argument that would be over by morning. It was also very icy and snowy out, so I didn't want to drive.

I told my sister that if things escalated to call me back. She said she thought Tyler had left anyway, so we went back to sleep. My boyfriend and I will regret that decision for the rest of our lives.

The next morning, December 18, 2012, at about 8:30 in the morning, my sister called me again. She was worried because Tyler hadn't come home. His car was still there, and he hadn't used his bank card to get a motel room. It was freezing outside, so she wanted to try to find him. I said I'd come over to watch Tyson or help her call around looking for him.

Before I could get out the door, she called me back. This time she was screaming and crying, so I couldn't understand her. At first, I thought she said Tyler was hurt, so I assumed he was in the hospital emergency. I kept saying, "Okay, I'm coming so you can go to him."

She kept repeating, "No. He's dead in the garage."

I was confused. I called our dad, who lived closer to her than I did, and told him to get to my sister fast. My car was covered in snow and ice which I had to clear before I could leave. I don't even know how I made it to her house. It is a blur. All I can remember is saying over and over, no way could it be true. Did he have an accident?

When I arrived at my sister's house, I saw an ambulance, so I thought maybe he was still alive. As I ran into the house to try to make sense of things, a police officer stopped me. He said I couldn't go inside. He said that it had to be treated like a crime scene.

I told him I had to get to my sister who was hysterical, so he allowed me to go to her. She calmed down for the sake of Tyson. Then she told me she thought Tyler had left, but he had really gone out to their detached garage. What she thought was the door slamming had been the sound of a shotgun going off.

Tyler had completed suicide. I couldn't believe it. I wanted to break down, but I had to be strong for my sister and nephew. I don't recall much of the rest of the day.

That night, the first of many such nights, my sister and baby nephew both slept in my bed with me. As we lay there, I just looked at them and tried to wrap my mind around the fact that Tyler was gone and that my three-month-old nephew will not remember his dad. He will never get to feel the pride and love his dad had for him. Someday, he'll know that he lost his dad to suicide.

I made a promise to myself, God and Tyler that I would make sure that his son would never feel ashamed or believe that his father's death was his fault. I would educate myself about suicide prevention. I would do everything I could to make him understand that his daddy loved him. I would share every memory I had of his dad with him. My heart truly broke that night.

After Tyler's aunt, uncle, and cousins heard the news of his death, they immediately drove from Idaho to Washington. Even though it wasn't how I imagined meeting them, they were as loving and kind as Tyler had said they were. They were grieving too, but they still offered so much love and support, not only to my sister and nephew but also to my boyfriend and me.

Despite the pain my sister was in, she knew that Tyson needed her more than ever. No matter how hard it was, she somehow gathered the strength to keep moving forward.

I learned through this tragedy that no matter how bad you don't want it to, life keeps moving on. You have to face the reality that someone you loved is not only gone from your life but from the world.

It has been five years since we lost Tyler. So much has changed. My sister moved away and has remarried. Her husband is a great dad to Tyson and has even adopted him. Tyson now has two little sisters. He's the best big brother to them.

Tyson is not only a spitting image of Tyler, but he also has his dad's personality. He does and likes so many things that Tyler did; there are many times that he has said something or had a facial expression that is exactly like his dad. It takes my breath away, so I have to walk away for a minute.

Tyson and I have a special bond like his dad knew we would. He is my pride and joy.

Tyler's aunt, uncle and cousins have been so supportive. We have all become family. Recently, we traveled to Idaho for Tyler's cousin's wedding. It was the first time they'd seen Tyson since he was a baby. They also saw so much of Tyler in him. It was such a wonderful time. Even though our visit was short, I think we all healed a bit.

I've learned a whole new set of emotions. Happiness is no longer just joy. It is also bittersweet. Sadness is so much deeper. The world lost a beautiful soul when Tyler died. I won't ever let him be forgotten. Honestly, I would trade places with him in a minute if I could.

I still struggle with guilt and the what-ifs. I go over every conversation we had. I think that if only I'd seen a sign. Maybe I should have listened to his problems more, given him better advice. Maybe if I'd gone to my sister's that night when she called I could have saved him.

I also try to answer the why question, even though it's a question I'll never know the answer to. The only person that knows is Tyler.

I am going to end this with a poem I wrote for Tyler. When he was alive, he was the one that encouraged me to write poetry.

Tyler,

someday my nephew will ask me
to tell him about his daddy
i can't wait for the day
there are so many wonderful things to say
I'm not sure where i will start
maybe i will begin by telling him about your golden heart
Then i will tell him about your smile and flair
and your crazy blonde hair
i will tell him how u were a friend to all
It didn't matter if they were rich, poor, big, or small
i will tell him how you use to play him the guitar
always joking about him being a rockstar
i will tell him u were one of the best man i knew

so strong,real and true
i will tell him u gave him his big feet
good for kicking goals and running in a track meet
i will tell him how u were willing to stand up and fight
for what u believed was right
i will tell him his eyes are the same color of blue
and how much he reminds me of u
i will tell him even though u are not here to watch him grow
ur daddy loves u more than u know
R.I.P AMIGO

About the Author
Doria Adams is Tyler's sister-in-law. She lives in Aberdeen, Washington. She is an advocate for suicide prevention. She formed a team called "TEAM TYTY" that walks their local Out of the Darkness walk and raise funds for the American Foundation for Suicide Prevention.

Cindy Marie Carroll

27 April 1957 - 13 June 2011
Tennessee

Cindy Marie Carroll
by Stephanie Candler (Daughter)

Mom was the type of person everyone loved. Unfortunately, she didn't love herself. I remember growing up watching her constantly pick apart her looks and her body; she cut her hair for hours on end and obsessed over things that no one else thought were wrong. Even though most of her funeral was a blur for me, I'll never forget hearing my dad say repeatedly that day, "She had no idea how beautiful she was."

When my brother and I were little, we were Mom's entire world. She was a stay-at-home mom for the most part, but she was very involved in our school and would even show up as the "reading lady" in full costume based on whatever book she was reading that day. I remember always having homemade meals, and we never went without what we needed.

Things weren't always great, however; I can remember times when Mom had to go away for a little bit and come back later. I didn't quite understand it until I got older, but I was told that Mom suffered from bipolar disorder and was getting inpatient treatment when she went away.

Even then, I still didn't really understand it until I was much older and had experienced more of these episodes with her. When Mom was first diagnosed, bipolar disorder wasn't as commonly understood as it is now. She became sort of a guinea pig for doctors to try out new medications and treatments that were supposed to help with the extreme behaviors and severe depression.

The real turning point in our lives happened when Mom's dad died. My grandpa was my best friend, and he was the person I felt most connected to in the whole world. Even more than twenty years after his death, everyone still remembers him fondly and misses dearly. He was also Mom's rock, and he loved her unconditionally. I can remember watching them interact; their bond was evident to me even when I was very young.

His death didn't seem to affect Mom at first. She seemed to be holding herself together, and her focus was just on everyone else. At that time, my brother, who tended to follow the wrong crowd, was having some struggles and got himself in trouble regularly. Also, Dad was away with the military serving in the Gulf War, so Mom was dealing with all these things on her own.

After the war and as years passed by, things kept getting more difficult for Mom to handle. The fact that she never really grieved her dad's passing finally caught up with her, and she fell apart more frequently than before. My brother continued to spiral out of control, and Dad's job in the military required him to be away a lot.

After Dad retired, we moved from Boston, Massachusetts to Knoxville, Tennessee, where all our extended family lived. There was still a great deal of turmoil within our household. The turmoil included fighting between my parents, manic episodes coupled with drug abuse, a constant barrage of medication trials and hospitalizations for Mom, and so much more.

We had some good times too, but these years were a perpetual roller coaster of events and emotions. I felt like I was walking on eggshells during it all. I didn't understand why Mom couldn't be stronger and couldn't be there for me like my friends' moms could. I almost resented her at times for it, but I was just a kid and didn't understand.

All of this led to the beginning of an even darker period, one which I never imagined was possible. Mom's first suicide attempt was when I was sixteen years old. Only Mom and I were at home that night. I woke up to the sound of my aunt banging on our door because she had talked to Mom and sensed that something was wrong.

After spending all night in the waiting area of the emergency room, I actually went to school the next day because I really didn't know what else to do. It was the only thing that felt remotely close to normal for me, but that day was so surreal. I couldn't quite process what had just happened, and I felt like I was walking in a tunnel all day with life moving all around me.

No one knew the events that had just transpired in my world. I couldn't talk about it. I felt like no one would understand and didn't even know how I would bring up the topic. Walking through the halls at school that day was like something out of the movies.

It felt like time was standing still yet moving at one hundred miles a minute around me. Everyone was just going about the day and laughing, while inside I was crushed and didn't know why Mom wanted to leave us.

Mom eventually rebounded and got back on her medication. This became a short-lived pattern, because she would often feel better and stop taking the medications. This would cause her to have another manic episode and continue the cycle all over again. She would cling to people who enabled her self-destructive behaviors and would often create drama where it shouldn't have existed.

Even through many hospitalizations and all our ups and downs, Mom and I continued to grow closer as I became like a caregiver for her. I was her rock for so many years when my brother and Dad were gone.

While I fought to have my own identity in my younger years, I finally understood how to deal with it as I grew older. My brother and I both had children, so there were many years where Mom was okay because being a grandmother ("Nana", as she would proudly call herself) seemed to finally ground her and give her a purpose in life.

Mom was the ultimate nana. She lived for her grandkids and would move mountains to see them and spend time with them. When the children were little, it was as if Mom had a purpose again like when my brother and I were young. She was able to better manage her bipolar disorder for longer periods of time.

She still had some ups and downs throughout that time, and even a couple more suicide attempts and hospitalizations, but her motivation continued to be her grandkids and she did whatever she could to be a positive part of their lives.

We grew closer throughout that time as I began to lean on her for help in my own life. I finally understood how to interact better with her and how to deal with the instability. This solidified a bond between us that could never be understood by others or broken by anything.

Mom really started in a downward spiral again after the grandkids grew up. They were needing her less and less, and her purpose in life was diminishing. She isolated herself regularly and became addicted to things like food, shopping, and even over the counter sleeping pills.

Mom had a seizure one year while on a concoction of medication that we didn't even know existed. She had been a guinea pig for so long that it seemed the medication had permanently affected her brain and changed her personality.

After the seizure, she had uncontrollable tremors; doctors wanted to do brain shock treatments (electroconvulsive therapy) on her. I was opposed to this, but I couldn't make the decision for her. It's a tricky situation when an adult has mental health problems yet makes her own medical decisions.

One cannot be involved unless the suffering person wants that involvement. Sometimes I wondered if she even told her doctors the whole truth before they tried out new treatments. After the shock treatment, Mom's tremors stopped, but she was forgetful and was never the same. She would repeat herself, asking the same questions over and over.

She continued with self-destructive behaviors and had trouble with some of the simplest things. Navigating around the town she had grown up in and lived in for over ten years became hard for her. It spiraled so far out of control that I felt like I watched Mom die long before she really did.

Deep down, I always knew how Mom would die; I just didn't know when. I even thought at one point that it wouldn't affect me because I had mourned her death already. I felt like the mom I knew before had died, and this new mom was a product of years of turmoil, medication, and experimental treatments.

Then I got the call. I was with a friend at the time; my friend got the call because my dad was afraid to call me if I was by myself. When my friend answered the phone, my gut knew immediately. I can remember standing at the gas station with wide eyes saying over and over, "just say it." I was finally told that Mom was gone. My friend didn't tell me how she died right then, but I already knew.

The events that transpired after that call changed my life forever. The range of emotions I felt - grief, shock, confusion, anger, and despair - were all very prevalent for the first year after Mom's death. I cried every day for six months, sometimes seemingly out of nowhere.

One minute I would be fine, and then a memory would trigger tears that couldn't stop. It felt like things would never get better. Then time slowly started changing things around us. As positive things began to re-emerge in our lives, the pain began to lessen.

I still have moments where the pain of losing her is like a fresh wound, and I feel angry or sad all over again, but life has proven to me that the future can be brighter than I ever imagined.

In the years since Mom's death, I found my one true love and got married, had another baby, and graduated from college twice. My brother's life also changed for the better; he eventually had another child. I know Mom never imagined being "Nana" all over again. I have missed sharing all these things with her, and I wish she could have known how many great things were going to happen in our lives.

There is a huge void in my life that resurfaces with each memory of the things I shared with Mom, especially birthdays, holidays and family events. The bond between a parent and child is like no other, so I understand now that void will always exist. I'll feel it when I see other women with their mothers, I'll feel it when I get the urge to share something new or exciting in my life, and I'll feel it when my kids venture out into their own lives and I am reminded of what Mom is missing.

Mom was beautiful inside and out. She was a talented artist who could draw the likeness of anything she saw. Mom was creative, funny, witty, and adventurous. Her smile was huge, and she could light up a room. One could feel how much she cared for others.

She was a mother, nana, wife, and friend to everyone. I wish Mom had cared for herself more, and I wish she had known that our futures would become so much brighter than it must have seemed when she finally took her own life. Even though I will always miss her and wish we could talk again like we used to, I like to think that she's with us in spirit always. In memory of my mom, Cindy Marie Carroll, never forgotten and forever loved.

About the Author
Stephanie Candler is Cindy Carroll's daughter. She lives in Knoxville, Tennessee. Stephanie has been married to her soulmate for five years. She has two beautiful daughters, Alex and Ava. Her family is very adventurous and loves to fish, hike, camp, swim, canoe, and do anything outdoors. She also enjoys reading. She considers herself a writer at heart and hopes to find a path to write more in the future when her kids are older.

Sheryl Champagne

14 July 1942 - 6 July 2012
Washington

Sheryl Champagne
by Virginia Phillips (Daughter)

On the night of July 6, 2012, I was in my bedroom getting ready for bed and picking up my phone to call my mom to see how things were going. My youngest daughter came into my room and said there was an officer at the door to speak to me. The officer introduced himself and the chaplain with him. I was still naïve and never imagined I'd be told that there was a murder/suicide and that my mom was the shooter. I was also not surprised.

Mom was the middle of three girls in a tumultuous marriage. Her parents were hard partiers and hard drinkers. Her dad was an aspiring country western singer/guitarist. Her mom was a looker and loved men.

Momma was born in Los Angeles, California. She made a quick entrance just as her mother arrived at the hospital. When my mom was three years old, her mother left. Though she often came back saying she was going to stay, she never did.

A man in the mid-forties raising three small girls all under the age of four was unheard of. They had moved to Albuquerque, New Mexico by now. The family lived nearby, so my mom was often looked after by her beloved grandmother.

Mom's grandfather was a horrible, violent man. It was often not a good idea to have little girls underfoot, so as the girls grew, they were left to themselves at the house.

Her dad was often on the road playing in various bands. When he was home, he'd go to the bar and come home in a drunken stupor. The girls were required to keep the house, cook, sew, grocery shopping, and do other normal wifely duties.

Mom developed early and those wifely duties included unspeakable acts by her father. I was twelve, the same age she was when these acts started, the only time I ever met her father. He was dying. My mom brought him out to visit so she could confront him about her childhood. He apologized and she forgave.

Momma met my dad when he was in Albuquerque training; she did some ironing for him. My dad was her first marriage. I believe she loved him, and he loved her. He took her out of poverty and gave her stability for the first time in her life.

I came along just over a year into the marriage. By the time I was a year old, my mom had given birth to seven children and adopted out three of them. She was only 24 years old, but four children at home and infidelity by both took a toll on the marriage.

My mom was alone then in a new state, Virginia, with an eighth-grade education and struggling to contain her bipolar disorder. My mom spoke her mind. She let us call her Mom or Momma, Sheryl, and Grandma but never Mother, Shirley or Mimi. Her mom was Mother, and she always called mom Shirley and an ex's wife was Mimi.

My mom was up for anything and never met a stranger. She gave hitchhikers rides and would give her last dollar to anyone in need. A hitchhiker once remarked to her that he could stab her and take everything she had. she advised him that was true but that he'd have to do it before she reached for her gun.

Mom could strike up a conversation with a cashier and walk out having exchanged numbers with plans to meet for lunch the next week. She made friends easily, but I think her depression was so bad that she didn't see it. I've lived in the same small town for over twenty years and she had more friends than I did.

I think what a draw for my dad was my mom's vivacious personality. She was the light in the room. She could make anyone feel comfortable and included. She loved to entertain and make a great impression. I think that was to hide her lack of book-smarts, as she would say. My mom was always open about practicing safe sex and about the fact that she had given up several children for adoption.

My sister found herself pregnant at nineteen years old. The first grandchild was my nephew, Cary. He was the cutest little boy. Cary's father was never told of his existence. I'm not really sure why, but it became a point of contention between my sister and mom and Cary as the years went on. (We did eventually discover that Cary's father had died by suicide many years before.)

My mom always told us to marry the first time for love and the second time for money. She did love my step-dad and he offered financial security, though they never comingled their finances. Money was a recurring contention between them over the years. She gave. He saved. They argued.

The house became an empty nest so my mom and step-dad moved to Florida. They bought a beautiful piece of property with the most luscious landscape. They joined the local church and became very active.

They both worked on the landscaping. My mom also worked for the jail ministry. Having had a tough upbringing, she could relate to the inmates. She went on to sponsor many of them into the Catholic faith.

Things were great. My sister now lived nearby with her husband and children. Mom always had a soft spot for Cary. He asked; he got. She never denied him anything.

Eventually, there was a falling out at the church and my mom felt shunned, ostracized. They were actually told that their services were no longer needed and they were not welcome to worship there. That was a massive blow to her.

She was looking for a new start while I was battling my recent diagnosis of Epilepsy. I was unable to drive, and the constant medication changes made things very difficult for my family. Mom and step-dad moved to Texas to be close to me. This was the first time I had been around her for an extended period of time in seventeen years.

My mom's unpredictable behavior and anger were very noticeable. The tension between her and step-dad sometimes caused massive crying jags. She finally confided that she got sad three times a year coinciding with the adoption of her other children. She didn't worry about them; she just wanted to meet them again. Did she make the right choice type thing?

Adding stress to my mom's life was my nephew, Cary. He was an adult by now and at times uncontrollable. Cary wasn't able to make it in the military service, so my mom was supporting him. There were many instances of homelessness, evictions, firings from jobs, etc.

We all tried to help Cary, but mom was always there with money and a new place to live or a bus ticket home. This caused conflict with my step-dad and my sister. He would randomly hop on a bus and travel across the country on a whim. He had no place to stay and no job. He had no money half the time. He'd just leave all of his things in whatever place mom had him set up.

The stress of helping Cary weighed heavily on my mom. Momma worried about who would take care of him when she was gone. He got along with my family, mostly. His siblings didn't understand him and often made fun of him to his face. Things were hard for him. He had trouble making friends and never had a girlfriend.

Eventually, Cary was arrested for domestic violence against his step-dad and thrown in jail. I bailed him out and made sure he had somewhere safe to stay. Mom and I went to pick him up several states away. She had just moved to Washington and was trying to start over again.

On August 30, 2010, I received a call from my oldest child early one morning asking about my mom. She relayed that my mom had called and left her a message telling her goodbye. My daughter had struggled with depression years before and attempted to take her life five times, so I think my mom thought she'd understand.

After I woke my husband, we practically flew over to my mom's house. I unlocked the door and went straight to her room. My step-dad came out of his room asking what was going on.

My husband had to break into mom's room. She was lying on her bed. I called 911. Mom had taken every pill she had. She was so mad at me for saving her that she wouldn't talk to me for two weeks.

After spending three weeks in an inpatient psychiatric facility, Mom seemed fine. I was leery though. In October, she took a road trip with a friend who was moving from Florida to Washington. While she was away, her mother died in a nursing home.

Mom came home saying that they were moving. I thought it was too soon after her failed suicide attempt, but they packed their things and were gone by December.

In February of 2012, while mom was visiting for my daughter's baby shower, we were informed that her godson had gone missing in Florida. Mom knew he had taken his own life. She envied him because he had decided when he's leave this world.

When my granddaughter was born in April, my mom came back to town. It was a pleasant visit and full of so much love. When I took Mom to the airport, she cried as she left. She'd never done that before. I asked her why. She said that she was happy, although they didn't seem like happy tears.

The end of June brought the arrest of my nephew, Cary. Mom came again, and we drove to Florida to bring him home with her to Washington. She was very tense and on edge. I'm glad I was along for the moral support because she was carrying her gun, and I worried that she might do something drastic.

Mom and Cary flew to Washington on July 3, 2012. They were discovered deceased on the morning of July 6, 2012.

I don't remember much of the first few days, the first six months actually. My mom had asked me not to tell my sister when she died. She made me promise. This was three days before her death.

I called my sister the day after as I hadn't heard from her, only my brothers. She was unaware of what had happened. I do remember telling my sister her son was dead as well as mom.

The primal scream is one you never forget. No one had told her. No police came to her door. The police later said that there was a disagreement on which department should go out.

During the investigation and trying to piece together what happened, we've discovered she was off her medication. She always had a handful of pills, so I assumed her prescription pills were in there.

When she attempted previously she had left a note. She did not this time. In the note, the first line is, "If you have to ask why, you didn't know me."

She railed a lot about Cary and my dad. She was hopeful that if she was gone, my sister would have no choice but to parent Cary. And she was just still very hurt about my dad.

I've pieced together that on July 5, 2012, mom took Cary to the library and a convenience store to fax documents for his probation officer. She made a wonderful meal and even made a blueberry pie. They had a nice dinner with my step-dad.

He went on to bed and they stayed up watching a movie rented from the library. Sometime after 1:00 a.m. my mom took a pillow from the bed, covered my nephew's head and fired twice. She left the pillow covering his head as he was stretched out on the couch.

She then went and got sick in the toilet. She locked her bedroom door and pulled it closed. She went back to the living room, sat in her rocking chair, right next to the couch, said a prayer and pulled the trigger on herself. My mom died about 1:30 a.m. on July 6, 2012.

My nephew, much to our horror, did not immediately die. He lasted till about 6:00 a.m. My step-dad found them later that morning after returning from walking the dog.

My mom was 69 years old and a week away from turning 70 and celebrating her 33rd wedding anniversary. My nephew was 26 years old.

My sister had a funeral for my nephew a week later. He was cremated; the ashes came the day of the funeral. We were unable to attend his funeral as I was still in Washington helping my traumatized step-dad with everything. I stayed a month helping him out.

My mom was also cremated. We had the ashes separated: some for each of us kids and one big container for my step-dad. Momma had told us that she wanted us to take her ashes to places we think she'd like. Leave a bit of her behind. The boys wouldn't do it, but I've embraced it. She's been to Germany, Notre Dame, the Champagne region of France, Cancun, Jamaica, the Golden Gate, London, Portugal, Spain, and Iceland. Great thing for her that my youngest travels a lot.

In 2014, we did have half her ashes interred. I always felt that everyone should have a headstone. A priest did a short service graveside. It was nice. It was the first time I had seen or spoken to my sister since the deaths.

Many harsh words were hurled at me in the immediate days after the deaths. It was easier to retreat to our corners and deal then to come out swinging at one another.

We've since made our peace. Maybe I've just accepted that my mom took the life of my nephew, whom she loved more than life itself, and that she was so depressed she couldn't understand the absurdity of it.

I spoke to her psychiatrist after her death. He told me Momma appeared to be in a good place. She was compliant, as far as he knew, with her medications and was hopeful for the future. He never saw it coming. Does anyone?

Over the last six years, I have struggled greatly with my mom's death. Our family was fractured for many years. My sister and eldest brother still don't speak. We've had to say goodbye to a brother who was murdered. My husband became suicidal and lost his job. I was never allowed the luxury of grieving. It's a very slow process when you have to keep it all together for everyone else. I don't recommend it.

I miss my nephew. He would call me and sing Frank Sinatra songs to me. He was always trying to make people laugh. He loved soccer and hockey. He had such dreams for his life. Grandiose dreams but they were his. He was not mental, narcissistic, but not mental. He did not deserve to have his life taken from him

I miss my mom. She was so healthy, so full of life. I helped nurse her after her knee replacement so I know she could endure anything. Anything but having to put Cary onto the street.

My mom did tell me in our last conversation that my step-dad said Cary couldn't live with them. She couldn't keep it up anymore and reached her breaking point.

I wish she had called me. I wish she had been honest with her husband. I wish I could have saved her. I didn't want her to move away from me. I thought it was too soon. But I didn't want to tell her how to live her life. I took every call from Cary so he wouldn't be bugging my mom. I did my best to keep her sane. I was successful for 23 months. I looked away for a moment and that's all it took. My first grandchild was three months old and I was fixated on her.

About the Author

Virginia Phillips is the daughter of Sheryl Champagne. She lives in Ennis, Texas with her husband of 31 years, her step-dad and their menagerie of pets, three dogs, three cats and a parrot. Her granddaughter has been her savior in all of this. Her life gives Virginia's life meaning. Though she has not written a book yet, she plans to do an in-depth book about her mom's life at a later date.

Kaitlyn Kimberly Cook

30 January 2003 - 15 September 2017
Tennessee

Kaitlyn Kimberly Cook
by Sylvia A. Bosma (Mother)

Meet my daughter, KK.

I was 34 when Jim and I got married on October 31, 2001. I wanted to get pregnant soon after, so on January 30, 2002, I quit smoking. A few months later we found out we were going to have a baby. Since I was considered high risk because of my age, my pregnancy was closely monitored. Everything went great, though. I exercised, ate right, kept a journal, and read every book about the subject that I could get my hands on.

When we found out our baby was going to be a girl, we were overjoyed. I absolutely loved being pregnant, feeling her move around inside me. That truly is one of the most amazing things, and I am grateful to have been able to experience that twice in my life. On Halloween, our anniversary, my husband painted my belly a Jack-O-Lantern. Her very first costume.

Kaitlyn Kimberly Cook was born in Hollywood, Florida on January 30, 2003, one year to the day after I quit smoking. We called her KK for short. She was a happy baby from the start.

We certainly were the nervous, first-time parents who second-guessed everything we did. We waited until 6 months to start her on solid foods, which she promptly refused to eat for probably a solid two weeks. I had nightmares about her never eating anything other than breastmilk supplemented by formula, but – of course – she finally caught on.

Conscientious about growth hormones, additives and sugar, we tried to eat organic and natural as much as possible. She ate a great variety of foods, and she was good at trying new things.
KK was a happy toddler, not much into dolls but certainly always surrounded by a variety of stuffed animals. She would constantly sweet-talk someone (grandparents, but certainly parents were guilty of this as well) into buying her yet another stuffed animal she simply

could not be without.

Even after we had placed a ban on the purchase of stuffed animals, the grandparents still managed to buy her latest must-have. They simply could not tell her no.

In the end, we compromised, telling her that for every new stuffed animal, she would have to donate one from her extensive collection. Dora the Explorer was the only doll she really wanted - and played with - for years after getting one for her second birthday. It was her favorite thing to watch on TV with Diego a close second.

The only time KK had terrible twos tantrums was when we had to leave the park. That child was crazy about swings and could easily spend at least an hour swinging back and forth. Even after having given her several heads-up that it was time to leave, she would throw a fit each and every time, literally kicking and screaming. When she was four years old, she abandoned an egg hunt because she saw swings at the end of the park. She promptly dropped her basket and made a beeline for them.

Seeing how much she loved riding ponies at fairs and festivals, I decided to find KK a place to learn to ride. She was hooked from then on. Beau was her first love, a gentle gray horse that she could not ride by herself since she was too young at age four. She would sit in front of her instructor, absolutely beaming with joy.

Even though on or around horses has always been Kaitlyn's happy place, she loved all animals, in particular dogs and cats. It took me quite a while to teach her to ask before petting anyone's dog on the street. She simply could not help herself.

I was born and raised in the Netherlands. We visited my parents several times when KK was very young. Every single time we saw a dog on the street – in Holland every other person owns a dog – she begged me to ask permission from the owner to pet the dog.

Her favorite camp was on a farm surrounded by farm animals from goats to chickens, from pigs to horses. That girl was simply happy there.

I think KK was around five years old when we made the mistake of watching the movie Marley and Me. It took me at least ten minutes before she quit crying hysterically because Marley died.

KK started going to daycare a couple of days a week when she was around 18 months. She made friends easily, and she loved to draw. I always carried a small notebook and pen or pencil in my purse so she could draw while we were waiting or driving somewhere.

I kept many of her little drawings. Thankfully I did not allow her to throw them out when she wanted to do so, around eleven years old. We would look at them and she would criticize her own work despite the fact that she had been a little child when drawing those. She was her own worst critic, finding fault in everything she did.

KK breezed through elementary school. She loved to read and learned quickly. She devoured books. We were at the library all the time checking out new books. Later on, she would get into the Warrior series – all about cats – and ended up collecting nearly all books in the extensive series.

In first grade, KK wanted to be called Kaitlyn. She thought KK was too babyish. It was the first or second day in third grade when I was called by the school that Kaitlyn was not feeling well. I went pick her up from school. Her teacher walked us out and said, "Feel better soon, Kate."

I looked at KK and said: "Kate?"

"Yeah, I wanted to try a little different name", she said.

I think it was in fourth grade that she begged me for an Animal Jam account so she could play online with her friend, Gracie, and her other friends. I finally agreed to let her have an account, but only after a lengthy speech about internet safety and protecting personal information. So, the account name she created was Alex Pinewood.

When I asked her where on earth she came up with that name, she said: Gracie is Leo Evergreen. As if that explained it. And when I asked her a couple of years ago to create a FaceBook account for our trip to Europe, she decided to be Alex Pinewood for that one too.

One of my aunts in Holland asked if KK was adopted, confused because of her FaceBook name. Some people know her by KK, Kaitlyn, or Kate, others by Kat, Katie, or Kitty. I don't quite know how she did it, but KK was able to know exactly who knew her by what name. Now, when someone talks about her, I know instantly by the name they use for her at what stage of KK's life they knew her.

Kaitlyn loved playing with Littlest Pet Shop animals, which naturally meant that she needed the accessories and houses of all sorts to go with them.

When she was in Kindergarten, we finally got a dog. She had been begging us for quite some time, but we would not commit until we had a yard big enough for a dog to run. Still, finally getting a dog was a big deal. We adopted him from a shelter, a sweet black lab, German Shepherd, pitbull mix that she decided to name Fudge. KK started researching how to train him right away.

Hootie, her childhood cat, passed away in our arms in May of 2011. A month later we opened our arms to Vader (as in Darth), a one-year-old kitten who looked just like Hootie.

Then, in 2014 we welcomed another rescue, Sadie, into our home. Sadie is a hound beagle pitbull mix, though we still aren't sure exactly how many different breeds she represents. I made sure that everyone in the family knew that she was the last rescue we would take in. After all, I was the one taking care of our little zoo for the most part.

KK loved her little brother, Zander, but absolutely adored her older brother, Aaron. He did not live with us for the most part but visited frequently during holidays and over the summer.

Her favorite holiday was Halloween, hands down. She was so creative and started planning her costume, complete with sketches, a month in advance. It always took a few trips to Goodwill and craft stores to get the supplies she needed to create her own costume.

Things changed gradually when KK – at that point she wanted to be called Kat – started Middle School. She started to become much more introvert. She became incredibly insecure and had difficulty speaking up for herself. Suddenly it was really hard for her to make new friends, but her old friends from elementary school were pretty much all attending different schools.

She started dressing in dark clothing, listening to depressing music. I tried to keep a dialogue going; I wanted her to know that she could come to me for anything and everything, but I found it very hard to connect with her.

Then, on May 1, 2015, I discovered that KK had been self-harming. It was a very tough, eye-opening period in our lives. Our long journey on the road of searching for the right approach, treatment, therapy, etcetera, began.

A week before Halloween I received a call from school. One of Kat's peers had reported that she talked about taking her own life; she had even picked the date of November 2nd. The school was obligated to call the crisis team. I drove to school in a daze. The crisis team tried to talk to her, but she basically refused to talk, and she did not want me to be present during the talk.

Finally, KK was released in my care. The team recommended checking her into the psychiatric hospital, but I was allowed to first take her home and pack a bag for her, provided I did not leave her out of my sight.

We drove home, each thinking our own thoughts. I tried to make sense of this, but I could not. KK was simply angry. She was so angry that one of her classmates had 'done this to her'. I did not find out about the level of her anger until much later. She simply was not talking much, and neither was I.

I was too stunned, trying to process that this was even happening, not knowing what to say to her. I so desperately wanted to make things better, but I had no idea how or even if that was still an option.

I took her to the emergency department where she needed to be checked in. Then, she was put on a wait list for a bed at the psychiatric hospital. She was given a room at Vanderbilt Children's Hospital in Nashville. We, her parents, were not required to stay with her.

There was, however, a 24-hour sitter with her. KK was not allowed to leave her room and all of her belongings were searched after she got to her room. Many things were not allowed in her room: phone charging cords, pens, pencils, etc. I could not even bring my purse into the room. We stayed with KK as much as possible, bringing things to occupy her.

After three very long days, a bed became available, so we were taken across the street to Vanderbilt Psychiatric Hospital to get checked in.

Kaitlyn was scared, and I was scared for her. Once again, I was at a loss about what to do, how to make her feel better. Phones were not allowed and neither were continuous visitors like at Children's. We were allowed to visit twice a day: once at lunchtime, and once at 6:00 p.m., each for half an hour. That was it.

My girl had such a hard time. I remember that she called me at 10:00 p.m. on the first full night she was there. She was so anxious, wanting to self-harm to take off the pressure. I talked to her, telling her I would bring her body markers the next day. Thankfully they had been approved by the nurses here as well.

On the second day, KK asked me to bring a razor so she could shave. The nurses gave her the choice to have me or one of the nurses watch her while showering and shaving. She chose me. They made it very clear that I had to physically be in the bathroom, keeping her in sight at all times.

During her exit meeting, the social worker and psychiatrist suggested starting her on medication to level out her anxiety. She had been diagnosed with clinical depression.

She was there for a week. It was a hell of a week, especially for KK. Missing Halloween made it so much worse for her. Finally, she was able to come home. We decided to have a Halloween party in November to make up for missing her favorite holiday. Most of her old friends and a few new ones were able to come, and the party was a huge success.

The next few months were really hard as we all tried to find our way in this new situation. I was constantly monitoring her social media. We had agreed that I would check her regularly to make sure she had not started self-harming again.

KK slept in bed with me, not ready to be alone in her room just yet. That was fine with me because it made me feel closer to her physically and emotionally. From the start, KK was very open about her struggles with self-harming and with depression. She did not care what other people thought. She felt that it needed to be brought into the open to break the stigma.

Slowly but surely things got better. She started to choose different clothing styles, not as dark as before. Individual therapy was going well. She began group therapy, and I had found a great farm for her to start riding again. Kaitlyn and I started to plan our trip to Europe which we were taking once school was out in May 2016. This was something she had asked me when she turned eleven.

Kaitlyn wanted us to go to Holland together for her thirteenth birthday, just the two of us. Thinking she might be bored if we would only visit Holland, I thought it might be fun to add a few days in Paris as well as London.

Because of Kat, her school decided to have an art class for the whole year, instead of just for one fourth of the year, so in planning our trip to Europe, we had included visits to several museums recommended by her art teacher, who thought Kat would be an ideal candidate for the Nashville School of the Arts. That would certainly look good on her application, plus it sounded fun to visit a variety of famous museums in Amsterdam, Paris, and London.

Kaitlyn was still struggling with the medication, though. We still had not found the right mix that worked for her. She was also having trouble sleeping. Our pediatrician was amazing through all of this and did his best to help but eventually had to refer us to a psychiatrist to help with the medication issue. He referred us to a female doctor. She and Kaitlyn formed an instant bond, so KK had no trouble talking to her. Another small victory.

Our vacation to Europe was amazing for so many reasons. I am grateful, now even more so, that we got to do this together. One of the most important things that happened during that vacation, was that we grew much closer to each other.

Once back, Kaitlyn resumed her weekly riding lessons at the farm. She had gotten really close to Kati who, from day one, was so much more than her riding instructor. KK started participating in competitions and did very well. She was a natural, and she simply loved spending time at the barn. Many mornings on the day of her riding lessons, Kati would come to pick her up at 6:00 and take her to the barn.

KK would spend all day there, helping with chores, regardless of the weather. Even if it was pouring rain all day long, she would want to go. That truly was her happy place.

Several times, KK flew out to California by herself to visit her grandparents for a week over the summer. There, she would ride Ama's horse, Snoepje. We also visited a good friend of mine in North Carolina on several occasions. When she was there, she would spend most of her time in the barn with their sweet horse, Molly, the other horses, and with the dogs and cats.

Kaitlyn's final year in middle school started out pretty rough. She had a hard time keeping up with math, falling back from advanced math in seventh grade to grade level in eighth grade. This caused her to be stressed about her other subjects, consequently falling behind in them as well.

We started tutoring lessons to help her catch up. Art was the only subject where she excelled. Thanks to her art teacher who gave her advice and helped her with her portfolio, Kaitlyn auditioned for Nashville School of the Arts High school.

In February we found out that Kaitlyn had made it in; she was thrilled. Art was her escape. For Christmas she got a Wacom Intuos drawing pad to use with her laptop and a Photoshop subscription so she could draw on her laptop. She was so incredibly talented.

She also loved music. One of her t-shirts read that it was her safe place. I cannot remember exactly when it started, probably at some point in 7th grade, when Lin-Manuel Miranda's Hamilton musical became extremely popular.

KK became obsessed with the songs from Hamilton; it didn't take long before she knew all of them by heart. Instead of listening through headphones, she would play her music on Bluetooth in our car, which meant that I, too, gained a pretty thorough knowledge of the songs. Then the movie Moana came out, which we both loved, and it wasn't long before we knew every single word to those songs as well. I loved those times, driving someplace listening to the music that she loved.

Depending on the song, we would turn the volume nearly full blast and belt out the words. We sounded terrible, but we didn't care. Even though I was not thrilled about some of the songs, at least this was something that we could do together in a way. Now I am so glad to have these great memories.

Sometime in early April I got another call from school. This time Kaitlyn had voluntarily gone to the school counselor and told him that she felt like she needed to go back to the hospital. I immediately contacted our psychiatrist. She arranged for an admission into the psychiatric hospital.

Things were so different this time around. She was there for about a week. She was then allowed to go into the out-patient program since she had volunteered to go into treatment. That meant taking her there in the morning where she would have a day of intensive therapy sessions.

Then, she was allowed to go home for the day at 2:00 in the afternoon. Kaitlyn liked this arrangement so much better, being able to sleep in her own bed. After about ten days, everyone believed that she was ready to go back to finish out the last few weeks of middle school.

Kaitlyn seemed to do better after the second stay. I think the fact that she was going to a high school she really wanted gave me more of a feeling that things were getting better. We were still playing around with the medication dosage, but both KK and her doctor seemed to think she was close. Where sleeping was concerned, she was doing a little better by using essential oils in a diffuser and a sound machine. It was still not great by a long shot, though.

I had to look through my pictures and notes (again, grateful they are plentiful – KK told me many times that I was being "such a mommy, taking so many pictures") to remind myself of the good things in her last year, her last summer with us.

Something that made her happy, even excited, was definitely our San Diego vacation in June. While visiting Ama and Poppy, she got to ride Snoepje, go to the beach, take a snorkeling trip, and fly in a hot air balloon.

Back home she helped Kati during a week-long summer camp, spending an entire week in her happy place. In July, Kaitlyn helped prepare for the move into our new home where she would have an enormous bedroom with her own bathroom, provided she share it with her 'boyfriend' Vader – our cat. She painted her room, drew a beautiful deer on her wall, and decorated it with fairy lights.

Earlier that year, right after Kaitlyn's fourteenth birthday, she asked me to start teaching her to drive. As soon as she would turn fifteen, she wanted to be able to get her learner's permit. She hated being dependent. She kept telling me she was sorry for me having to drive her all over creation even though I told her I did not mind one bit. I gave her some parking lot driving lessons; she caught on quickly.

August came, and so did the start of her first year in high school. KK was terrified that first day. I texted her around noon to ask her how things were going. She replied: better than expected. That's when I relaxed.

We were not aware that any of her friends were attending the school in her conservatory, which was visual arts. Thankfully Kaitlyn ran into one of her good friends from elementary school; that made that first day so much easier for Kitty – the name her friend knew her by.

It took a few weeks for Kaitlyn to get used to her new school, make friends with the kids in her classes, and to get to know her teachers. She was not happy at all about one of her teachers, but since it was not an option to change at this point, I asked her to stick with it for the year. I would help her with her homework and preparing for tests as much as possible so that next year she could request the teacher she wanted.

On August 21 we got to watch the solar eclipse, which, according to KK's Instagram post was "the best thing I've seen in my life." It truly was a spectacular once-in-a-lifetime event.

Towards the end of August, Kaitlyn said she didn't think her medication was working. I called the doctor to move up her appointment, but the earliest appointment I could schedule would be on October 2nd. I asked Kaitlyn if she'd be okay to wait for about a month; she said yes. I had her name added to the cancellation list, in case someone canceled.

As soon as September rolled around, it was nearly Halloween in Kaitlyn's mind, so she would start listening to – and watching - Nightmare before Christmas. Kaitlyn had been doing that for a few years now. She loved it almost as much as her all-time favorite movie, Spirit: Stallion of Cimarron. Another favorite thing was the Cheshire Cat.

Kaitlyn owned several shirts. Her favorite sayings were: "We're all mad here" and "If you don't know where you are going, it doesn't matter what path you take". (I just looked up this last quote and KK would have been fascinated to know that this is actually not a quote from the Cheshire cat.)

On September 14, 2017, KK did not eat dinner with us. Eating dinner together was a custom in our family that I insisted upon unless someone had a good reason not to be at the dinner table. KK had a good reason: This was her first group therapy after the summer break. The sessions would always last for almost two hours.

The girls would meet at a place called the house. (The therapy center wanted to feel like a home, not an office) They would talk a little at first, then they would all head out for dinner for a more casual atmosphere. KK really loved these therapy sessions. She also enjoyed them because they gave her a chance to eat whatever she wanted without me telling her to eat her veggies.

Kaitlyn always ordered mac and cheese if that was a menu option. All I had to do was make sure she had money to buy dinner. Kaitlyn had always been a great eater; she could put away huge amounts of food without gaining an ounce. My main goal was that she benefitted from the group therapy, which meant she felt comfortable with both the group leaders and the other girls. On the way home from the session, I remember her talking excitedly about the new girls that joined the group.

They seemed so kind, Kaitlyn said. She was already looking forward to the next meeting the following week. When we got home, KK went to her room. She had to catch up on homework since we had gone to group therapy straight from school.

My husband and I spent some time together watching a movie after I put our son to bed. I called out to her on my way to bed. I did not get a reply so I assumed she was asleep.

I woke up early the next morning, about 2 o'clock because I heard a noise. I checked on Zander, who was sitting up in bed. I put him back to bed, assuming that was what had awoken me.

My back was hurting, so I got an ice pack from the freezer. On the way back to my bedroom, I heard a noise coming from KK's bedroom. This time I went to her room to check on her. I did not turn on the light. I saw her shape in bed, so I asked her if she was awake in a whisper. Kaitlyn did not reply, so I thought she must have been dreaming and talking in her sleep. I went back to bed.

The ice helped, but I was unable to go back to sleep. I dozed for a bit and then decided I might as well get up. It was about 3:30. I turned on the coffee machine and took the dogs outside. I sat down to drink my coffee when I heard a noise again.

Zander was still asleep. His bedroom is directly across from KK's. When I closed his door, I distinctly heard a moan, coming from her room.

I turned on the light. I saw Kaitlyn on the floor, convulsing as if she was having seizures. I woke up Jim to stay with her while I called 911. I got everything ready for the Emergency Medical Technicians (EMT), and we waited. About half a minute before their arrival, we had to start cardiopulmonary pulmonary resuscitation (CPR) because KK had stopped breathing.

At that point, I still thought Kaitlyn had a seizure. When the EMT's asked about her history, Jim asked me about the pills I had gotten from my doctor for after my carpal tunnel surgery the week before. I checked and they were all there.

As the EMTs were trying to revive Kaitlyn, she was put on a stretcher. I told Jim to go with them while I got Zander ready for school and followed them to the hospital.

After they left, it occurred to me to check Kaitlyn's phone. She had had a conversation with a friend around midnight and mentioned that she was going to take pills. I found the empty bottles in her room when I went to look. She had taken two nearly full bottles of her medication for depression. I texted the information to Jim to pass on to the medical team.

After I woke up Zander and got him ready for school. I received a call from Jim's phone, but it was the social worker. She told me to just come and bring Zander with me.

When we got to the hospital, a couple of nurses took care of my son while they took me to a small consultation room. Jim was there, red-eyed, unable to speak. The doctor came in as well and told me they had tried everything, but Kaitlyn did not make it.

We were allowed to see her to say goodbye. I cannot for the life of me remember whether I kissed her goodnight or told her that I loved her on Thursday, the night before she died.

Due to health issues, KK's Oma – my mom – was unable to attend her service. She was cleared to fly a couple of months later, so we had a tree planting ceremony at the farm then, KK's happy place. I picked a white dogwood that Kati and I planted on top of a bio urn that contained most of KK's ashes. We went around the group and shared a memory of Kat, drank hot chocolate and ate mac and cheese.

I have been visiting the farm nearly every week since she died. I can just feel her presence there, when I sit by her tree, talk to Kati, pet the dogs, and most of all when I stroke the horses.

I have been writing her story, now nine months later, for a few weeks now. I have only dreamed about her twice, the last time only two nights ago, on June 22, 2018. I think that was because finally, after nine months, I got her laptop and iPhone back. Those items were taken by the police on the day KK died.

The detective was waiting in our driveway when we got home from the hospital. The CSI team came in and took pictures in her room. Any and all electronic devices were taken to be examined, to make sure she was not coerced or bullied.

I would receive a full report of what they would find if I wanted it. Of course, I wanted to know everything she was unable and/or unwilling to confide in me. Long story short, it wasn't until I contacted the local press that I finally got her things back. Nothing had been examined, her laptop and iPhone intact in their original evidence bags.

I need to let that go, though. I need to be grateful that I have her things back and that I saw her in my dreams the same night I got them back. I will spend the next week or so charging, backing up, looking through things. I do not have any hope of finding any answers, or a note. I just want to know more about her state of mind in the last few weeks, days on earth. I have most of her passwords, another thing for which I am grateful.

Then, when I think I have looked at everything, I will finally be able to cancel her phone and her Spotify account that I have been paying for since September. But not before I create a Spotify account with her favorite playlists. Then, when I need to feel close to her, I will get in my car and drive to the farm, while listening to – and singing along with - her favorite songs. And maybe someday soon I will be able to watch Moana again.

About the Author
Sylvia Annelies Bosma is KK's mother. She's originally from the Netherlands, but now, she lives in Nashville, Tennessee. Her passions are spending time with her family and friends, reading, photography, spending time in nature. She also enjoys going on scrapbook retreats, a time of remembering and documenting life, fellowship, and friendship in a peaceful environment.

Leah Renae Cox

12 March 1975 - 24 March 2018
Tennessee

Leah Renae Cox
by Janet Cox (Mother)
and Cara Perkins (Sister)

Leah was born in Kingsport, Tennessee at 12:15 p.m. on March 12, 1975. It was a gorgeous day; spring was early and the flowers were in bloom. Her first name was picked from a baby book from the 1930s, and her middle name was her great-grandmother's first name.

Leah was always a feisty little thing. She was constantly teasing her little sister, Cara, when they were kids. She was mischievous as a teenager and was rebellious as a young adult. Her small stature only helped her to have a larger than life personality.

Many of Leah's personality traits were at odds with each other, which made her restless. She was always trying to reach out and experience life, sometimes even before she really needed to. She was like a diamond that had a million facets; a description of her cannot do her justice. She was a wonderful, loving, eccentric, complicated person. She was ours.

Leah loved ballet. At a young age, she started dancing and showed great talent, later even soloing in The Nutcracker. She was always zipping down the roads, driving to the studio in her red Honda Prelude, music blaring and a Capri cigarette in her hand. Yes, she smoked, even as she danced to stay fit.

Leah's favorite holiday was Halloween. She dressed up and went trick-or-treating when she was young. Once she even dressed up and went trick-or-treating for her little sister who wasn't able to go. She dressed up as a fairy princess once on Halloween, but Wonder Woman was her favorite costume. Sometimes, as she got older, she still dressed up and we would hit the town in costumes.

Leah also loved the beach. It was her Zen place, so much so that she moved to the beach when she was a young adult, much to the chagrin of her family. She rented an apartment with her best girlfriend in Virginia Beach; they roomed together for six months. Leah did what Leah wanted, and we wouldn't have had her be any other way.

After living in Virginia Beach, Leah moved to Norfolk Virginia, where she met her husband.

She loved gothic things, black, ravens, Edgar Allen Poe, and the poet Oscar Wilde. A big history buff, she loved historical novels and movies. Leah had a mind that always needed to be fed. Before her death, she even tried to learn German, to add to the French she had already mastered in high school and college.

Leah went to Dobyns-Bennett High School in Kingsport, Tennessee. She went to college at East Tennessee State University. She transferred to Haywood Community College in Clyde, North Carolina, where she learned to make jewelry.

Leah loved the French language and always dreamed of going to Paris. She, in fact, always referred to her mom by the French word for mother: Mere.

Leah may have been a spitfire, but she was filled with love and a huge heart that would help anyone who needed it. She was fiercely loyal to her friends and family. If you had an issue, she was on it. Next thing you knew, you had twelve texts telling you how to fix it.

Her sister, Cara, got very ill at one point. Doctors couldn't figure out what was wrong with her, but it was Leah who figured it out after she had gone through a multitude of tests. The beautiful, smart, older sister, Leah, was always there when her family really needed her to come through.

Leah had been given her fair share of hard knocks in her life. She suffered the heartbreak of a failed marriage and divorce. She had waded through the misery of a sexual assault.

Also, she was involved in a car wreck at age seventeen when she pulled her car out in front of another car in front of the high school she attended. She suffered permanent injuries to her neck and shoulder.

Leah got married when she was twenty-five years old. She lived in Virginia Beach, Virginia during the six years she was married. Following her divorce, she moved back home to Kingsport, Tennessee.

Leah valiantly fought her way through each of these situations and came out on the other end. She shared with us that the past few months had been some of the happiest she had experienced in a long time.

The million dollar question is: How did we end up without her? Isn't that the question we all ask? How did this happen? She had struggled most of her life with depression, or as the doctors called it, a chemical imbalance.

Leah was diagnosed as chemically imbalanced at the age of fourteen. When she was a teenager, she holed up in her room and was rebellious. As an adult, she slept a lot. She went to several counselors and psychiatrists, but she never found a good fit. Her doctors tried her on almost every anti-depressant that hit the market. She went thru a lot of trial and error; some medications helped more than others.

The hard thing to understand about that is that many of us struggle with depression sometimes, so how does that lead someone to suicide? We don't know. For Leah, it just kept reinventing itself from a chemical imbalance to a chemical dependency to alcoholism to ending it all.

We think what got Leah the most was her heart. This world was too much for her. She was an empath; she could sense what anyone around her was feeling emotionally, and we think it just became too much. The emotions of the people around her, combined with her own personal struggles, finally won out over her own sanity.

Doctors put Leah on a new medication to help her sleep. Since she died, we seriously wonder if the sleep medication could have contributed to her death. You see, there were no warning signs, no red flags, no dinging bells, no signals, and there was no call for help. She just left one night and never came back home.

The days after Leah disappeared were maddening with anxiety as we and the police searched for her. Days passed in chaos. Three days later, our beautiful Leah's body was found on a riverbank by a man who had gone fishing. Police determined that there was no foul play, so her death was ruled a suicide.

That day broke our world apart.

You are probably wondering where hope comes in. Nowadays, hope comes in forms of therapy, drawing closer to family and friends, and remembering Leah and the love and caring we shared. We can't bring Leah back. We can't fix it. Yes, it's still going to hurt, and yes, we'll cry and scream and want to rage at someone or something.

The only way we know to bring something good out of Leah's tragic ending is to make sure that we never stop talking about her, never stop thinking of her, and that we never stop talking about suicide prevention. We must live to honor our loved ones. We need to live lives that are worthy of our loved ones who are gone, to carry their flame and when our time here is done, we can go ahead to meet them, knowing that they continued on through us and the legacy left behind.

About the Authors
Janet Cox is Leah's mother. She lives in Kingsport, Tennessee, but is originally from Virginia. She is retired now and loves retirement. She has a passion for community theater. She has a 14-year-old Jack Russell named Maggie, or as Leah liked to call her, a weird little dog.

Cara Perkins is Leah's younger sister. She lives in Knoxville, Tennessee. She is happily married to her husband, Trent. She has a passion for adopting stray animals. She is an interior decorator.

William Charles Dehmer

31 July 1981 - 2 April 2016
New York

William Charles Dehmer
by Karen Davis (Mother)

This is the story of my youngest son, Billy Dehmer, who had a heart of gold. Billy was truly the light of my life, my best friend, and my go-to everyday person.

He was born July 31, 1981 and took his own life April 2, 2016. To this day I find it so hard to write those words. You learn to manage the flow of pain and camouflage the shock of this heartbreaking reality of suicide. These are the things that happen to other families. Things you are not educated in nor want to read or know about until it happens to you when it is too late.

I remember the day my son was born 34 years ago, it seems like it was yesterday. Billy was four weeks late and it was a hot summer day. I was only 22 years of age and I just gave birth to my first son 15 months prior.

Back in the 80s, you did not know what sex you were having so the birth of a child was a wonderful surprise the moment you heard the first cry. I hoped in my heart that I would have a girl but when they showed me my son, I must admit I was not even surprised. Boys were common in my family.

Little did I know that day even though God decided not to give me a daughter, what he gave me was so much more. He gave me a boy that would love and protect me all the days of my life.

My Dad fought in World War ll and had a strong value of savings. He took Billy to the park when Billy was a little boy. Dad gave Billy two new quarters. Billy met two boys at the park that he wanted to be friends with.

The first thing he did was give his quarters to them. It did not matter what Billy gained for himself. It was more important for him to make the two boys like him and feel happy. This was a quality that would stay with my son throughout his whole life. Why we always called Billy the Heart of Gold.

Where do I begin to write about my son Billy? What words can I choose to tell you the profound impact he had on my life? For the rest of my life, I will never have the answer to why he decided to leave me. I will never know why Billy was so sad inside himself and felt he was never good enough to stay here on this earth.

I knew from the minute my sons were born the only thing that mattered to me was to love and protect them every single day and to shelter them from harm and pain. To let no one on this earth hurt them. How did pain and harm creep its way into my son's life and come under the cracks of Billy's soul?

Billy was always acting silly in school. Every report card would say he needed to practice self-control. He would make everyone laugh in class. Billy loved to laugh about everything. To this day people share some great stories about how he would quote all the movies he watched and funny lines from them. He truly was so funny and loved to make people laugh.

When Billy entered the ninth grade he was on the honor roll. He decided to get serious about his life; I was so proud of him. Billy stayed on the honor roll until twelfth grade. He won best dressed in the class yearbook. He went on to college but dropped out after the first year.

My son was so ambitious. When Billy was fourteen he would shovel snow in the winter around the neighborhood. One winter he made $200.00. At fifteen years of age, he went to the florist and swept the floors and then to the bagel place to clean the grills on Saturdays.

He went to work at the age of sixteen to various jobs. Billy always had a job. At age nineteen he started working in Manhattan as a concierge, which was a union job. Billy worked there for fourteen years and was so loved by everyone there. This was his job until he died.

Without a doubt, Billy's heroes were Jim Carrey and Robin Williams. He loved how funny they were and how they made everyone laugh. He saw their movies a million times. I think Mrs. Doubtfire was his favorite movie. When my grandchildren and I still watch it, we always think of Billy.

My son told me I was his hero. I have several cards from him and he always wrote that in them. Billy was Best Man at his brother's wedding. His speech was about how I raised two boys as a single mom. He said, "We are the men we are because of Mom". I will always remember that speech.

Billy was always artistic, loving, charming - always the funniest person in the room throughout his whole life. No matter who knew Billy or who he met for the first time, he was so charismatic. I do not think Billy had any enemies.

He would meet strangers and become instant friends with them. His love for his family was his world. It was Billy's purpose and gave him his breath every day. I truly believe if you took one of us out of the equation, it would set Billy's world off balance. There is no doubt in my mind about that.

I believe Billy never felt he was good enough for anyone. He often told me he felt like he failed in his life as he got older after he married. We live in a tough world where owning a home and providing is very difficult for young people. Billy was always being so hard on himself. He saw the good in people but never in himself.

Billy loved nature and because of this he saw beauty in the simplest places and things. He loved to go fishing and he loved to draw.

Billy was an incredible artist. My son started drawing at the young age of three. He used to love to copy characters from cartoon magazines. He seriously started drawing while he was married. I had never seen Billy so serious about his art.

He went as far as purchasing drawing tools and started an Instagram account with 4500 followers called Disney Art. He managed competitions. Billy asked me to follow his Instagram. He drew so many amazing photos.

Then one day Billy deleted everything. I asked what had happened? He said that he thought his art was taking too much time away from his responsibilities at home.

He then started tattooing himself with tattoos that he would sit six hours for. Billy started competing in tattoo competitions and won first place in several contests. I was told Billy gave all his trophies away to the tattoo artist who drew them within the two months before he died. I never knew about that. Giving away prized possessions can be sign of suicide.

As a little boy, Billy often spent time in special places on Long Island. Sand Point Nature Preserve was absolutely his favorite place in the whole world. It is a place on Long Island sound with many nature trails. It is called the Gould Guggenheim Estates. They often host medieval festivals, which he went to as a child.

Billy also loved going to Westbury Gardens, Planting Fields and Old Bethpage village restoration. There was a nature preserve in Oceanside where we both lived.

Billy was the best father to his little girl. He brought so much laughter and joy into her life every day. He took her on his adventures to all his favorite places on Long Island. My son watched his daughter three days a week and worked a full-time job. On his days off he loved to take her to these places. Billy loved to take photographs. I bought him a camera and he used to send me a million pictures of his little girl through the three and a half years he was with her.

Billy was raised loving fishing. His grandpa often took him on his boat and his dad always took him fishing. Billy fished as a recreation, so I think this was calming in his life. He often went out on the boat with his childhood best friend or stepdad. I have a picture of Billy on the boat holding a fish. I cherish this picture of him and when I look at it I know that Billy was so happy.

Billy made me feel cherished every single day of my life. If I was sick he was right by my side. Billy spent his life making sure I would always feel loved.

I would look at my son and wonder how did I create such an amazing person? How did this little blonde-haired boy grow up to be this sensitive thoughtful caring soul that saw other's pain so deeply who had so many talents that he never felt worthy enough to own?

There were events that happened in the last four years before Billy took his life. I truly believe each one of them contributed to his anxiety and depression. I do know that his life changed and all the things that meant everything to him were slowly becoming unbalanced. Whatever Billy needed to balance his life became unstrung.

Billy lost both of his grandparents in 2011. His grandmother died one month before his wedding. He was very close to both of them. They had a huge impact on Billy's life after my divorce in 1991.

My parents were very active in his life and he continued to see them every week on his days off as they aged at 90. The day before Billy took his life I was told he sat outside of their house, which had already been sold, and cried in the car. He was with his wife.

Billy was married in 2011. At the same time, there were problems in the family, so Billy was not able to speak to or see his brother or his nephews for three and a half years.

In 2013 Billy started to see a therapist. He told me he did not like the way he was feeling inside. His daughter was born in 2012 and this brought a lot of changes to Billy's life. He adored her; she was the love of his life.

His marriage was often up and down with conflicts and arguments. I think Billy wanted a successful marriage. He did not want to replicate what he saw with his own parents.

Billy often told me he felt like he failed in life because he could not afford a house for his family. He started to suffer anxiety over several health issues after four years of being married. To us, it seemed like it came from nowhere.

After a few family problems, I went to visit Billy and his family on Easter. He acted very strangely that day, almost as if he was in a dark tunnel with no expression. I thought he was just still angry; I was so sad to see him act this way. I was never focused on something being wrong mentally, but rather that something was just wrong with us. Billy took his life five days later.

You never forget the day you find out your child is gone or the day you are right there when they find him, when you hear the words, "I am sorry; he is gone."

Time stands still. The best friend I have loved every day of my life for 34 years would not walk beside me anymore. My body was frozen in time, back to a time where death could not happen to someone I love. I remember I had to go home. I had to go lay down and never get up again. I could not eat or drink.

It was as if the lifeline running through my body was pulled out from me and I was trying to survive with little air. I was not sure if I even wanted to. From the days and months that followed, I remember feeling like I was in a fog or zombie state of mind. Everything was happening around me and I was walking through this long tunnel filled with pain. Will this ever go away? Will I ever stop feeling like I too want to die?

The first year for every holiday and birthday were the worst. The anticipation of the days that lead up to the day was far worse than when the day arrived. I became obsessed with photographs. I had to save and print every photograph that I could find. I started a memory website and would post picture after picture.

I became the obsessive mother who lost her child. The one where people feel bad when it happens, but after a year become exhausted supporting her. Or that's how I felt. My rock, my best friend, the one who would make it ok, who would buy me a little thoughtful gift or a note in a card, my biggest cheerleader, was gone.

My strength was gone too, and I felt so empty and alone. The added grief that Billy left me from sadness was compounded onto my daily struggles.

You wake up one day, if you are lucky enough, and say, "I am either going to forget my life or I am going to do something to survive." I became someone else. Suddenly it was as if I was seeing the world with my son's eyes. Everything was so sharp and clear.

I have learned how to manage my pain for the most part. I have learned that on days when I want to really cry, I do. This is love. Love becomes grief. Love never leaves this earth. Love lives on in another form and we must learn how to figure it out individually in the best possible way.

About the Author
Karen Davis lives in Oceanside, New York with her husband. She is the mother of Billy Dehmer. She also has an older son, and three young grandchildren. Karen walks in honor of her son for the AFSP Out of the Darkness Walk on Long Island. She raised $2,000 in 2017 and will continue to walk in honor of her son and raise money for Suicide Awareness to help others who struggle with mental illness. She joined online websites of support and met other women who lost their children the same way. They continue to support each other. Karen has a child-loss blog to help grieving parents. You can see some of Billy's drawings there.

Dennis James Ewing

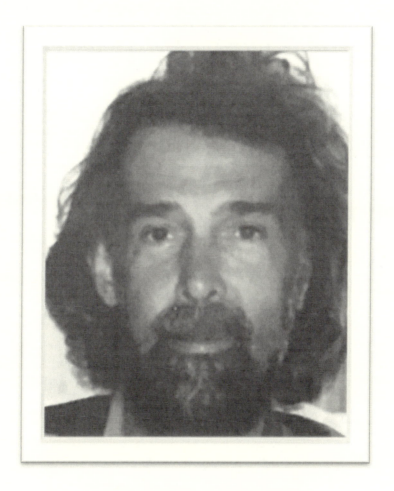

**27 August 1955 - 10 June 2003
Pennsylvania**

Dennis James Ewing
by Rebecca Parr (Friend and Lover)

June 9, 2018

This is a difficult story to tell, especially as I write now, just one day from the fifteenth anniversary of my friend's departure. Dennis was so much more than just a friend.

How do you describe a relationship that spans many years and is interconnected through family and layers of events? How do you describe love, loss, the moon, howling, dancing, light, kisses, tears, regret, pain, pardon, passion, relationships, passing, pulsing, vibrancy, more kisses, and unspoken goodbyes? How do you describe a moment and a lifetime? How do you describe the point of no return?

When I met Dennis, I was thirteen years old. He was a friend of the man who would later become my stepfather. Dennis liked motorcycles, drugs, dancing and being the life of the party. He liked work, fast cars and most people he came in contact with.

I didn't really become very close to Dennis in those early years. He had a crush on my beautiful sister as did most men when we were growing up. Dennis was like a member of our family. When we moved away, my parents stayed in contact with him, though not with frequency. Dennis also moved away. I believe my parents went to visit him once in his new town.

As life happens, Dennis had two daughters in his new town. He also had sons from a marriage prior to me meeting him.

Over the span of twenty years or more, we would periodically hear from Dennis. He spent time in and out of jail and living a wild life. The life of my family, on the other hand, had become rather normal or routine. For those twenty years, my life continued with very little thought of Dennis. From time to time, my parents would tell me he'd gone to jail and they were sending spending money to him, or they would say that they had sent a letter with encouragement and shared memories.

I cannot tell you much of the story of his life throughout those many years. I cannot tell you why he went to jail, what were the names of his friends and women, where his family lived, or if he had contact with anyone from his past outside of my parents. I cannot tell you of his pains or joys during those years, other than what he shared with me later, because this story has a continuation following those years of absence. This story has the prodigal son's return to the fold, a restoration of the pack, and a whirlwind of life in our midst, followed by his death.

Dennis showed up at the family home pulling his camper with an old Ford pickup truck; he had his sidekick in tow as well. His sidekick was sullen and followed Dennis around as if he were his god, his keeper, or even perhaps his lover. It was a difficult relationship to witness, but you could tell there were many years and layers to that relationship that weren't ours to understand or unravel. His sidekick stayed for a few months I believe, but I only had met him a few times before he left.

Dennis stayed. Not too long after his sidekick left, Dennis got word that he had shot and killed himself. I don't know what Dennis suffered from that loss. He kept those feelings mostly to himself.

I thought Dennis would leave after that, but again he stayed. He had found his way to something he could call family and a place he could eventually belong. He was in the fold and was part of a pack again. The pack was small but strong and provided shelter from the things about Dennis and his story that he was unable to share.

It happened without warning that Dennis and I began a relationship. It happened under moonlit circumstances, dancing and stolen kisses. It happened so suddenly that I wasn't sure if it would continue or had just been a moment's fancy. It happened so abruptly that I wasn't even aware that my heart had been mixed in and that I would be sharing the next three years in this dancing and spinning, with consequences that would change who I am forever.

It happened that we began a love story with intensities I hadn't considered possible in my makeup ever again, nor since. We sometimes carry wounds that can close us from possibilities until something happens that awakens the exiled parts within, and we find ourselves allowing the freefall. That's how it was for me that fateful night with Dennis. I allowed his touch to awaken me. I allowed his body to fold with my own, and I allowed the possibilities to re-awaken the headiness and intoxication of oneness with another.

Do I regret now that allowance? No. I don't regret the beauty and chaos of my time with Dennis. Still, fifteen years later, I feel the whisper of his voice on my neck and hear the long howling of his pains unspoken. I only regret that I didn't know how to reshape his suffering into a space of completeness and belonging. There were many incidences in those three years of drama and then the many spaces of quiet and peace.

Dennis had issues with addiction, and unfortunately those issues spilled over into our life together.

June 10, 2018

Today marks fifteen years. As I write, my limbs feel heavy and my throat constricted. My eyes are filled with tears and my heart still laden with grief. I had mentioned regret in writing yesterday, so I wish to explain where that rests in me. I wish to express, like so many before or after me who live to tell the story of a loss to suicide of a loved one, how difficult it is to shed regret and guilt. There is always the continuation of thought: What could I have done differently that day?

Could I have said or done something to change the outcome, if at least for another day? How do I live with the consequences of not having seen or known what was going to happen on that ill-fated day? How do I find a path to self-forgiveness, even if I know in my heart and mind I'm not responsible for his choice to depart? What if I had just said something, anything that would have kept Dennis from making that choice?

That day lives like a very bad movie in my memory. The memory plays out in slow motion and in a sickening color with a very heavy air. The haunts of the things unsaid or said have a way of remaining like a lead blanket that will not allow movement. I have gone to treatment for PTSD, but that doesn't remove the reality of that day. It does help with my immediate response to certain objects or images, but it doesn't take away the weight of pain that still exists.

Still, a slight smile comes to me when I remember Dennis in his many hours of play and light. How he would yell my name from across a crowded room just to let me know he was there and was thinking of me. I remember the day before his passing, how he pulled up on a bicycle with what was undoubtedly a stolen rose bush, and how adamant he was to get it planted right away.

Dennis often brought gifts to me. One gift he brought not long before his passing was a large mosaic heart that I still keep in my yard. He said he bought it, but I will never really know.

The house and home I bought a few years after he died is just two blocks from where he took his own life. We were both at home that day when a friend stopped by for a visit. Dennis wouldn't sit to watch a movie with us, but he kept coming in and out. At one point, Dennis asked me where the dog leash was. I found it odd at the time but didn't think much of it. It was where we'd always kept it.

Now I wish I had questioned my feelings more. I remember that day I had concerns for his safety and how relieved I was when he pulled up in the yard on his bike after having gone somewhere for a short ride. When I saw him pull into the yard, I knew I didn't have to worry about his well-being anymore. He was home and safe.

The last few months of his life, Dennis had gotten rid of most of his few belongings. He had everything down to what would fit in a small backpack and a locked box of old memorabilia and photos – mostly old car and motorcycle pictures and his birth certificate. I've kept those items tucked safely in a drawer. Sometimes I look at them, but mostly they're just there. They were special to Dennis, which makes them special to me.

A few months after his passing, I found Dennis's daughter's phone number and called her. That was perhaps one of the most difficult conversations of my life. How could I explain what had happened when I really didn't know myself? I told her how much her dad loved her and her sister and how often he spoke of them. I don't know the circumstances of his relationship or parting with their mother. I do know the burden of having the final moments of Dennis's life and any final words between us being mine to carry.

Oddly my last words to Dennis were, "I just don't want any trauma or drama."

His reply was, "There will be no trauma or drama."

Shortly after, I looked out my window and saw Dennis hanging from a tree in the front yard. I couldn't save him. That moment will forever be the most traumatic and dramatic of my life.

Today will be a day that passes slowly. Today I'll think of Dennis and our sweet hours of lovemaking and the many spins across the dance floor. I'll think about his love of animals and plants, and I'll even think about what a bad boy he liked to be.

I'll think about his love of cars and motorcycles, but most of all, I'll remember the people he cared about most, those he considered family. I'll think about his children that I never met.

I'll also think about how Dennis loved to go to work as a painter, and how he would explain to me the knowledge of his craft. I'll think about how he loved to sit in the sun and drink his cold beer, and about how he could make friends of strangers in just a moment's time.

I won't think about what could have been because it is too painful to live in "what ifs." Instead, I'll remember the love and take the time on this very long day to honor what was and shall remain forever in my memory and heart. In the aftermath of all that has happened, Dennis still lives, if only in the sacred spaces of my being and in his story, however limited in the telling.

Though I no longer dance, when I close my eyes and remember our movement together, it is as if I am there still, and this I will always treasure.

About the Author
Rebecca Parr works in her community to help people find recovery options for addiction and bring about hope for marginalized communities through the use of mindfulness, art, connection, and organizing with our local government and supporting agencies. She also works as the Production Manager for the University of Tennessee School of Music Opera Theatre program. Her greatest joy is helping to raise her great nephew/son for the last five years, and writing.

Deborah Ann Martinie Hardin

20 December 1954 - 30 March 2017
Tennessee

Deborah A. Martinie Hardin
by Deborah Lynn Bradford (Daughter)

Born in Sardis Mississippi, December 20, 1954, my mother, Debbie was the second born of four children. I don't have a lot of information to share about her childhood because Mom didn't talk a lot about it.

It's difficult to write someone else's story, especially when that person didn't leave anything behind they wanted to be told. What I do know, I don't believe I have permission to share. Mom either didn't want to tell her story, or she didn't know how to tell it. Either way, hers is not my story to tell. I can, however, share some of Mom's adult story because much of it included me.

You see, my mom was my constant. A constant is someone who has been with you since birth. She was my very first constant.

Mom tried to give me her best; I see that now. She loved to introduce her kids to her friends and coworkers. I smile about it now, but it really did annoy me then. Mom would just get so excited, but only because she was such a proud mom.

She was an independent woman who always worked hard and loved her job, or at least the people. I believe her love was expressed through gifts and words of affirmation. She lit up like the sun when someone gave her a compliment.

We took quite a few family vacations growing up. Mom's favorite vacation trip was fishing. For a woman so girly, she sure didn't mind getting those manicured nails dirty. I have many memories now that Mom is gone. I really took them for granted growing up.

Suicide is different from any other death because when a suicide occurs, the person has made an irreversible decision. My mom made that fatal decision on March 29, 2017.

My mother was surrounded by a family that loved her very much, not just in her life, but also in her death. On the day she died, Mom was living with her husband, sisters, sister-in-law, dogs, cats, iguanas and a turtle that she'd found.

One of Mom's last Facebook posts read, "I have decided that driving home so many times after dark, that all of God's little creatures out and about just need our headlights to guide them quickly across the street." She loved all of God's little creatures; I loved reading that post.

There is nothing under the sun that will prepare you for something like this. I was out prom-shopping for my daughter. On that day, I got a phone call from my aunt. The last time I had seen my mother was just a few days prior; she had come to my daughter's school to watch one of her performances. We took some photos afterward. I hugged and kissed my mom goodbye, and then I never saw her again after that.

I'll never forget that phone call I received, the call informed me that my mother had put one self-inflicted bullet through her head. I was frozen. The thoughts running through my mind consisted of how to remain calm because my daughter was with me. I thought, "How am I going to tell my kids about this? Does my brother know? What do I do? Can she come back from this?"

I left the store and was on my way to pick up my son from work. I couldn't cry. I couldn't scream. I couldn't go to her. My aunt assured me that they had already called 911. I knew there was no way for me to get there before the ambulance took her.

I drove straight home and told the kids I would be right back. I then drove back to the parking lot at the entrance to my neighborhood. I stopped there to get all of my thoughts together and catch my breath before returning home to tell my kids what had happened. I didn't want them to find out any other way, so I needed to tell them before heading to the hospital to check on my mom.

I needed to go home and prepare my family for what might be the hardest thing we have ever gone through together. My mother was their grandmamma, and they loved her very much. I waited for my other son to arrive. I called to tell my brother what had happened. He has always been my other constant.

Police and ambulance arrived on the scene. They took Mom up the hill from where she lived so a helicopter could life-flight her to the trauma unit at a hospital in Nashville. When we arrived at the hospital, we were taken into a room to discuss her condition with the doctor. We were informed that there was very little brain activity. We had some decisions to make.

We made the decision to remove the machines so she could fight on her own if she wanted to. I wanted to tell her goodbye. I just couldn't bring myself to go in to see my mom like that. That remains one of my most solid decisions, yet one of my greatest regrets. I didn't want that memory of my mom to be my last. I miss her so much and if I could have just held her hand, told her I loved her just one last time, kissed her forehead or painted her toenails for her, I would have. Her fight ended the next morning. Mom was pronounced dead on March 30, 2017.

The family was given the option to donate her organs. We didn't have a chance to decide that though; Mom did it for us. My mother had already signed the back of her driver's license to be an organ donor.

Everything seemed to be moving fast, but I wasn't ready to let go. I stayed at the hospital until every organ that could be donated was. There were happy stories during our grief and pain and for that I am thankful. One day I would like to meet her donor recipients. I know my mom would be proud of the lives she saved.

Those days, weeks, months and the entire year following my mother's death have been difficult. While the rest of the world had to move on, I didn't want to.

My daughter's sixteenth birthday was the day before the memorial service. Mother's Day and my brother's birthday were also right around the corner. So were my 40th birthday and what would have been my mom's 63rd birthday. My mother also shared her birthday with her youngest granddaughter.

I took time off work on my mom's birthday so we could spend the day remembering her. Just nine months after her passing, my mom's sister lost her son. He was diagnosed with stage-4 cancer, and in less than two months, he too was gone. We went to be by his side, so when Mom's birthday came around we were with him. There were moments during his passing that I will never forget, one being when he sang happy birthday to his Aunt Debbie. It was on the morning of her birthday, which also turned out to be the morning of his passing.

In 2008 my mom's other sister lost her son. It took me nine years to accept that his death was also a suicide. It took the suicide of my own mother.

The hardest thing for me to process as a daughter, as a mother, and as a sister, was her choice to leave. My mom was the only one of her siblings who hadn't lost a child, yet she chose to leave her children. I don't blame my mom for that.

I did seek counseling after my mom passed and I do appreciate how it helped me work through some things. I think most people have experienced some anxiety at least at some point in their lives. What I experienced after my mom passed was beyond your typical anxiety though. I was having panic attacks. I had never experienced those before.

I could usually get through them and calm down pretty quickly, until one day I couldn't. I pulled into the parking lot at my counselor's office. I shut my car off and started to get out. When I looked up toward the front of my car, I saw a helicopter that had just landed on a helipad. It was picking up a patient waiting to be life-flighted to a hospital. I was so close to that helicopter that I could see the patient on the gurney as the first responders were taking them to the helicopter. The panic attack started; I could not catch my breath.

I didn't understand it, but I could see my mom in that same situation. The pain and grief of not being there with her when she was put on the helicopter came crashing down on me. I managed to make it to my counselor's office. When I did, I lost all control. I was having a full-blown panic attack. My counselor managed to walk me through it. I was so thankful to be in the right place and at the right time.

A few days after Mom's passing, my brother, stepfather and I all went to a nearby park to discuss arrangements and details for the memorial services. As we wrapped up and I got into my car to leave, I couldn't go. At this point, I hadn't been able to look at any pictures of Mom or listen to the voicemails from her that were still on my phone.

As I sat there, I opened the pictures of her that I had saved on my phone. I listened to the voicemails that Mom had left me. It was hard. I cried. I cried out to God, and I asked Him why.

It wasn't the first time I had prayed that prayer, but this time was different. There was a field in front of me. I felt like I needed to walk across that field, but I looked down and realized I was wearing flip-flops; this was not going to be a comfortable walk.

In seeking answers, I went anyway. I got to the other side of the field, walked down a small roadway, and I saw water. There was a river. I sat down beside the river and looked across to the other side. I noticed a silo. I didn't know why, but this silo was comforting. I carried that comfort back to my car with me and drove it home.

As I pulled into my neighborhood, I saw it. I live in a neighborhood on a fairly busy street in a fast-growing town. My neighborhood is in the middle of two other neighborhoods. In the center at the entrance to my neighborhood, next to the parking lot where I had met my brother that day, there is a silo. It is an unusual place for a silo but when the builders built the neighborhood they left it and built the pool and neighborhood around it.

We had just moved into a new neighborhood a couple of weeks before my mom took her life. My mom had helped me pack up the old house to move. I was excited to be living close to where she lived and worked. I looked forward to spending more time with her. Mom was going to come over to help me unpack, put the house together, and arrange furniture and pictures.

Since we moved so much while I was growing up, this was exciting to me. It was what my mom and I always did together. We lived in nine different states, and I went to fifteen different schools all in an eleven-year period. We were experienced movers.

For multiple reasons, my mom was cremated. We didn't have anywhere to go to sit or to set up flowers like we would have had if Mom had been buried in a cemetery.

As I mourned, I would often go up to the end of the road I live on and walk up a hill overlooking the city. In this quiet place, I would seek answers, healing, and guidance. I would talk to my mom. I kept a notebook with me so that I could write down things I was feeling or things I wanted to say to her, like, "I'm sorry. Forgive me. I forgive you" or just to tell her, "I love you." At the base of that hill, there, too, is a silo.

I drove home after having dinner with my brother one night. I probably should have pulled the car over since I couldn't see the road through my anger, pain or tears. I screamed at God and reminded Him that it just wasn't fair. This was tough. I felt so alone.

When I drove home another night, through the side-view mirror of my car, I saw a silo. I began to feel like I was never alone.

After the day at the park when I first noticed the silo, I did what every human does when they need information, I googled it. Of course, I already knew what a silo was used for, but I thought there was probably more to a silo than just to store grain. One of the definitions of the word silo was: to isolate from others. As I continued to study the word silo, I found multiple translations. One translation from Hebrew is Shiyloh, (she-lo') also known as Shiloh.

This caught my attention because in one of the photos in the slideshow of my mom and my aunt during her memorial service, my aunt was wearing a t-shirt that had the word Shiloh on her front pocket. We had two separate memorial services for my mom, one at a local church and a second on the property where my mom had lived. On the day of the second memorial, I walked over to pet the horses in her backyard and it came to me again. One of those horses was named Shiloh. That was it. I then began to study the word Shiloh.

Since I believed God was answering my prayer, I looked up Shiloh in the Bible. Shiloh is a place in the Bible where the Ark of the Covenant was kept.

In the Ark of the Covenant was the presence of God. Genesis 49:10 says, "The scepter shall not depart from Judah, nor a lawgiver from between his feet, until Shiloh comes, and unto him shall the gathering of the people be."

That was the answer to my prayer. The difference between the presence of God and the manifestation of the presence of God is our acknowledgment of it. Silo can represent isolation or the presence of God. We have the choice of which to seek.

According to those present at the time my mother took her life, she got up from where she was sitting on her back porch. She walked through to the other side of the house past family sitting on the front porch and her sisters who were painting in the hallway. She walked into her sister's bedroom and shut the door. The next thing they all heard was a loud noise. This noise turned out to be a gunshot. Isolation brings death and destruction, but relationships bring life and abundance.

My mom was so good with people and they absolutely loved her. She did, however, tend to isolate herself at times, even from those closest to her. Mom really was such a beautiful person. If I could go back and do one thing it would be to tell her how beautiful she was. The love and excitement in the sound of her voice when she would see someone she loved walking into a room was contagious. Mom's smile could light up the dark and I miss that smile.

On June 25, 2017, I was standing in church and I had an "Aha" moment. My pain didn't go away, but I realized that even with all my pain, I was still standing and I was praising. It wasn't because I was happy or that I was content without Mom; it was because I had comfort. Mom is gone and will never be forgotten, but in the meantime, God is always with me. He is my Comforter.

About the Author
Dee Bradford lives in Spring Hill, Tennessee. She is the daughter of Debbie Martinie Hardin. She is married with three biological children, four stepchildren, and one grandchild. She now has a new constant in her life. That constant is grief, but she also has hope.

Kevin Alexis Hiciano

4 July 1994 - 20 June 2017
New York

Kevin Alexis Hiciano
by Vince Milack (Partner)

I first met Kevin on September 18, 2011. He came into a store I managed in Manhattan, New York, looking for a job. He was persistent in coming back and asking, so I hired him. I trained him to become an efficient worker; he then moved up to a corporate store. Having a relationship with him was the furthest thing from my mind, but he made it known he was interested. He was very persistent in making it happen.

Kevin was born on July 4, 1994, in Santo Domingo, Dominican Republic. He described Santo Domingo as Heaven. It was so beautiful, he said. He loved swimming in the ocean, catching fish, and running up and down hills with friends. He was the oldest of three siblings.

Kevin lived in Santo Domingo with his mother until his pre-teens. He then came to America to live with his father and grandmother in Washington Heights, Manhattan. Kevin stated that coming to America was very scary but exciting. He believed that being educated in America was a privilege that he was happy to have. In school, he studied photography and learned how to skateboard professionally. Kevin was a very quiet but playful child. His cousins said that Kevin was the one to decide what and how to play; he was always right and in charge.

Kevin had several passions. He was never without a skateboard. One could always find him in Canal Street Skatepark, New York; Washington Square Park, New York; or just bumping to local hills around his hometown at One hundred Sixty-Eighth, New York, near Presbyterian Hospital. He was quite the professional.

Kevin's other passion was cooking; he loved to eat. He and I would have cook-offs in my kitchen. He was very neat and articulate when making a dish. He used onions and cilantro in everything; his cooking was an art. We liked to walk around New York City and on Riverside Drive in Manhattan. Kevin often joked and laughed. We liked to dine out in many restaurants.

Kevin and I had a lot of fun together. My life felt so complete with him in it. He was very thankful to me for everything I did for him. Our relationship lasted seven years. He got a kick out of people when they asked me, "How old is your son?" There was an age gap between us. Never in my life had anyone ever chased me the way he did or become so persistent about being with me.

Kevin was an old soul in a young body. He was very strong-minded and determined in anything he did. He knew exactly what he wanted in his life. Several influences in his life weren't healthy for him, yet he believed he had to listen to these influences. This caused him to become very confused and depressed. He made bad choices, but knowing what he wanted, he would snap out of it and do what he wanted anyway.

Kevin sought approval and love from some of these people who influenced him, and he took rejection and fighting with them to heart. As time went on, I noticed certain confusion and crying outbursts; I would just sit by him and assure him all was going to be okay and remind him that I was always there for him. His depression grew as time went on.

I remember Kevin telling me twice that he wanted to die. Something was telling him that he had no self-worth. I talked him out of it, telling him how it would kill me if that happened and that it would really hurt his family. When he had the reassurance of love, he would seem okay.

In the early morning hours of June 20, 2017, I was told that he texted his cousin in Santo Domingo, stating there would be no more pain, rejection, or fighting. He asked his cousin to please take care of his mother. It was the last time anyone ever heard from him.

Kevin's lifeless body was found three days later in a boiler room in the apartment building where he lived with his family in Washington Heights, New York. Kevin died on my birthday, June 20, 2017. He left this earth on the anniversary of the day I was born. I will forever blame myself for not being there to stop him. I know I could have.

About the Author
Vinny Milack, Kevin's friend, partner, and soulmate, lives in Long Island, New York.

Carter Michael Howard

16 June 1996 - 9 February 2018
Iowa

Carter Michael Howard
by Karlee Howard (Mother)

On June 16, 1996, my first born baby boy, Carter Michael Howard, was born. It was Father's Day. How could there ever be a better Father's Day gift than that, right? He brought in a crowd; he was the firstborn grandbaby on both sides of the family. What an amazing gift from God that he chose us to be Carter's parents.

Carter was a good baby and was very smiley. He had beautiful big blue eyes that sparkled. When he started getting a personality with the dramatic facial expressions that he started to show, we knew he was going to be full of energy and passion. When he started to crawl and then walk, he was a busy boy. He was such a curious little guy that we always had to keep an eye on him.

Carter loved the outdoors the minute he was old enough to express his wants. Cold, hot, rain, blizzard, it didn't matter; if he could be outside, then he was.

In the summertime, he would sit in his Grandma Howard's garden and eat the vegetables right out of it. He loved going through that garden.

Carter started fishing at a young age with his dad, catching many of his own fish before he was even three years old. He went fishing with his grandma Pam often; he would tell her, "Grandma, you don't know how to set your hook right," so he showed her how to set it.

She said it almost always worked for her. He fished with his grandpa Howard occasionally, as well. Carter would pretend to fish in the puddles; if that's the only "fishing" he could do that day, then a mud puddle would have to do.

He tagged along with his dad to hunt, as well. Carter developed a passion for hunting at a young age that you don't see in many. He learned to blow a duck call very young, as well, and he was extremely good at it, better than some adults.

When he was young, his grandpa Dave, a runner, had Carter signed up in some youth runs. He did very well in them, so that made his grandpa proud.

We had a lot of fun with Carter. He had a great imagination, so there was never a dull moment in our house. He had all sorts of activities and ideas planned for us at all times. I also loved the down times, in the mornings and late evenings, as he would always crawl up next to me to cuddle. Carter liked to stay busy, so as long as we gave him something to do, he was a pretty easy young boy to entertain.

Carter loved to swim; he started private swimming lessons at age two. I wanted him to be comfortable in the water, and I wanted him safe, as curious as he was. The sooner he learned to swim the better. He loved to be in the water, and he loved to go out on the boat with his dad. The first time he rode a jet-ski, he was nothing but smiles. He was a daredevil; not much scared him.

He always loved the fourth of July; it was his favorite holiday. From about the age of three, he would enter different contests at the Independence Day celebration. He always got a bag full of candy at the parade and something to eat at the food stands. He enjoyed watching the fireworks lying flat on his back on a blanket so he could look straight up to the sky.

I remember Carter even comforting his little brother, Trace, as I covered ears during the fireworks because he was scared. He got up, hugged Trace, patted him on his back, gave him a kiss on the forehead, and then lay back down to watch the fireworks show.

One day at age four, just after he had started pre-school, Carter had a baseball-sized lump bulging from his abdomen. We rushed him to the emergency room. The doctors said that he had a blockage in his urethra, so he spent several days in the hospital as they slowly drained his bladder with a catheter. He then had surgery to remove the blockage.

After the initial arrival at the hospital when the pain subsided, he was a good little patient. The hospital staff seemed to enjoy him and always gave him extra tender loving care.

Carter recovered from his kidney problem with most of his symptoms subsiding. Due to the amount of urine that had backed up into his kidneys, he had some kidney damage that had to be watched since one kidney was worse than the other. He just had to see a urologist occasionally for a checkup.

Carter had a rebellious personality as a young boy and would sometimes get himself into mischief. At one point, he saw a pediatric psychiatrist and was diagnosed with an oppositional defiant disorder. They gave us tools on how to deal with him, because we did not want to medicate him at such a young age. Sometimes, we chalked his behavior up to just being an ornery boy, however.

For a while, Carter did seem to respond well to the tools we used from the doctor. He attended Morning Sun Elementary School in the town we live in. He usually did well throughout grade school academically, but his teachers reported that he had issues with attention and sitting still a bit more than the average kid.

Carter was diagnosed with Attention Deficit Hyperactivity Disorder (ADHD), but again, we chose not to medicate yet. We continued to use different tools given to us by the doctors with the agreement that if his grades started slipping, then we would try medication.

Many of the teachers at parent-teacher conferences would have a funny story or two to tell us about something he had done. Some teachers told us that though he was a handful, they enjoyed him very much and definitely would not forget him.

Carter played little league baseball, and then he joined a travel team from out of town that went to state championships and won second place. He was a valuable player on that team. He played flag football and soccer in grade school, as well. He was talented at everything he did.

When Carter was in the sixth grade, we started to see changes in him again. The rebellious behavior intensified; he was even more defiant and hyperactive. He seemed to always get into some sort of bad situation. This is the age where the real struggles of his life began. Academically, he was slipping.

We then decided to try medication for ADHD, but Carter hated it. He said it slowed him down to where he even believed his motor skills were slower. Sometime, we would find his pill in his pocket that he had claimed he had taken.

I then started handing Carter's pill directly to him and watching him take it. Sometimes he must have hidden the pill in his mouth, claiming to have swallowed it. We knew when he hadn't taken the pill because he couldn't concentrate or sit still, and he would almost always get into some kind of trouble that day. Sometimes he'd admit to spitting out the pill.

Carter's poor choices continued. Though I was defensive at the time, I know the teacher was truly trying; they all were. He was desperate to be accepted so that was when he would make these poor choices. Then, he'd tend to panic because he felt that some looked down on him.

It got to the point that I knew Carter had a definite problem that he couldn't control. You see, this boy's heart was bigger than ever. I knew that my troubled son's sensitive side was sincere and strong with so much remorse for his actions.

Carter had mourned over other people's pain and problems since he was a young child. It consumed him so much that he forgot about himself and appeared to express his troubles with mischief.

He did have a lot of fun times in elementary school. To this day, his classmates have many stories to tell about Carter along with stories of him always protecting someone in the class. He was a protector at heart from as far back as I can remember; that never changed.

After Carter completed the sixth grade in Morning Sun, he went to a nearby town to the Wapello Community High school. He seemed to really like it there; he had many friends in Wapello even before he started school there.

At age thirteen, the doctor said "I don't diagnose or treat bipolar until about age sixteen, but I do strongly believe that's where this is heading."

I began to educate myself on bipolar disorder in the meantime. Carter continued to see his psychiatrist who was treating him for ADHD every couple of months. He was doing decent academically, especially when he complied with taking his medication.

He played baseball and basketball through junior high. Then his grades started showing some trouble again when he entered high school.

Finally, right before he turned 16 years old, Carter was diagnosed and treated for bipolar disorder. During his freshman and sophomore years, he played basketball, but suddenly, he lost confidence in himself. He also seemed to lack commitment to what was required to play, so he didn't continue playing on the team.

Carter, again, was on and off his medication. We could tell that he wasn't taking his pills. He didn't play baseball his freshman or sophomore years. During his junior year, he took better care of himself as far as his bipolar was concerned, at least for a while anyway. He participated in events with his classmates; he went to prom and other school functions

Carter then returned to play baseball his junior and senior years of high school and he loved it. He received an honorable mention in baseball in his senior year. He golfed all through high school and was pretty darn good at it, too; he was their top golfer on the team his senior year. Over his high school golf career, Carter received a conference award and an honorable mention.

During his senior year, he was able to play baseball and golf with his younger brother, Trace. Carter stated that it was the best time he had ever had getting to play sports with his younger brother.

Carter had been struggling more in high school with his grades, though he was capable of getting good ones. He was smart, but he tended to come across as someone who just didn't care. Much of the time, he struggled to concentrate.

Surprisingly, this loud, outgoing boy couldn't get up in class to give a speech anymore; he'd avoid it at all costs, even if it meant getting an incomplete or almost failing the class. Carter's teachers worked with him to write out his speeches online or they gave him additional assignments so he would at least pass his classes.

The high school principal and staff were very willing to work with Carter. They tried to accommodate some of his struggles to get him through so he wouldn't give up at school, even though he was absent a lot.

During the Christmas holidays of his senior year, his Grandma Howard took the entire family to Mexico. Carter stated that he had the time of his life, and it was clear that he did. It was great to see him happy. He always had said he wanted to go back to Mexico.

Carter went through a relationship struggle, mostly due to his behavior and his wrong actions. He never told us that he was suicidal, but police officers showed up at our house telling us that they had been called because he had threatened suicide. We made him see his doctor for an emergency visit.

He continued to struggle with his bipolar disorder the rest of his way through his senior year, but as far as we know, he didn't threaten suicide again.

In May of 2015, Carter graduated from high school. What a great day it was. I could tell that he was proud of himself, so that made us happy. We were proud of him.

Our son talked about going to college. Then, he decided that he wanted to go to school to be a lineman. As the time grew closer, he was less able to get himself to go. He had a hard time committing to things like school and work.

Since I had educated myself on bipolar disorder, much of his behavior didn't appear to be a surprise anymore. I was a defensive mother over Carter all of his life, but I was much more so as I learned about his illness and as he talked to me about how he was feeling.

Even when I knew Carter wrong, because I understood the struggles that others didn't, I defended him. We didn't talk about it to everyone because Carter was ashamed of it. He didn't want to be looked down upon for being different.

He didn't even attend local ball games after graduation because of the insecurity and shame for some of the things he'd done. He believed that everyone there would look down on him. He went to a few games after he graduated, and that was it.

We encouraged Carter to go to the ball games. Even if there were a few people who judged him, we encouraged him to just try to stand tall and do this for himself. We told him to not let it destroy him inside.

Usually, to me, Carter would show remorse and the desperate side, but to his friends, he would show the more wild and daring side in the way he expressed his problems. His friends say that he continued to be there for them no matter what he struggled with.

Carter moved out of our home for a while to live in the same place where some of his friends were attending college. Then he returned back home in the spring of 2016. In May of 2016, Carter got drunk. While he was drunk, he rolled our truck. He was charged with operating a vehicle while intoxicated. His blood alcohol level was three times the legal limit.

He broke his foot in the accident. His friends, who were in the vehicle with him, were okay except for a few minor cuts and bruises. Carter felt really bad about the accident. He said he wouldn't have forgiven himself if something worse had happened to any of them.

After the accident, he went to jail and had to complete a weekend substance abuse course. He also had to pay fines and lost his license. Later, he was arrested again for driving without a license just a few days after it had been revoked.

Carter's manias came out in all sorts of behaviors: paranoia, euphoria, hyperactivity, rebellion, lying, illegal, reckless, and impulsive types of behaviors. He would do wrong things that would betray someone, and many times it was to the people he cared for the most.

Then he'd be in distress, not knowing why or how he could do that to someone he loved. He'd say to me, "I don't know why I am like I am. I don't know why I do the things I do. I don't want to hurt anyone, Mom. I don't want to lose my friends, but it's like I'm not me when it happens."

Carter physically fought others a lot. Sometimes it was over protecting someone, fighting for what was right or defending the underdog, but other times, he fought simply to fight for the thrill of it. Fighting appeared, at times, to be like a drug for him.

When Carter was in a low, it was like crashing off a mountain for him. The smallest thing would fuel the decline or just simply his illness. With no reasoning behind the emotional downslide, it would just happen. Life events that are hard for people were devastating for him. He didn't handle difficult situations well.

When it came to hard times for others, he was almost always there. He occasionally reached out to his best friends when going through common rough patches in life, and they were there for him, but when it came to the issues of battling bipolar illness, that's when he hid it from them.

One of Carter's friends told me that if they were having a bad day, he would be there for them changed their moods in five minutes; then it was time to have fun. His friend said that he hardly ever talked about his own problems; he just always made sure we were okay.

Carter had many friends that stuck by him through it all. They may have gotten frustrated or they may not have understood him, or they may have even felt betrayed by him, but many never left him. Carter's bipolar put strains on many of his relationships with others many times through his lifetime, such as family, friends, and girlfriends, but his shame in it kept others from understanding him

One day, Carter said "Mom, you have to stop defending me and getting into my business. I'm an adult now and I'll have to deal with it myself."

I started to back off and just told him I was always there for him. Many times, Carter didn't follow the doctor's orders he was given, so he was accountable for his actions just as anyone else.

Carter couldn't hold a job. He would give it all he had for the first few weeks, but then it would start to dwindle. He couldn't function long enough to do the work. He went through a period of time where he started lying to everyone about working or lying about the reasons he was not working.

Carter loved hunting and fishing. He liked being outside. He once told me that hunting was also like therapy to him. Hunting was something he was confident and pretty good at. He would hunt every day for several consecutive days. He really got into catfishing the last few years of his life.

When Carter went on and off his medication, it had terrible effects on his moods. He drank alcohol a lot. Sometimes, the drinking would intensify, and other times he seemed to control it okay. He was never supposed to drink excessively due to his kidneys, but that never stopped him.

At the end of the summer of 2017, Carter felt ill all the time. After several tests, doctors told him that he was getting over pancreatitis. Luckily, it didn't get really severe, but it took a long time for his symptoms to subside, especially since he didn't follow the diet and instructions he was given.

Carter's behavior was very unpredictable so it put a major strain on his relationships with other people. He told me that his behavior had gotten to where he couldn't control it, and he expressed remorse.

Since Carter was an adult at this time, I reminded him what he needed to tell his doctor and to get to his appointments. He actually appeared to be more comfortable when I took him to see the doctor.

In November of 2017, Carter overdosed on his bipolar medication. He stayed in intensive care at the hospital for the night, but then he was released.

Carter wasn't admitted into a hospital or held for evaluation. They just sent him home to call his own psychiatrist to set up an appointment. He continued to worsen with his unpredictable behavior.

We planned another family trip to Mexico for December of 2017. Carter backed out of it. The entire family wanted him to go and everyone missed having him there. When we spoke to him over the phone every day while we were gone, he seemed to be doing okay.

One day I missed his call, so I called him back. He was sobbing; he sounded overwhelmed and expressed regret for not going with us. I begged him to cheer up and stop being so hard on himself. My dad went over to check on him.

Carter had a few parties at our house while we were gone, but he promised that we'd come home to our house all in one piece. Fortunately, our house was fine when we returned home on Christmas Eve, except that our lilac bush was missing. We all got a laugh out of that.

We had Christmas dinner as usual with his grandparents. He left early that day saying he didn't feel well, but otherwise, he seemed okay.

A few weeks later, Carter made a bad decision one day, a decision that he immediately regretted. He said, "I didn't mean any harm in it, I didn't even think about it being a big deal and didn't mean to scare anyone, but yes it was a bad choice."

Police were called. The officers did a wellness check on him. Carter asked the officers to take him to the emergency room; he even asked to be handcuffed because he was suicidal. The officer took him to the emergency room and had a long talk with him on the way there. He really wanted to help Carter. Later, Carter told me how much he appreciated that talk with the police officer.

After Carter's death. That officer told us, "I really was hoping we could help him that day", but he was released from the emergency room just hours later, once again not being admitted for psychiatric care and released with the diagnosis of "acute reaction to stress and hyperthyroid."

Even after Carter had overdosed a few months prior, there was still no admission into the psychiatric unit. He would want help one minute and then try to back out of it the next.

The hyperthyroid diagnosis explained his weight loss and some behaviors, along with having bipolar disease. I made an appointment for Carter to see his psychiatrist as soon as possible after that. He was put on new medication.

He also saw a local physician for his thyroid. She got the appointments set up for him but later told us he didn't show up for any of them. He suddenly seemed rational and passive, which was not his normal, so I thought maybe these new psych medications were finally working.

Fifteen days after Carter started his new medication, he took his own life. It was the calm before the storm.

Like the verse in Elton John's Candle in the Wind, "Seems to me you lived your life like a candle in the wind, never knowing who to cling to when the rain set in." That candle flickered, almost burning out several times, and then it would brighten back up again. The candle went out the night he took his own life.

Through the struggle, we all have many great memories of Carter, and we miss him so much. He has a village of friends that have kept his memory alive. His friends, family and our community celebrated his first heavenly birthday together. They raised enough to cover all expenses, plus scholarships.

About the Author
Karlee Howard is Carter's mother. She lives in Morning Sun, Iowa with her husband. She and her husband want to be advocates to share information about Carter's struggle with bipolar disorder in hopes it will encourage others to have no shame in it and always take care of themselves.

Matthew Tyler Hudson

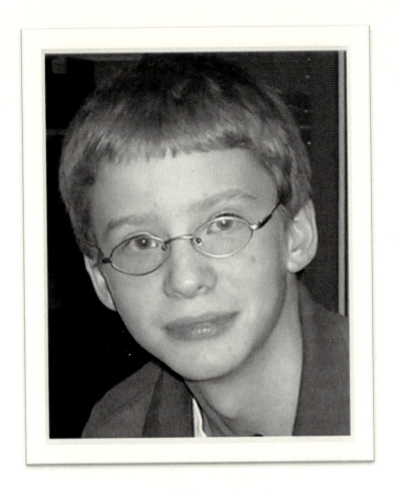

22 January 1990 - 29 March 2008
Oklahoma

Matthew Tyler Hudson
by Robin Hudson LeBlanc (Mother)

On January 22, 1990, my husband and I drove to the birthing center in preparation for Matthew Tyler Hudson's arrival. Tyler was born in Anaheim, California, across the street from Disneyland. It was amazing to see and hear the fireworks before his birth. He was born with great characteristics that allowed him to be a great actor. I can remember after he was born and everyone had left, I lay awake all night just watching him breathe. I was in such awe of his beautiful face that I didn't want to miss a second.

Tyler first moved to Texas when he was just a year old. We lived in Carrollton, Texas. We moved to Webster, Texas, for six months when he was three. We then moved back to Carrollton. Right before Tyler started kindergarten, we moved to Tulsa, Oklahoma in 1995.

When Tyler was little, he loved costumes and would sometimes pretend to throw himself down the stairs. He would watch movies over and over until he knew every word, so he could reenact the parts. He was the littlest kid at school, but he didn't let that hold him down.

Tyler would stand up against anyone who was mean to other people. He was always kind. We would get comments from his teachers on his report cards like, "I wish I had more students like Tyler in my class."

On stage is where Tyler had his biggest achievements. He was the lead actor in the play Pinocchio, and he played various roles in The Christmas Carol. He was written up in the paper for his acting abilities. In middle school, he challenged other middle school kids to "pay it forward" and write letters to the troops. As a result, several radio stations across the nation called him to help with his challenge.

Then the attack on the World Trade Center and the Pentagon happened on September 11, 2001, and Tyler's world changed. It was as if the light inside him weakened. That's when he realized that the world could be mean and cruel. He began to believe that one person couldn't make a difference. I wish he would have seen the strength within himself that everyone else saw; what a difference he could have made.

As Tyler began to spiral down and get depressed, he also began to slowly isolate himself. He was no longer the happy-go-lucky kid that he was when he was younger. He was now hurting deep inside. It was as if he took on the weight of the world all by himself.

Tyler missed many days of school due to medical appointments and counseling. He needed only English and one other credit to graduate, so he took the needed classes in the summer. He was bored at school, so he did his work online. That allowed him to do his work faster, and it enabled him to graduate a year early. (It was a decision that was easy for him because it was getting harder for him to be around crowds of people.)

Tyler graduated from Memorial High School in Tulsa, Oklahoma. He was proud of graduating early. His dad and I were proud of him too because he had struggled so hard through his depression.

When he was in high school, Tyler ran on the cross country track team. I think he could run and get some of his frustrations out. He once told me that the best thing for him was being outside. He said somehow that seemed to heal him just a little.

He was fortunate enough to have been able to climb to a top of a mountain, Hermit's Peak, at Las Vegas, New Mexico. He fed deer from his hand on a deserted island, Out Island Adventure Seabase at Key West, Florida. He also got to kayak at the island.

These adventures were with Boy Scouts. I went with him to climb the mountain and took him to the island. He and I also went parasailing in Florida. These are special memories. Tyler and I drove back from going to pilot season in California. That's when he would do his commercials and modeling.

We stopped at the Ice Cave, where they were tagging hummingbirds for the Federal Department of the Interior, Fish and Wildlife Service. Joan Day Martin, one of only sixty people in the world authorized to tag hummingbirds was there. She allowed Tyler to hold one of the hummingbirds while she tagged it.

Tyler loved the outdoors and all animals. He traveled from one coast to the other, and he loved to be at the beach. He loved Huntington Beach, Newport Beach, and Balboa Beach in California. He loved Key West and Naples in Florida and Galveston in Texas. Our last trip was to Myrtle Beach, South Carolina.

Tyler first went to the West Coast in 2000; we went to California two years in a row for pilot season. It was always just Tyler and me. In 2004, we drove to Key West, Florida, for Sea Base with the Boy Scouts.

On March 28, 2008, Tyler had a single car accident; he hit a pole head-on. I almost believe that it was a suicide attempt, but I don't know for sure because I can't ask him. No one was hurt. He walked away from the accident and left the car. The car was towed, and we were not notified. I wanted him to know that wrecking his car was not the end of the world; things would be taken care of as he was getting back on track.

Tyler took his life the next day. As he talked on the phone to someone, he became upset. He was in the backyard at the time, pacing. He seemed angry and left the yard through the gate.

I called out to him. He replied, "People are mean. I'm sorry, I love you."

I thought at that point that he didn't have a car, he had no money with him, and he had nothing that could hurt him. But I didn't know that he had a gun.

Tyler had an appointment set up to see a doctor on Monday; he needed to get back on his medications. Tragically, he didn't make it through the weekend. I think that's one thing that makes it so hard. There are so many whys, ifs, should haves, could haves, and whats.

At 9:30 that night, I was on the computer when the doorbell rang. Tyler's dog, Booker, was going crazy barking. I went to the door and held Booker back when I opened the door, even though inside, I knew. I put the dog up before I let the police officers in.

There were four officers. When I opened the door, I said, "He's dead, isn't he?"

They asked me who I was. This made me mad because they had come to my house and had rung my doorbell, yet they want to know who I was. They asked me how I knew, and I fell to the floor.

I told them that he had attempted suicide five times previously. I asked where he was. They told me that I probably needed to call someone since I was home alone. I asked how, and they told me with a gun.

I told them that Tyler didn't have a gun or own a gun. I asked when, and they said they didn't know when. They said he buttoned up his coat with his arm out of the sleeve to hold the gun in place so it wouldn't move. It still seems like a dream, like it can't be real, but we know it is.

I never thought it would be me who would have to go through something like this. However, suicide doesn't discriminate based on who you are, how much you have, or anything else. It just kills. Depression is real and it hurts.

If our hearts or kidneys are malfunctioning, we take medications. It seems to me, however, that as soon as someone says something about depression or some other mental health issue, no one wants to hear it. If one's brain doesn't work right, the rest of the body cannot work right. If a person needs to take a prescription for the mind to be balanced, then the whole body will be balanced. Wow, what a concept.

At Tyler's memorial, there was standing room only. I couldn't believe how many people were there. We played all his favorite music; probably things that had never been heard in a church before. One song we sang was "You Are My Sunshine."

At the end of the service, we released four hundred rainbow balloons in his honor. It was gray and misting outside, but it was if Tyler pulled the clouds apart and reached down and grabbed the balloons that day. The sun shone just for those few minutes.

Tyler was a beacon of light in this world; without him here, my ship can no longer find the harbor. It is lost at sea without Tyler's light. He will always be my sonshine.

My heart is truly broken and is beyond repair. There is no pain that will ever be greater than this for me. There's nothing in this world now that could hurt me anymore. My life felt like it stopped the day Tyler died, and some days it still feels like the world continues to go on without me.

About the Author
Robin Hudson LeBlanc is Tyler's mother. She lives in Tulsa, Oklahoma. Since Tyler's death, she has remarried and has adopted a beautiful daughter. She also raises butterflies. She takes time to watch the sunset, which Tyler loved, and the clouds, looking for shapes like she and Tyler did together when he was little. She also watches for rainbows to feel a little closer to him.

Dewey Vantroy Johnson

29 May 1938 - 2 November 2016
Tennessee

Dewey Vantroy Johnson
by Nancy McVicker Johnson (Wife)

Little did I realize that Sunday morning, so long ago, that the most handsome man wearing the Air Force uniform would make such a lasting impact on my life. Just before the service began, I, a naïve sixteen-year-old girl, was sitting quietly when this handsome man came in and sat in front of me. My heart flipped. I knew who he was because his family were members of our church.

But alas! He had a girl with him. Never did I imagine he would even notice me; I still do not know if he noticed me that day. Months went by and I thought about him no more as I went on with my life as a sixteen-year-old girl does.

Later that year, early in winter, he showed up after discharge from the Air Force. Then my story really began. He started to search me out and talk with me, which totally amazed me. After a little while of talking at church, he asked me out. Of course, I had to have permission from my parents, who consented.

Our first date was a normal small-town date, and we got to know each other a little more. As I learned more about him, I realized that he was a very deep thinker who searchingly analyzed everything.

Before long, he discovered I was only sixteen. He was twenty-three. It was a while before I heard back from him, and I was beginning to think all was lost. Then, one day he called me. As it turns out, he thought I was older when he asked me out, and he had thought to himself, "What am I doing robbing the cradle?"

Apparently, I had made a deep impression on him, and he couldn't forget about me. He even had gone to my dad's place of work to ask permission to continue to date me. Though I had thought all was lost, we dated regularly. As months progressed, I turned seventeen.

As time moved on, I realized that he had a deep-seated anger and hurt from his childhood. I also learned that he had a strong perception of how he thought life should be and how he wanted it to be. Even though it disturbed me, I continued to date him and began to love him more and more. It was apparent he felt the same about me.

In late summer I had the misfortune of a visit from the mumps. He had already had the mumps, so he visited me while I was sick. One afternoon, he began to speak about marriage. I couldn't believe it. I still had my senior year of high school to finish, and at that time you had to have parental consent to marry before eighteen. I also knew that my dad would not consent if I didn't finish high school. It was also required to turn in a notice to the school that you would be married in order to continue classes at school.

As it turned out, my Dad would not sign the consent, but my mom did it for us; she had to answer to my dad for that. We decided to marry at his classmate's home. This classmate was a pastor of a church. This was February 1, 1963. I finished school, graduating in June of 1963. Our first year of marriage was really a tough one. No way were we in the "honeymoon" stage.

We were from totally different backgrounds. I was family oriented, and he was family "alienated." I was just a backward, young, inexperienced girl, so he became my teacher and leader. His ideas were so different, and the ongoing inner problem was always evident.

In fact, before our wedding, I was afraid I couldn't handle the differences in thinking and the way he thought about things, so I called off the wedding. However, I couldn't let him go, so I sought him out, and the wedding was back on.

We were blessed with two beautiful daughters and a son that God wanted to bless us with; we had planned to stop at two children. During the years of child-rearing, there were many times of turmoil between Dewey and me, though we did love each other deeply. There were times I didn't know if we would make our marriage last.

As he struggled with unforgiveness and hurt festering inside, he developed a perceived "breathing" problem. He underwent all kinds of testing all through the years, even as recently as 2015 and 2016, but nothing could be found physically. Doctors at times suggested a mental problem, but Dewey would never acknowledge the possibility. I knew that he definitely had a mental issue, and the children now agree with me.

As the years progressed, he gradually got worse. The perceived breathing problem became an excuse, a crutch to withdraw from us. He became eccentric, and at times, he tried to force his thinking and beliefs on others. At the same time, he turned more and more to God's word, becoming almost obsessed with Heaven.

Because of the years I had spent with him, neither I nor the children thought a lot about what he was doing and saying. He established rules and boundaries due to his breathing problem, and I had to live by them. I thought by doing so, I was helping him and honoring his request to be able to breathe. I wanted to do whatever was needed to help him get well.

After retirement, he progressed toward almost total isolation. The children and I were obviously concerned but didn't know anything else to do. We continued to pray and honor his requests.

On November 2, 2016, I left the house at 7:30 a.m. He knew I would be gone all day and what time I should be back. I got home about thirty minutes later than I had thought, and I found him lying on the floor with a gunshot wound.

As is common to those who experience the suicide of a loved one, I was in complete shock, and I could not fathom what he had done. Never in a million years would I have guessed he would do such a thing. He left notes, and as we look back, we can see a pattern of probable planning. As I write this in June 2018, the unbelief is still so strong.

What would convince a Godly man who loved his children more than life itself to go this route? What would cause him to be so miserable that he would be convinced this was the thing to do?

Of course, there is no way for us to know. One thing I do know, however, because of his ability to deeply think things through; he thought this was the best thing to do. Some suggest he may have done it because he loved us and wanted to spare us more heartache. There are many possible reasons, but to heal, we must let go of those questions.

Dewey had a loving heart and concern for all he met. If someone needed help, he would do all he could to meet that need. Never was there any reluctance to provide for his family, even when it meant doing something he absolutely hated to even think about doing, such as selling sewing machines.

He was not a person with an outgoing personality; this was extremely hard, and he probably lost sales because he wouldn't force anything on anyone. Dewey worked hard and always went the extra mile to do a good job. The same principles he applied at work he applied with any project at home.

There was never a question about whether Dewey Johnson would do a great job. He was extremely creative. In his mind, there was always a way to get something done. We still come across some of his "inventions" unexpectedly, and this always brings a smile.

Will I ever completely accept the reality that he is no longer here with me? Will I get past how he left me? I don't know. I do know that with my Lord's help, I am moving forward, but always with my "forever love" in my heart. I am and will be eternally grateful God brought Dewey Johnson into my life for fifty-four years.

My heart knew a love that I don't expect to ever know again. There was never any doubt in my mind that God placed us together. A love that deep only comes once in a lifetime. My one comfort is knowing that the "love of my life" is no longer in that deep, dark place he was in, but in Heaven; he is healthy and whole and knows a love that cannot be described with words.

About the Author

Nancy McVicker Johnson lives in Tennessee; she was Dewey's wife. She helps care for her one-hundred-year-old dad. She is active in several organizations and stays busy with household chores. She attends church in Murfreesboro, Tennessee. Her oldest daughter lives in Fort Worth, Texas. Her youngest daughter, grandson and granddaughter live in Bowling Green, Kentucky. Her oldest grandson lives in New Orleans, Louisiana. Her son, daughter-in-law and grandson live in Athens, Alabama.

John Trenton Kirby

9 February 1999 - 18 January 2016
Nebraska

John Trenton Kirby
by Sherri Kirby (Mother)

John was born on February 9, 1999. I had to be induced. Let me just say that he always ran on his own schedule, even prior to birth. Several years later when signs of Attention Deficit Disorder (without hyperactivity) became apparent, I teased John that he always needed to be nudged to get things done—including being born.

John was always so laid back. He didn't seem to worry or feel anxious about anything. As one friend said, John seemed to "put a lot of oil on his back in the morning," meaning that things just seemed to slide off of him; he never seemed to let anything bother him. I talked to him about this several times, wondering how he was able to be so relaxed. He told me that he didn't see any point in worrying about things that you have no control over.

When John was in fifth grade, he was able to start playing in the elementary band. We were fortunate to have a band director who was remarkably talented and did a wonderful job of passing on her passion for music to her students.

John latched onto that passion for music and put his heart and soul into adding the trumpet to his musical repertoire. Just like playing the piano, he caught on quickly. He played the trumpet in the band until shortly before he died, halfway through his junior year of high school.

John lived up to his initials (JK or just kidding in texting language). He loved to make other people laugh. He was described by other parents as the "heart of the student section" at games. He'd make sure the others were cheering their classmates on. John once told me that if it weren't for him, there wouldn't be a student section. I believe that to be true.

At the start of every fourth quarter of a football game, he'd stand in front of the fans and holler at the top of his lungs like a carnival barker. "Ladies and gentlemen, are you ready for some fourth-quarter Eagle football?"

His classmates loved John, and so did the other parents. They looked forward to seeing what he would come up with next. One time at a basketball game during a timeout, he performed a series of cartwheels from one end of the gym to the other. I smiled at the other moms and said, "Yes, that's my son." Even the opposing team's fans enjoyed his antics.

John was a talented musician; he was mostly self-taught on the piano. He was around nine years old when he started playing the piano. He didn't want to take formal lessons, so I took out the piano books that his older brother and sister, Phillip and Abby, had used and started teaching him to play.

Apparently, I wasn't taking him through the book fast enough, because John worked ahead on his own. He soon told me he needed the next set of books.

When he was thirteen years old, John decided he wanted to learn to play Canon in D by Johann Pachebel. I had the sheet music, so I took it out for him to practice. Not only did he learn to play the song, but he memorized it.

When John was in eighth grade, the music director asked if anyone wanted to play the pre-service music at our church's Christmas program. John volunteered; Canon in D is what he played.

He was the last out of maybe four or five other students playing a song. The others were mostly beginners playing a short song from their level one or two piano books. When his turn came, John sat down at the piano, no music in front of him, and he started playing. People still tell me they remember John playing that song and how impressed they were, not just with his talent, but that he had the song memorized.

I recorded a video of his performance at both dress rehearsal and the night of the program. I put the video on Facebook after the program. Every year it comes up on my memories for that day, so every year, I share it. I cry and I smile at the same time at this bittersweet memory.

Another activity John loved was playing basketball. Starting in fifth grade, he played on our school's elementary team. He played basketball until two weeks before he died when he suffered a concussion.

This was his third concussion in just over a year's time. It was also his most severe concussion. John loved sports, but I would have to say that sports didn't love him. His junior high English teacher and I used to tell him that God was telling him he should stick with music.

One thought that came to my mind in the days following John's death was that he was probably sick and tired of being sick and tired. I must have taken him to the doctor more often than his four siblings combined.

In seventh grade, John fractured his wrist while he was riding a bicycle. The brakes were faulty, so he literally ran into the corner of a brick wall. Ironically there's a small chip in the corner of one of the bricks. He told me that he put that chip in the brick. I have a picture of him standing next to the wall with his blue cast.

When John was in eighth grade, he fractured his hand playing football at school during Physical Education class. During his freshman year of high school, he decided to play football. He never made it on the field for a game.

It seemed there was always an injury. First, He was injured while he was lifting weights. Next, he sprained his ankle. Then, he had another weight-lifting injury, this time to his shoulder which later required surgery. Then before we could schedule the surgery, he fractured his ankle playing basketball. After his ankle healed he finally had surgery on his shoulder.

In John's sophomore year, he had two concussions, one during a basketball game and the second while hanging out with friends. Neither concussion seemed to cause him much difficulty.

In his junior year on January 4th, John suffered his third and final concussion. This was more severe than the others. In addition to headaches, he experienced some memory loss. He didn't even realize that he'd hit his head until a couple friends told him at school the next day. He thought he just had a migraine. Because we didn't realize that he had a concussion until almost 24 hours after it happened, there was no immediate medical attention. He just needed to take time for his brain to heal.

My husband Dan and I asked John every day how he was feeling, if he still had headaches, and if the headaches were less severe. He always said he was feeling better. He did say he still had headaches, but that they weren't as severe as they had been.

Just three days before our son died, he told me that the athletic trainer had administered the concussion test again. John had passed the agility portion but had failed the cognitive portion of the test. His brain still needed more time to heal.

Since this was on Friday, I planned to call the doctor on Monday to have John checked out again. He also told me that he was going to ask the C Team coach if, in the fall, he could help with their basketball practices rather than playing basketball.

January 18, 2016, started like any other day. I got out of bed, get the two younger children, Tucker and Sherridan, up for school, and made breakfast and lunches for the kids to take to school. My oldest son Phillip was awake and in the kitchen waiting for John when I got up.

Phillip said that the night before, John had asked him about going to school a little early so he could finish a Spanish assignment. He had left his book in his locker. Phillip was getting impatient because he hadn't seen John yet nor heard the shower running. He wasn't in his room, either.

When I went to the laundry room where we kept the snacks for the school lunches, I noticed that the light was on in the basement. My hands were full so I returned to the kitchen and asked Phillip about the basement light.

Phillip was certain that he and John had turned the lights off the night before, but he headed to the basement to turn the lights off downstairs anyway.

Phillip wasn't gone long when I heard him call out for me. In an extremely panicked voice, he yelled for me to come downstairs. I met him on the steps and asked what was wrong.

He insisted that I come downstairs; he even took my arm and led me downstairs with him. As we stood at the bottom of the stairs, he told me to look where he pointed to in the next room, the furnace room. The light was on.

Even though I had never been aware of any suicidal thoughts in John, I remember wondering if I was going to see him hanging. Instead, what I saw was John lying on the floor by the furnace. In the poor lighting, it looked as if he were sleeping. I couldn't figure out why he'd be there. Then I saw the rifle next to him.

I called my husband Dan. Phillip and I went back upstairs. Dan went downstairs and told us to call 911. Phillip told the two younger children to go upstairs to his room to protect them from knowing what was going on. The children went upstairs without questioning why.

I said to Phillip, "He wouldn't do that."

I barely remember calling 911, but waiting for the ambulance to come was unbearable. Now, we live in a small town with a volunteer fire department. Everyone knows everyone, yet the rescue team went to the wrong door. I had to go outside to show them which door to use to enter the house, and then, I lead them to the basement to where my son was lying.

Then I went back upstairs to sit with Phillip praying that they could do something, hoping that this was all a nightmare and I would wake up at any moment. I wanted it to be a terrible but fixable accident. I wondered if this could just be one more injury to add to John's long list of other injuries. At the same time, I knew. I knew my son was gone.

We decided that the younger children should go to school since they didn't realize what had happened to John. This gave them one more normal day and gave us time to make arrangements and plan how to tell them.

Thank God for a small town. I didn't have to tell anyone which church or pastor to call. Ginger, Mike, Tim and Jeff, all members of our church and of the volunteer fire and rescue department, were among the first to arrive.

Ginger called the church office to let the pastor know to come see us. Then, she called the high school to tell them that the boys wouldn't be at school that day. Jeff and Tim gave us hugs before they left. Mike offered for he and his wife to pick up our oldest daughter, Abby, from Lincoln where she went to college. Everything was falling into place. The funeral home was called.

I went to John's room to search for a note or anything to give us some clue as to why he would do this to himself, to his family, to his friends. Phillip joined me. He had already looked and hadn't found anything. I looked for clothes. I knew I'd need to take something to the funeral home for John to wear. I grabbed some clothes from the floor and took them downstairs to wash them.

When the two officers from the sheriff's department came, we discovered that there was a note lying on the floor next to John. He wrote the note to the students and staff of his school. He told them he was sorry. He told them to not keep things bottled up like he did because it isn't healthy. He encouraged them to find someone to talk to. He finished his note by saying not to forget that he loved them all.

One of the officers commented that on his way to our house, he had heard on the radio that it was Blue Monday, the third Monday of January, the most depressing day of the year. The officer took the note with him and went to the high school to let school authorities know what happened.

Pastor Schmidt came over to visit and pray and offer words of comfort. He assured us that God doesn't punish someone for taking his own life. John was God's child on earth, and now he is God's child with him in heaven. Before the pastor left he offered to go to the elementary school to inform the staff there of what was going on.

Now it was up to us to call our family and tell them that our precious John was gone. We cleaned the house, we cried, we screamed.

The next several days went by in a fog. I'm sometimes surprised by the things I remember and then by the things that others tell me that I don't remember.

We have many precious memories of my son, but now, I'll share just one more memory.

John always dressed up on the third Tuesday of the month for no other reason than that it was the third Tuesday of the month. He'd send out a message on Twitter a few days before to remind everyone to dress up with him. Usually, they all forgot.

John had just sent out the reminder on Saturday or Sunday about the third Tuesday dress-up day. Unfortunately, he wasn't here to see that third Tuesday of January. The students from the public high school in our town all dressed up. The students from the Catholic school in Norfolk all dressed up. The students at the Lutheran school in Norfolk (his school) all dressed up - in honor of his memory.

I want to end this story by saying that even though my son isn't with us here on earth anymore, he's in our hearts. I told his classmates prior to their graduation that he'll always remain in our hearts.

We need only to keep his memory alive. I believe that God gave us John for a reason. I don't know what that reason is and may never know. Even in his short life of almost seventeen years, John made an impact on those around him. I'm always finding out things about how he made a difference in someone's life. I believe that everyone who knew him will never forget the difference he made in our part of the world.

About the Author
Sherri Kirby lives in Battle Creek, Nebraska with her husband, Dan. She is the mother of John Kirby and also of Tucker, Sherridan, and Phillip who attends college in Lincoln, Nebraska, and Abby. She enjoys quilting and spending time with her other children. Much time is spent going to Tucker's games and practices and to Sherridan's dance lessons and competitions. Dan works on his motorcycles for a hobby and recently had an adventure riding his motorcycle from Nebraska to Alaska and back home. He was gone for five weeks on the open road.

Ryland Joseph Louis Kresse

10 November 1994 - 26 May 2018
California

Ryland Joseph Louis Kresse
by Teri Rose (Mother)

Ryland was a wonderful, cheerful, loving, and compassionate boy and adult. He always tuned into the feelings and thoughts of others. These traits were to remain with him throughout his life in good times and bad.

Although I knew of the deep pain within Ryland and that the drugs he took helped him to escape that pain, I never could have imagined he would choose to end his life and leave the people he loved. I now realize that perhaps he stayed much longer than he wanted because it was so hard to leave the people he loved.

Ryland was born on November 10, 1994. His father and I were thrilled to be present at his birth. Both he and his sister were adopted. From the moment Ryland was born, he seemed unhappy to be part of this world. He began his life crying and seemingly angry. He seemed so angry that I asked a nurse if a baby could be born angry. Little did I know that day would begin a 23-year journey of trying to comfort Ryland, help him find peace, and help him to live in this world he seemed to never want to join.

Ryland's first year was one of discomfort with continuing agitation and angst. He was so uncomfortable and agitated that he landed in the hospital at six weeks old because they could not identify the source of his discomfort.

Ryland had extreme neuro-irritability. Even though the screaming, the nurses and staff were charmed by Ryland because even in his discomfort, he was a sweet and loving baby.

Upon returning home and on all subsequent and frequent doctor's visits, I was encouraged to try and help Ryland self-soothe, as babies who don't learn to do this are unable to later on, which often leads to things like addiction.

In looking over the journal I kept during his first year, there are many entries that show the frustration I had trying to comfort and get Ryland to self-soothe. Each page was also laced with how sweet a soul he was.

Thankfully, several angels who remained in Ryland's life until the end helped me get through those years. Beth, Maureen, and Mona, all dear friends, loved him and took turns caring for him when I couldn't. They helped us both throughout Ryland's lifetime.

He always seemed to have an angel on his shoulder whether one of those lovely people or others in the form of friends and teachers. People fell in love with Ryland despite him trying to keep people out. He had a quick wit and a lovely smile that charmed the pants off people and endeared him to them.

Ryland started preschool at two and a half years old and made fast friends of the teacher and students. He was a favorite for playdates. During this period, we took him to a behavioral pediatrician. At preschool, he developed a love of drawing. During Ryland's childhood, after bedtime stories, we would talk about big subjects for such a little boy.

Ryland was an old soul from the beginning. We talked a lot about God and what happens after you die. Bedtime was a time we discussed very heavy subjects for such a small child. We often talked about God and what happens when you die. Ryland told me many times over the years that he did not think he would live to be old. This always struck me as quite odd because it's not something children often discuss.

From a very early age, Ryland displayed a compassion for others. If a friend or even an adult were hurting, Ryland wanted to help ease the pain. In retrospect, he always lived with pain inside his head. That pain turned him into a loving and empathetic soul.

Ryland's learning issues began to surface in elementary school. Although he tried many different sports, he was not a fan. In later years, Ryland played rugby and loved it. He also became a skilled diver while living in Samoa. I tried desperately to find something Ryland could feel successful doing.

The thing Ryland truly excelled at was making friends. He was beloved by his classmates and friends. He began having solid school issues in the fourth grade, so I ramped up the tutoring schedule. The professional tutors loved Ryland so much that they cut their fees in half. Ryland also saw different therapists because I thought that he needed to talk to someone other than me.

I knew it was hard for Ryland to see that the other kids were doing well while he was struggling. He was fortunate to have several classmates who helped him with his work and rallied to keep him on track and in school.

By the sixth grade, Ryland was introduced to marijuana by friends who were a few years older. He later said that he liked pot because "It makes me feel relaxed, helps me sleep, and puts my mind at rest."

I continued my quest to help him. I always thought the next therapist or tutor could help him. One day Ryland asked why I was always trying to fix him. I told him I was trying to help make his life easier. Ryland's response was that nothing could do that.

Generosity began for Ryland at an early age. He saved his money, so when we would see someone asking for money, he would give his money to them because he said they needed it more than he did. Ryland was particularly taken by homeless vets. He couldn't understand how we, as a country, could not provide for those who served us.

It was Ryland's dream to one day go into the military. He was proud of the fact that he was born on the birthday of the Marines. As Ryland got older, our discourse increased. I was frustrated with the drug use and the seemingly lackadaisical attitude. Ryland was frustrated with school and life. It was around this time that his creative life flourished.

Ryland began doing graffiti on buildings - which I explained was not okay. He saw a blank building as his canvas. We had a very unusual bond that was created in the car. We spent a lot of time going to therapy, tutoring, and other classes so we really got to know one another in the car. It was our sacred time with no fighting or arguing.

One of Ryland's biggest disappointments came when he didn't get into the Catholic high school with his friends. He had been in Catholic elementary school his entire life.

At age fifteen, Ryland's pot usage increased. He was failing in school and very depressed. Ryland said he had lost hope for his life ever being better. His father and I sent him to a wilderness program for ten weeks. We thought if he got away and got outdoors, he could find himself.

Ryland was always a spiritual kid and had a deep relationship with God, often enhanced by the marijuana. Ryland's therapist in the wilderness program said he needed a therapeutic boarding school. We let Ryland choose his school, so he chose a school in Samoa for an adventure.

Even though Ryland complained about being away in Samoa, when I visited him ten months into the program, he was happier than I had ever seen him. He loved diving. He did a lot of volunteer work, and he played rugby. Of course, Ryland made lots of new friends, including some of the villagers.

Ryland still struggled with school, but I was more interested in him learning to be happy and finding things to do that he loved. He was a student of the world and could tell you everything about Samoa's history and culture. I wish he could have stayed there.

A few days shy of his 18th birthday, Ryland returned home. We had three good days, but then the drugs started again. It took Ryland eight years from start to finish to earn his high school diploma, but he did it with a lot of help from some wonderful teachers.

Ryland still struggled with the demons in his brain. He got heavier into drugs, but those angel teachers did everything possible to help him. He could be awful, but they liked him so much that they continued to work with him. We all wanted him to succeed.

As the drug use escalated, his father and I knew that we had to get Ryland into rehab again. We sent him to a wonderful friend in Georgia who runs a drug rehab program. Ryland did well. Unfortunately, after he returned home, he relapsed immediately.

Ryland began a four-month journey of living on the streets. One of the lowest points of my life came when I saw Ryland panhandling. He was ashamed and embarrassed, but he kept his quick wit about him. Ryland told me to leave as I was ruining his business. Then he said, "I love you."

August of 2017, Ryland knew he needed rehab again so he went back to Georgia. In Georgia, he had friends who cared about him and a girlfriend who shared his struggles and love. Ryland flourished this time and was the happiest to date.

At the end of January 2018, Ryland again relapsed. This time Ryland overdosed as he had a serious addiction to heroine. He landed in the hospital. He said it was an accident, but he would not go back to rehab. He was again on and off the street.

As Ryland's drug use increased, so did his paranoia and hallucinations. He said people were after him trying to hurt him. Our friend in Georgia tried to help, but Ryland wouldn't let him. Ryland lived his last days in a shack being tortured by his mind and those around him who were also serious drug users.

His father and I were working with someone Ryland had met who was trying to make sure he ate and was safe. We were taken for a ride.

The day before he died, Ryland called me and was so happy. He was out for a run; he said it was a beautiful day. He was excited to start a new job. I felt hopeful for the first time in months. Our call was breaking up, so he told me he would call me that night. Ryland told me how much he loved me and how grateful he was to have me in his life because I never gave up and always stood by him.

Ryland never called again, but the next morning his father received a text saying Ryland was happy and having a great day.

Two hours later the phone rang with the news that Ryland had hanged himself in the shack. He had been talking with others earlier and appeared to be happy. The others went back to the shack two hours later and found Ryland: he was dead.

I had always prepared myself for the fact that Ryland might overdose. He was a serious heroin addict. Nothing could have ever prepared me for this, though. My heart stopped and broke on that day. The light had left the world.

I returned to Georgia to see where my son had been living and to try to retrace his steps and get some answers. I was able to meet some great friends Ryland had lived with earlier in the year; they warmed my heart with their generosity of spirit and stories. They helped me to see a side of Ryland I didn't know.

His girlfriend told me that Ryland wanted to die. She said that his suicide was his decision and he was solid on it. She said that Ryland couldn't take the pain of his mind any longer. The depression, homelessness, and drugs were too much. Ryland said he was done.

He told her he had a happy life more than one could expect. Ryland loved and was loved. She said that Ryland could do rehab again, but he could not do the recovery again. I did gain some understanding while I there. As a mother, I understood his pain. I am forever grateful I was able to see him one last time.

I was so troubled that he died hanging in a shack. He deserved a better life. The shack was situated in the woods; my friend pointed out the beautiful trees and the birds singing. This is what Ryland saw as he left this world.

Ryland looked at peace. For that, I am also grateful. Ryland struggled with depression and anxiety his entire life, and with addiction for eleven years. His mental health issues, addiction, and suicide will never define him. Ryland was so much more than that.

My sweet loving boy was just too sensitive for this world. Ryland was a loving, funny, caring, creative soul. This world was too much for him. He simply no longer had the resiliency needed to cope with his life. I am so grateful to have been Ryland's mom and to have had the time with him. I am also profoundly grateful to all those who loved and helped him in his short time here.

About the Author
Teri Rose is Ryland's mother. She lives in Alameda, California where she works in palliative care. She likes to walk, garden and read. She is fortunate to be surrounded by many loving people who are helping ease her pain. She will love and miss him all of her days.

Ethan T. Meetz

29 April 1990 - 16 April 2008
Wisconsin

Ethan T. Meetz
by Colleen Olsen (Mother)

Ethan, my first-born son, was a delightful, helpful and happy child who enjoyed helping others. Ethan was a talented musician who played in a band with some of his high school friends. He was a self-taught drummer, guitarist and bassist. I always found that amazing since neither his dad nor I had any musical inclination; I can't even read music. He aspired to attend a local technical college for music production.

Ethan was born on April 29, 1990. I remember that we had a snowstorm on Mothers' Day that year. Coincidentally, this year on the ten-year anniversary of his death, we also had a snowstorm.

When I was a young teenage girl, I did not particularly want to have children, though I can't remember why. However, the day Ethan was born was one of my best days. He was a beautiful boy who brought joy to my heart. Being a young first-time mom was the most rewarding and exhausting time in my life, as it is for many women.

However, Ethan was a delightful, happy baby who seemed to alleviate some of the exhaustion. I lovingly called him "my guinea pig" (not to his face, of course, just in discussing with others), as he was my experimental child.

I learned to be a mom by experiencing all the firsts (good and bad) with Ethan. I feel sad that I have missed out on many firsts because of his death at seventeen. I did not get to see my first child graduate or become an adult.

When I was pregnant with Ethan, "Thirtysomething" was a popular television show that had a character named Ethan; I fell in love with the name. Ethan was an extremely sensitive child who showed others much compassion. He always looking out for others, especially those with disabilities or other difficulties.

When Ethan was three, I got sick with stomach flu. I also had another child, Jared, eighteen months old, to care for. I was separated from my ex-husband and living with my parents. Unfortunately, my parents also caught the flu. Ethan was doing his best to help all of us with whatever we needed. I had to call a friend to come over to help take care of us; Ethan became her personal assistant. I loved him with all my heart; his generosity and kindness were infectious.

Somewhere in Ethan's late teen years, his personality changed; he became sad and difficult to deal with. Finally, near the end of 2007, he was diagnosed with bipolar disease. This was after his second suicide attempt. I remained optimistic about his treatment and was supportive of him during his many counseling appointments.

The last time I spoke with Ethan was the night before his death. I was doing dishes in the kitchen when he came home from a friend's house. He came into the kitchen, talked to me for a few minutes, gave me a hug, kissed me, and went off to bed.

Unfortunately, Ethan succumbed to what he called "demons taking over his mind and soul" on April 16, 2008, when he hung himself in our garage. Ethan was not a fan of medications and didn't put them to use effectively in his life. The day Ethan took his life was a Wednesday afternoon; he had come home for lunch from school and was alone at home.

When he did not return to school after a while (unusual because he did not like to miss school), his brother and girlfriend became suspicious. I received a call from school. By that time my other son and his girlfriend had already taken it upon themselves to search for him. Sadly, they were the ones to find him. Our garage door had been jammed somehow, and they heard our phone ringing in the garage. (This was me, calling constantly).

Shortly after Ethan was found, I got home to find police officers in my driveway. They explained the situation to me and asked me to identify my sweet boy, Ethan. This was one of the most difficult things I had ever done. It was hours before the crime scene was cleared and his body removed because of waiting for a coroner.

By that time word had spread through our little town, and family and friends had arrived to support us. The scene in front of our house was one filled with at least fifty of his friends waiting to hear the horrific news.

I took such comfort in seeing them all there; some of his friends are still there for me. Ethan was a senior in high school and a member of the choir. At his funeral, the whole choir sang; this still gives me chills. I remember looking at each and every one of the kids' faces so I could remember them.

Here is my Facebook post which I shared on April 15, just before his tenth-year death anniversary:

Ethan; 04/29/1990 – 04/16/2008. Don't stop believing. So, tomorrow marks the 10 year death anniversary of my boy . . . WOW. Completely unbelievably hard to believe sometimes but unfortunately a reality. Sometimes I struggle to come up with the right words to express my feelings, know how I want to say it but it does not come out right. What I've learned is there is no right or wrong to express feelings and grief truly sucks at times."

Thankfully, I have made it out the other end of that horrific pain as unscathed as humanly possible. It's been said that time heals all wounds; I can attest that is true to a certain extent. I have found through each passing year the grief and loss get easier to handle. I'm not sure if that means time is healing the wound. The hole in my heart has become smaller each year, but the loss of a loved one changes us forever in some way.

My suggestion is do whatever it takes to help you heal and be able to move on. Of course, do so with no harm to yourself or others. I am a firm believer in feeling the pain in order to work through it, even though it is sometimes unbearable. I used to feel guilty laughing after Ethan died as if in some way I was having fun and shouldn't be. Now, my life is filled with laughter again.

I have had many wonderful things happen in my life over the past ten years. Today I will do my very best to honor Ethan's life by remembering wonderful memories of him. If you have a loving memory you would like to share, it would be wonderful to hear. I wear his memory as a badge of honor in my life.

E (our nickname for Ethan) was a true light in my life. I am trying keep the light bright by making choices that honor his life and memory. I feel so proud he called me "Mom," and I was so lucky to have had him on earth with me for seventeen years. Ethan was a funny, loving person, a talented musician and a perfect mess living in an imperfect world. He will remain in my heart forever.

Thank you to all my families' and friends' constant support and love. I am forever grateful for every one of you and appreciate all that you have done for me. You have been on this journey with me all along. Those of you who've endured your own personal struggles along the way have given me the inspiration I needed, and I am in awe of your courage and strength.

I wish my path in life had lead me somewhere else, but unfortunately this is what I have been dealt. I have chosen to rise above and heal myself, keeping him forever in my heart and mind, while choosing to help others.

About the Author
Colleen Olsen is Ethan's mother. She lives in Mayville, Wisconsin. She is married with two grown boys and four step-children. She is currently enrolled in the Master Counseling Program at Concordia University. She enjoys fishing, camping, wine tasting, going to rummage sales, and spending time with family and friends.

Lisa Elaine Mewbourne

23 September 1965 - 23 April 1991
Georgia

Lisa Elaine Mewbourne
by Faye Mewbourne Martin (Mother)

Lisa was born on September 23, 1965. It was a pleasant fall day in Decatur, Georgia, a suburb of Atlanta. When I felt those all too familiar labor pains, my husband and I packed up a few things and drove off to Emory University Hospital. Having had two other children, I was well acquainted with the routine.

This delivery, however, would be special in that my new baby would be born where I grew up. My first two babies were born in Riverside, California, and Plattsburgh, New York. My husband had been an officer in the Air Force and his assignments took us to these and other places. Finally, it was exciting that I would have a baby with relatives and friends nearby.

Lisa's birth was an easy one with no complications. When they brought her to me, I felt the love for her well up in my heart. She was so pretty. She was smaller than my other two babies and had rosy picture-perfect skin. Her features were so delicate that she looked like a little china doll. She nuzzled into my neck with little mewing sounds and was already looking for her dinner.

My mother hadn't been able to be with me when my other babies were born, so she relished the fact that she now could be with her only daughter as I gave birth. My mom's bright smile was the first thing I saw when I awoke.

Her whole countenance conveyed her pride in me and in her new grandbaby. She asked if I had decided on a name and I told her I hadn't. She suggested the name Lisa and I agreed. Before I signed her birth certificate, I had a middle name selected. This child was Lisa Elaine Mewbourne.

Her brother and sister, David and Denise, thought she was their very own baby, so they wanted to take turns holding her. They dressed her like she was a little doll but made a fast retreat when it was dirty diaper time. Sibling rivalry didn't come until much later.

Thankfully, Lisa was a good baby who cried very little and slept through the night in just a few short months. She was a happy baby who laughed all the time. Her stunningly blue eyes reflected her laughter. Not even the blue of the sky could compete with the blue of my beautiful baby's eyes.

She was an early achiever, crawling at five months and walking at nine. And, oh my goodness, she was into everything. One time she sneakily grabbed her sister's toy and ran with it as fast as her little legs could carry her. She crawled under the kitchen table and sat holding the toy and peering out at her wailing sister.

Around age four, a fuzzy white stuffed lamb entered Lisa's life. She loved that lamb passionately, so they became best friends. She carried her lamb everywhere and snuggled close to it at night. She called it her Widdle Wamb. The lamb and a soft pink blanket were all she needed for bedtime security. She carried that lamb until it was worn smooth with love like the Velveteen Rabbit. It earned her the family nickname Little Lamb, a nickname that she carried for the rest of her life.

At age five, Lisa started kindergarten at a nearby church. She loved the music and art and especially loved her teacher. She mastered her ABC's before the year was out and was doing well with her numbers. She was developing quite a sociable personality and seemed to really enjoy making friends at school. Even so, she was still shy and always wanted to cling to me.

Elementary school got off to a bad start. All of my children attended the same elementary school. The other two had been blessed with great teachers. But, sensitive little Lisa was not so lucky. Her first-grade teacher was a loud, angry, authoritarian woman who yelled at and criticized the little ones in her class. Usually a happy child, Lisa began crying when it was time to go to school. She would beg me not to make her go.

Determined to find out what was going on, I got permission to sit in on one of her classes. I was shocked when I heard the way the teacher talked to the children. Even with me present, her treatment of them was harsh and demanding. If someone couldn't answer a question, she ridiculed them in front of the whole class.

One little boy cried, so I got up and went to comfort him regardless of what that teacher thought. I realized that this was the kind of treatment my child had been receiving.

Lisa was visibly shaken by that incident. When the class was over, I picked her up in my arms and went straight to the principal's office. I asked the principal to give Lisa a different teacher and take her out of that class. She agreed and made the change the next day.

Unfortunately, by this time the year was half over and damage had been done to Lisa's once keen desire to learn. Her reticence led to a diagnosis the next school year of learning disabilities. I was puzzled because her kindergarten teacher had said she was gifted, but this teacher believed she had a learning disability.

For her second year, I drove Lisa to another school that had special classes. She did well in those classes. In third grade, Tucker Elementary began their own special classes in Specific Learning Disabilities so she returned to her previous school. Her teacher there was incredible.

I volunteered to help in the classroom where I saw first-hand how Lisa blossomed under this teacher's tutelage. Lisa began to love school again and was excited about learning. This teacher discovered that Lisa was slightly dyslexic. With her wonderful teacher's unrelenting help, Lisa fought it and quickly mastered the correct way of spelling words. Dyslexia had been her learning problem from the beginning even though no diagnosis had been made.

At the end of that year, the teacher and I threw a party. We had cake and ice cream and all the things kids love. Each child could select a gift from a box of reward items that we kept in the classroom. I watched as Lisa went to the box to select her gift.

She pulled out a pretty necklace but instead of putting it on, she walked up to me and handed the necklace to me. "This is for you, Mama," she said. She didn't want anything for herself, just for me. I accepted it with tears in my eyes. I loved this precious child so much. I still wear that necklace today.

Lisa's vivacious personality skyrocketed at Tucker High School. She made cheerleader and spent her days learning new cheers and hanging out with her cheerleading buddies. Our house rang with laughter as they practiced their jumps and cheers. Lisa was never happier than she was then.

We went to all the ball games where she cheered; I loved watching her. Her enthusiasm and cheerfulness were things of beauty. If I went up to the fence, she would run to me and share something she thought was funny or give me a big hug. She was never embarrassed to show affection for her mom.

It came as a surprise to me that Lisa was very athletic. I definitely hadn't been, but her father played high school football and was captain of his gymnastics team at Georgia Tech.

We lived in a great neighborhood in Tucker. It boasted a nice neighborhood swimming pool and tennis courts. During the summer, Lisa spent every day at the pool. She became a proficient swimmer and brought home lots of blue ribbons from swim meets.

She took gymnastics and track in school and excelled at both. Many early mornings would find Lisa running through the neighborhood. I attended some of her competition events and cheered her on. Quite often she won a first or second place ribbon. I was proud of her for this and for so many other reasons.

She made friends up and down the streets of our neighborhood when she ran. One neighbor was a well-known runner; he encouraged her every time he saw her. Lisa was thrilled when he made a special trip to China to run the Great China Wall. It was in the news and she kept a newspaper clipping showing him on top of the Wall. When he returned he brought a Chinese coin and gave it to her. She was thrilled. She kept this coin in a small wooden box with a few other treasures.

Unfortunately, my husband and I divorced when our kids were still young teenagers. My life became much harder, so I had to ask the children to help around the house. Lisa and Denise tackled housecleaning and cooking with gusto, and David was handy with the lawnmower. I was grateful to have their help and hoped that I could maintain the kind of life they deserved.

At age 14, Lisa accepted Jesus as her Lord and Savior. It changed her. She had been visiting her father in Florida and attending a Christian youth conference. She watched as an ex-Vietnam soldier named Dave Roever told his story and gave his testimony of being burned beyond recognition when a phosphorous grenade exploded in his hand.

Dave described how his faith had pulled him through. His strength in the face of a disabling injury and his fervent belief in God spoke to Lisa in a powerful way. With tears running down her face, she accepted Christ that night. She wrote to tell me that she was going to be baptized while she was in Florida. She apologized for not waiting until she got home so I could be with her, but she said she needed to do it right then.

When Lisa returned home, she was a girl on fire for Jesus. She and I visited churches until we found one we wanted to join. It had lots of teens about her age that were actively involved in the church. Lisa jumped right in with these kids and I jumped in with her; all of us filled up the three front rows of the church every Sunday morning. To my delight, they called me Mama Faye.

Lisa had a new Bible. Every day, I would find her in her room deeply enthralled over some passage of scripture. She underlined any scripture that meant something to her. It seemed strange to me that she especially underlined many parts of Job. Did she have sorrows that I didn't know about? She eagerly learned passages of scripture and quoted them to me. I became more proud of her with each passing day. My most treasured possession is her Bible with all her marks in it.

One sunny day in 1980, I heard Lisa and her best friend, Pam, in our driveway. They were singing at the top of their lungs. I went out so I could see what all the merriment was. They were singing Lisa's favorite rock tune by Shaun Cassidy and dancing up a storm to his music. I can hear her singing this song today:

I met him on a Monday and my heart stood still
Da do ron-ron-ron, da do ron-ron
Somebody told me that his name was Bill
Da do ron-ron-ron, da do ron-ron

We had just come from church, so I teased her by saying, "Lisa, I didn't hear them play this song in church."

She gave me her brightest smile and kept on dancing. "Mom, don't you know that they will play all kinds of music in heaven." (Maybe she now dances to Da do run run in Heaven. I hope so.)

Lisa had always been sweet and loving towards me and now with her new-found faith, she became even more so. I was the broker and owner of Cornerstone Realty with more headaches than I could handle most days. Sometimes when I came home late at night, tired from doing paperwork or writing contracts, I would find a little note on my pillow. She wrote scripture verses on these notes to encourage me.

I will never forget a play Lisa was in. She was to play the part of a woman in the 1920's. I took her to The Junkman's Daughter, a vintage clothing store in Little Five Points where she found an appropriate dress that fit perfectly, a pair of frumpy shoes, and a pair of white gloves. The look was exactly what the script called for.

Lisa's role was that of a mother with four small children. She moved through the scenes easily and didn't miss a single line. At the end of the play, she was to stand all alone and sing a song that had been written to the tune of the song Amazing Grace. She wasn't a singer, so she was nervous about this.

However, when it came time for Lisa to stand up on that stage with the spotlight just on her, it was a magical moment. She sang the song with perfection and the curtains came down when she finished. There was loud applause that I knew was for my daughter. I had always known that Lisa was beautiful, but on that stage, she looked like a young Elizabeth Taylor.

Three years passed with Lisa loving Jesus more every day. Her older sister and brother, Denise and David, no longer lived at home so it was just Lisa and me now. She smiled at me once and said, "Mama, I always wondered what it would feel like to be an only child. Now I know and I really like it. I love being with you and being your only child."

Those years with Lisa were more precious than I could have ever thought possible. But, trouble hit and hit hard. She was by now a senior in high school. I noticed that Lisa was losing weight and having lapses in her energy level.

One evening we were at the home of a friend when she came to me very upset and said she needed to leave because she was sick. The next day, I obtained the name of a specialist. Lisa was diagnosed with Diabetes Mellitus, the worst type of the disease.

Her blood sugar was 550 and could have sent her immediately into a coma. The doctor phoned Emory Hospital and arranged for me to take Lisa there at once to be checked and admitted. He told us we were not to even go home to get clothes. I knew then how sick my baby was.

As I drove into the parking lot of Emory University Hospital, it hit me with deep sadness that this was where Lisa was born. Now, I was bringing her back in hopes of saving her life. She was only seventeen years old.

Lisa stayed in the hospital for seven days, and I stayed with her. They pulled a cot into her room for me to sleep on. I never left her side. They taught us both how to live with diabetes, to give insulin shots, to test blood sugar, and so much more that my head was spinning. Her diet had to change drastically.

She had always been an avid dessert lover. We baked cookies, cakes, and pies all the time. That was back when an ad spouted, "Nothing says lovin' like something from the oven."

Leaving off desserts was hard enough for Lisa, but keeping constant track of her blood sugar and having to take insulin shots every day was too much. One day, about six months into the disease, she became so ill that I had to take her to the emergency room. Her blood sugar had shot up to over 600.

With tears in her eyes, she confessed to the doctor and me that she hadn't been taking her insulin shots and that she had been eating desserts. It tore my heart out when she looked at me and said, "Mama, I just wanted to be like all the other kids."

My baby would have to live with this tragic disease for the rest of her life. But, Lisa persevered. While she was never a straight A student, she maintained a B average in her grades. Sometimes a grade of C got thrown in, mainly from her math subjects.

Her Scholastic Aptitude Test (SAT) scores were not high enough, so she didn't try to get into college. Those scores upset her, but she didn't let it get her down. She applied for a job at a bank where she was hired. She did well there and as always made a lot of friends.

At the end of a year, Lisa decided to change jobs and went to work for a company doing inside sales. She did so well that they promoted her to outside sales. She really blossomed in sales and soon had her own territory, making money for the company and herself.

Lisa wanted to go into straight commission sales where she could make some real money and asked if she could live with me while she got started. Of course, I said yes; she lived with me for about a year.

Lisa took a new highly coveted sales job for a computer supply company in the CNN building in downtown Atlanta. To coin a phrase, she hit the ground running. Her commissions were so good that she soon thought she could support herself. She moved into an apartment with a girlfriend. Once again, Lisa had proven herself. I don't think she ever failed at anything she tried to do.

She excelled at this new job signing up huge national accounts. Her territory was downtown Atlanta, and she came to love going down there.

One of her big national accounts was Home Depot. She became good friends with people there. They told her that if she could get her degree, they would hire her in their marketing department. Lisa promptly applied to Georgia State.

She also applied to Agnes Scott College in Avondale Estates. Always a class act, she even went so far as to take a woman from their admissions office to lunch. I teased her about using bribery; she smiled and said, "Whatever it takes, Mom, whatever it takes."

During this time, Lisa met and fell in love with a handsome blond-haired, blue-eyed young man. They met on Lake Lanier – Lisa on one boat and him on another. But their eyes caught as the boats passed, and it was an instant attraction. They managed to meet later that day and a romance began.

They later married and had a spectacular wedding. She and her new husband looked stunning together with their amazingly blue eyes. I remember thinking that I would have beautiful grandchildren.

Lisa's dress was white silk with a cathedral length veil. She looked like an angel. They held their reception at the Hyatt Regency Hotel in downtown Atlanta, also one of Lisa's top clients. The huge display of food was pure artistry as well as extremely delicious. The band was excellent and played her favorite dance music.

One precious memory I have is of her picking up a small child and dancing alone with him on the dance floor. Everyone watched the enchanting scene that unfolded before them. The girl knew how to make a statement.

She and her husband built a nice new house in Alpharetta. Lisa went overboard with decorating although her good taste might have exceeded her pocketbook because she ran up some bills that caused problems for her. The colors she used for decorating were purple and teal which went surprisingly well together. Once again, I was very proud of my daughter.

For Lisa's twenty-fifth birthday on September 23, 1990, I wanted to surprise her by personally delivering a flower arrangement to her office at CNN. I was amazed to see that she had recently been given the coveted corner office. She had earned that office by outselling even their older, more experienced salespeople. Her office had glass walls that looked out over the luxurious CNN lobby.

The little girl who used to say that she was a chip off the ol' block (meaning me) had outdone anything I had ever hoped for in my own career. That same day she made a statement that gave me high hopes for her future. She said, "I've got the world by the tail, Mom." And she did, too. Or so it seemed.

But, things somehow changed for Lisa. I don't know exactly how or when it began, but she started showing signs of despondency. Her pretty face, usually lit with a smile, reflected sadness rather than happiness. And feelings of anger began to surface.

Her marriage of three years was faltering; her husband had reluctantly moved out of the house. He still loved Lisa. She told me sadly that she didn't she believe she would ever have a successful relationship. I sensed that her depression went much deeper than this break up of her marriage. How much deeper I wouldn't know until a day of terrifying horror and anguish that would tumble me over the cliff of unending grief.

On April 23, 1991, I received a phone call at work from Lisa's father-in-law. He was so choked up that he could hardly speak. He told me to get to Lisa's house right away because she had been hurt. He instructed me not to drive. I called my son and told him to meet me at her house.

I got someone to drive me to Lisa's house. When we arrived, I thought my heart would stop beating. There were many police cars and ambulances and those awful yellow ribbons around her house. Uniformed people were swarming all over the yard.

I jumped out of the car and started running across her yard calling out her name. It was then that I saw her mother-in-law with a face red and swollen from crying. Her words will forever haunt me, "Faye, she didn't make it."

Didn't make it? What did that mean? Didn't make it?

I kept screaming Lisa's name and trying to run to her door when I felt strong arms holding me back. A paramedic was holding one arm and my son was holding the other. I screamed and fell to the ground. I came to with a shock as a paramedic held smelling salts to my nose.

I awoke from the faint sitting on the ground unable to get up and walk, still trying to comprehend what was happening. My son, who was also crying, sat with me. He said that Lisa's husband was at a neighbor's house down the street. I desperately wanted to see him so I got up and started running towards that house.

My son-in-law saw me coming and rushed out to meet me. I had never seen such horror on a person's face. We hugged and wept together. His face confirmed to me what I agonizingly sought to deny. My angel was gone. It could not be. How could my beloved daughter be dead?

Two weeks after Lisa's death, a letter came in the mail from Georgia State University. They had accepted her. I wonder if it would have changed the course of events if she had seen that letter.

I won't go into the unspeakably horrific days, weeks, months, and yes, even years that followed. Suffice it to say that as I write her biography right now, 27 years later, I cannot control the sobs. I can no longer deny that Lisa took her own life. Why, dear God? Why? This happened in the face of so much happiness and the promise of so many good years ahead for her.

I was with Lisa the night before she died. I will never forget two things my daughter said to me. She told me that she wanted me to know that she still loved the Lord and still had a relationship with Him. She also told me that she had always known I loved her and that she had always loved me.

Her kind and considerate comments gave me the only solace I could find for a very long time. Even knowing that her death was near, she wanted to give the mother she loved some words of comfort.

That night we had some serious conversations about things that were grieving her. Lisa told me that her diabetes was getting out of control. She had passed out several times, and she feared that the disease was damaging her eyes and kidneys. She said it was like living with a nightmare. She cried and held onto me for a long time. It would be the last time I would hold my darling daughter in my arms.

The only parts of my baby that I was allowed to see the day she died were her feet, cold and hard and clad in lacy white stockings. The medical examiner had denied my pleas to see her; that was probably for my own best interest.

But, when I asked to see her feet, the doctor wanted to know why. I told her that because as Jesus hung on the cross, His mother must have been able to kiss His feet. I now wanted to kiss the feet of my own dead child. They brought Lisa out all covered up except for her feet. I kissed those precious little feet and bade her goodbye.

Was Lisa in heaven? Do suicides go to heaven? When I couldn't go on for wondering where my beloved child was, I wrote to Billy Graham.

He wrote back with words that gave me the strength to keep on living. He said that the brain is an organ of the body like any other and that organs can get sick. He said it is no different than a heart attack, or liver failure, or lung cancer, or any other bodily sickness.

Rev. Graham assured me that because Lisa had given herself to God earlier and professed her love for Him, she was with Him in heaven. What good news from a man I respected so much.

I also found an article by Father Ron Rolheiser confirming Dr. Graham's words. He validated the beliefs of Dr. Graham. He reiterated that suicide is a disease and the most misunderstood of all sicknesses. It takes a person out of life against his or her will, the emotional equivalent of cancer, a stroke, or a heart attack. The brain is an organ of the body like any other and can get sick. Suicide is an illness, not a sin. God healed them from their pain after they crossed over into His loving arms.

A part of me died with Lisa - a part that can never be restored. My grief for my daughter has changed my life. It is a living, breathing part of me. It softens with the passing years but surfaces unbidden with the slightest provocation.

The same memory that brings a smile one day might well bring tears the next. Jayne Newton, the editor of the Atlanta Compassionate Friends newsletter, said of the loss of her son, "It is not my guilt that won't let me forget my child; it is my love for him."

A parent's love doesn't diminish, neither does the desire to see and hold our child. We feel a responsibility to forever protect our children, and when that responsibility is denied it turns our world upside down.

Life does go on whether we want it to or not; and all these years later, I am still here. It took most of those years for me to even begin to recover from my loss. If we let it, life can go on in many ways.

In 1996, I married a very special man. His name was Robert Jeffery Martin. I met him only one year into my bereavement when I was still nearly insane with grief. He supported and loved me through it all and helped bring me to the point where I could love again and be almost normal.

I believe in my heart that Lisa sent Rob to me, knowing that there would be big, empty holes in me that needed to be filled. He brought to our marriage a cute little seven-year-old daughter named Melissa. I was given another chance to be a mom to another little girl. What are the odds? I thank my Heavenly cheerleader, Lisa, and a loving God. My precious husband died in 2010, another devastating loss.

Lisa is still with me in the strongest sense of the word. She began her physical life inside my body, and now that that part of her has gone on ahead; she is still inside me in spirit. We will never truly be apart, either in this life or the next. I thank God for the gift of my daughter, Lisa Elaine Mewbourne.

If I could speak to her one last time, I would say, "Dearest Lisa, my baby, Little Lamb, my beloved child. I'll always love you and forever yearn for you. We'll be together one glorious day where there will be no more tears, no more sadness, no more sorrows, no more death. Only the love of each other and Christ. Until then, He'll take care of you. You were my baby for a while, now you belong to Jesus."

I know that Lisa's love shines down on me from Heaven. Her love, like her memory, will never fade. If she could hear me she would give me a wink and a smile as she joyfully skips off to Glory.

About the Author

Faye Mewbourne Martin, Lisa's mother, lives in Atlanta, Georgia. She's also the mother of Denise, David, and Melissa. She has four lovely grandchildren from David and two from Melissa. Faye is a published writer of short stories. She has written her memoirs of the first thirteen years of her life.

Dennis Lee New

5 March 1970 - 13 May 2000
Michigan

Dennis Lee New
by Christine Marie New (Wife)

When I first met Dennis, we were both in ninth grade at a middle school in Ann Arbor, Michigan. The first time we met, we didn't like each other very much. I had just graduated from a private school. As I looked at him, I could sense that he was trouble. He didn't like me very much either. We didn't have any interaction at all. I had my group of friends, and he had his.

Then in our junior year of high school, eleventh grade, we had a class together. I believe it was British Literature. Now, you may say you did not like each other, but if your friends have other classes, which both of ours did, and we knew each other, why not be friends?

So, Dennis and I sat next to each other in this class. Dennis used to bring a different book to class with him every day. He would sit and read while the class was talking about the book we read or watched a video about the book.

One day, the class took a test on Hamlet by Shakespeare. I had read the book, watched the movie, and studied for the test. Dennis never read the book, never watched the movie because he was reading his book for the day, and he never studied. Dennis got an A on the test, and I got a C. I was so mad at him.

During our junior year, I had a boyfriend who was a senior and very popular. One day, Dennis came up to me at my locker and asked me out. Dennis says I laughed at him. I said I only laughed because I had a boyfriend and everyone knew about him. Dennis never asked me out again.

Our senior year, Dennis had a locker that was not where he wanted. His locker area was with sophomore students. I shared a locker with my best friend on the senior floor. I asked her if we could share our locker with Dennis, and she said sure. Dennis was not at the locker very much.

Dennis and I became the best of friends our senior year. That summer after our senior year, he enrolled in the military. He had enlisted into the United States Army, 82nd Airborne Division.

I was dating a different guy. One day, a letter showed up for me at my house. The letter was from Dennis.

The letter was the first one I had received since he had been gone. In it, he told me how much work it was, and how he had lost weight. Then he said something very weird. Dennis closed the letter by saying "I love you."

I thought this couldn't be true. Dennis knew I had a boyfriend, so I figured he was just saying it because he was lonely. I wrote back to him. I told him about what I had been doing, how my boyfriend was, and I asked him why he wrote that he loves me.

He wrote back that he had said that because he does. He also said that he had been in love with me since our junior year.

I was shocked, confused, torn, and completely in love with Dennis, although I didn't tell him. We continued to write to each other every chance we got. But, I refused to see Dennis, because if I did see him, my true feelings would come out, and I didn't want that.

Then one day after my first year of college and Dennis's year of service, my boyfriend and I broke up.

I knew that Dennis was coming home. I was so excited to see him. I could hardly wait until he got home and we saw each other again.

Dennis asked me to go to a movie with him, his parents, and his sister. I said yes. When he took me home that night, we kissed, and I knew I loved him. I loved Dennis New.

We went through some very difficult times after that, but we did end up together.

One night, this was in 1990, right before Desert Shield took place, I went over to his parents' house. I took them some cookies I had baked at work.

Dennis called. At first, his mom, Judi, answered and talked to him for a few minutes. Then, she handed the phone over to me. She then left the room and went into the back.

I gave Dennis a hard time about painting their vehicles desert colors. Then his mom, dad, and sister walked into the room with a card and a box. They put him on speaker phone. I thought the card was addressed to his sister, Cherie, but it wasn't.

I opened up the card and it read, "The legend of the wedding ring". I opened the card up, and there was this big long letter from Dennis which I said I would read later when I was alone.

Then I turned to his dad, David. David was holding the box open with the engagement ring.

Dennis asked if I would marry him, and I said yes.

David put the ring on my finger. The next day Dennis went over to Desert Shield, and I did not see him for nine months. I talked to him a few times, especially on Christmas.

We were married on December 14, 1991. I was the happiest I had ever been. I looked forward to moving down to North Carolina where Dennis was based. I knew I would finish my degree when we got back to Ann Arbor, and I did just that.

But, the war had changed Dennis. I didn't know that when we got married, but it did. The change was ever so slight at first, I missed the signs. Now, there was nothing I could do.

In 1994, Dennis and I found out we were pregnant after three home pregnancy tests later. We were thrilled. Of course, I was only 24, but the thought of a baby thrilled us both.

On March 15, 1995, our son, Kyle was born. He was six weeks early, and only weighed 4 lbs. 5 oz. Then in 1997, our daughter was born. January 3, 1997, Kaitlin was brought into our lives. Our life was complete. We had a boy and a girl, and we had each other.

In December of 1999, Dennis was working at a jail in Indiana. He told me he had to move to be in the county where he worked because we didn't live in that county. I asked him if we were separating, and he said no.

So, Dennis moved to live in the county in which he worked. Sometimes I would not see him for a week or more, but Dennis did see his kids when he had the chance. The weekend of May 7, 2000, he took the kids to Kings Island, a fun amusement and water park.

When he brought the kids home, Dennis pushed me down the stairs and left. Then, he said that he was sorry and that he would see the kids this next weekend.

That was the last time the kids and I saw him. Friday night, May 12, 2000, just before midnight, I got a call that he was across town. I got the kids up and put them in the car. I went over to see him, to talk to him.

One police car was there when we arrived. I was told Dennis was not there, but they had spotted him. I sat in the car with my children, who were five and three years old. The chaplain came and told me that they found Dennis and that he was no longer with us.

I fell to the ground and could not move. Someone drove me and the kids home and waited there until someone showed up from his family. He died on May 13, 2000. He took his own life.

Dennis was cremated and his ashes spread in Montana, where his grandparents lived. He has a veterans marker at a cemetery in Holly, Michigan.

About the Author

Christine Marie New was Dennis New's wife; she became a widow when she was 29 years old. She lives in High Springs, Florida. Her children are Kyle and Kaitlin. She volunteers at the High Springs Lions Club three days a week. During the school year, she volunteers with a local pastor. She likes to read, watch movies, cross stitch, and just relax.

Scott Anthony Parise, Jr.

7 January 1996 - 20 July 2017
New York

Scott Anthony Parise, Jr.
by Billie Jo Jenkins (Mother)

My precious boy was born on January 7, 1996. I remember that day like it was yesterday. If you live in New York, you should recall the Blizzard of '96. Scottie and I were hospital bound for five days due to a state of emergency.

From the day I brought Scottie home, he was at my hip. He was definitely mama's little boy. He was a very loving, caring and funny child. He had a smile that would melt your heart. He was an easy child. Scottie was always well behaved. He never gave me or his dad a hard time about anything, at least not as a small child.

Scottie was very family oriented. Family meant the world to him. He and his sister, Nichole, were extremely close. Scottie was about two and a half when his dad and I divorced. His father remained in his life, taking Scottie for visitation and helping with the things he needed throughout the years. They had a close relationship as well.

Because Scottie was so young at the time, the break up did not have much of an effect on him. It was not until he was older that he began to ask questions about why his dad and I were not together. As Scottie grew older he began to express his disappointment in his dad and me for not making the marriage work. He never really understood why we just did not stay together.

In 1999, I began dating and met my second husband, whom I married in August of 2007. My husband was there for my children from day one. Scottie was the Best Man at our wedding. My daughter was my matron of honor

We were a very close-knit family. We went on family vacations and went camping every summer. My husband and I made it a point to involve my children in everything we did. We did a lot of hiking, boating and skiing, both snow skiing and water skiing. Scottie also spent a lot of quality time with his father and grandfather. He really enjoyed their time fishing and hunting together. He was always spending quality time with his grandparents.

Scottie was extremely outgoing as a child. He was well liked through school. He got along with everyone and had many friends. Many of them were females. He would always win the class clown awards. Scottie had a personality like no other. He was so bubbly.

Scottie was a chunky little guy until he hit high school. Once he hit high school he had a growth spurt and turned from cute to handsome. Boy, was Scottie handsome. He was loved by the girls, although he only had two serious relationships. If you ask me, girls were Scottie's ultimate problem in life. I would always tell him to focus on himself and his needs and wants. His heart was broken at a very young age. Scottie moved on to a second relationship, which was very toxic from the beginning.

From a young age, Scottie loved to cook. I guess you can say it was his passion. He worked at a friends' family restaurant when he was fifteen years old. Scottie started out just keeping the kitchen clean. Within a year or so he began cooking and catering. Scottie worked there throughout his high school years.

Scottie struggled when it came to actual school work. He did the best he could to keep his grades up so that he could participate in wrestling and football. Scottie participated in both these sports through middle and high school. He enjoyed both very much and earned quite a few medals, awards and patches for each.

As a mom, I wanted to see my children go to college. Scottie did not think he was cut out to be a college boy. He would always say, "I will never go to college. I'm too dumb to go to college." Truth being, he was very bright but just could never see it in himself. Scottie did graduate high school and received his Regents Diploma as well.

After graduation, Scottie began working at a well-known resort in New Paltz, New York as a cook in the kitchen. Cooking was a hard job and he wanted to try out a new field, so he took a BOCES course (Board of Cooperative Educational Services) to become a Certified Nurses Aid. Scottie received his license and began working at a local nursing home. That did not last very long before he realized that he wanted to go back to cooking. Scottie was always struggling with where he wanted to go in life, I guess to find his niche. He always went back to cooking.

Scottie began smoking marijuana at a young age. Once he turned 21, it was alcohol. I was so against this since alcoholism ran in my family. Scottie would become a different person when he was drinking, not always bad, but different. This was very worrisome to me. I stressed day and night.

Scottie went through a rough patch. We thought he was getting back on track when he was eventually hired as a dishwasher at a local restaurant. After his first week working Scottie was promoted to the chef and within a couple of months, the executive chef. The job was demanding. Scottie was working day and night.

I think it was a little too much for Scottie to handle. He began hanging out with co-workers at the restaurant bar when his shift ended. That is when his drinking got out of hand. Scottie was struggling with work, his new apartment, paying his bills and his personal life.

Scottie and his girlfriend were on and off for quite some time. They had dated since about the tenth grade. I soon realized that they weren't good for each other. They were both good people, just not good for each other.

As Scottie grew into a young adult he struggled with the transformation. He felt as though he was a burden. He really hated to ask for help with anything once he was out of the house on his own. I never wanted Scottie to move out and I made that clear time and time again.

Scottie's bedroom remained his bedroom, with the hopes that he would soon come back to live with us. Not a day would go by that I would not say, "you know, you can always come back home." I do not know, maybe I should not have pushed the subject so much. Deep down, I think me doing that made Scottie want to be on his own even more. Like he had something to prove. I guess I will never really know.

In mid-June of 2017, Scottie had scratches on his face. I immediately thought his girlfriend caused them, but I was wrong. He never really admitted doing it to himself, but from our discussion, I knew Scottie had scratched himself. That is when I realized that his issues and problems were much deeper than him just struggling financially. That is when it hit me, Scottie was depressed.

I took my son out to dinner the next night and we had a deep conversation, at least as deep as he would allow. I expressed to Scottie that I thought he should probably talk to a therapist or psychiatrist since he would not open up to anyone else. Scottie told me he would think about it. He promised me that night that he would never hurt himself again.

My husband and I, together with Scottie's dad, talked about having an intervention with Scottie. Little did we know that we had no time to set up such a thing.

On Wednesday, July 19, 2017, I took the day off from work to spend time with Scottie. We went out to lunch and did some shopping at the mall. He bought all new clothes. Everything was great.

Later that night, after he left, Scottie was arguing with his girlfriend. They had decided they were going to try to make up. Before he left the house, he raided my fridge to get a few ingredients so that he could cook her dinner at his place. Scottie kissed me goodbye, said, "I love you" and walked out the door. That was the last time I saw my baby boy.

I got a phone call on Thursday, July 20th at 4:45 am. It was Scottie's sister. She was saying that Scottie and his girlfriend were at her house arguing. This was a continuous thing.

I tried to call Scottie and got no answer. My daughter called me back and said that Scottie's girlfriend had brought him home and then gone back to her house to avoid the fighting.

I called Scottie again and finally got to talk to him. This was at about 5:45 am. He sounded like he was tired but okay. Nothing different in his voice. Scottie told me he was in bed and not to worry. He was going to sleep it off and call me later. I asked if he wanted me to come over. He lived only ten minutes down the road. Scottie said, "no Ma, I'm fine." I told him to call me if he changed his mind. I told him I loved him. He said, "Okay, I will. I love you too."

My phone rang again at 6:37 am. It was Scottie's girlfriend, screaming so loud that I could not even make out what she was saying. Finally, she yelled, "I found him hanging!" I screamed, "call 911" and dropped to my knees.

My husband and I arrived at Scottie's place within minutes. The paramedics were just arriving. My husband ran upstairs to see what was going on. To this day, I regret not going up the stairs to at least say goodbye to my baby boy. I really believed that he was going to be fine. The thought of him not surviving was not at all in my mind.

The police came over to talk to me and get my side of the story. I told them that there is no way this was happening. Just the day before Scottie was happy go lucky. I still just do not understand.

Finally, the paramedics talked with my husband. They had worked on Scottie for about 45 minutes, but there was nothing they could do. They did not even have the decency to come to talk to me, his mother. Not that I was in any state of mind to talk at that point.

That morning will forever be implanted in my mind. Every day is like Groundhog Day. I wake up and think to myself, "Oh my gosh, here we go again with another day of sadness and heartache."

My life has come to a halt. It's like I cannot move on. There is no way that life can just go on without my baby boy . . . just no way.

We had Scottie cremated, and he's in a beautiful urn that sits in our living room. Each of us, my daughter, my husband and myself, as well as Scottie's father and grandparents, have a pinch of his ashes in a keepsake necklace. I wear my necklace every day, keeping Scottie close to my heart.

I cannot seem to look at pictures of Scottie, and I feel terrible for this. I am not sure why because he is such a beautiful sight to look at. I am hoping one day soon I can get out of this funk I am in. My heart feels empty. There is a void in my soul. I miss my son every second of every minute of every hour of every day. I love Scottie so dearly. I talk to him all the time in hopes that one day he sends me a sign that he is at peace.

A little poem I wrote on the 1 year anniversary of Scottie's death:

You left this world one year ago,
why oh why, I'll never know.
On that day I lost my heart, and since then I fell apart.
I miss your beautiful smile and your handsome face,
Your hugs and kisses I cannot replace.
I long for your presence, how I miss you so much,
I wish I could hold you, or just feel your touch.
Are you finally at peace? At least that much is true?
The price I have paid since my hearts broke in two.
I pray your soul lives on happy, and your pain is no more.
For the pain that I'm feeling is too much to endure.
I ask God to take you into His loving arms, to guide you and teach you, and bring out your charm.
Every second, every minute, every hour that's passed,
Each day that goes by, I miss you more than the last.

About the Author
Billie Jo Jenkins is the mother of Scott Anthony Parise. She lives in Highland, New York with her daughter, Nichole, her grandson Dezmond and husband Henry. She thanks God for them. Her family planted a garden in the backyard in memory of Scottie; there, they placed some of his ashes as well.

Erick Plunkett

22 October 1975 - 18 September 2017
Tennessee

Erick Plunkett
by Rachel Anne Brennan (Wife)

"We found him," said the officer standing on my porch. I knew what his next words would be, yet I was hoping against hope that I was wrong.

"And...," I said, with a quiver in my voice as I sat down in the red folding chair on the porch.

He lowered his head, looked back up and said, "He's dead."

"Are you sure?" I shook as these words fell from my lips.

"Yes ma'am."

Odd questions flew out of my mouth before I could even think about what I was saying. "Did he shoot himself?" "Did he suffer?" "How many times did he shoot himself?"

These questions must have seemed ridiculous to the officer. In hindsight, they seem ridiculous to me.

I remember asking the officer how I was supposed to tell our children, ages eleven and six, that Daddy was gone. They were in their bedrooms making crafts and cards to give Erick upon his return. The officer could not advise me on that subject.

I asked him to stay for a little while and he agreed. He stood there while I made the hardest phone calls of my life. My first call was to Erick's father. My second call was to my mother. After that, I don't remember much.

Erick was 41 years old. He was just a little over a month shy of his 42nd birthday. He was born in Indianapolis, Indiana, on October 22nd. He was the only child of Fred and Vicki.

Erick's mother had three children from a previous marriage, but they were teens or preteens by the time of Erick's birth.

Erick's father describes the day of his birth.

"The story of Erick's birth must start the day before, October 21, 1975. The day was an ideal fall day. The sky was clear and the air warm but not hot. I owned a dune buggy at the time. Erick's mother and I spent the entire day running around in the buggy.

It was a sight to see Erick's mother (nine months pregnant) climbing in and out of the buggy, as it had no doors. It was impossible for her to look graceful. All that bending and contortion probably had Erick thinking 'I have to get out of here.'

At roughly three o'clock in the morning on October 22, we found ourselves on our way to the hospital. Erick was the fourth child for his mother. Because of this, I was told it would not be a long drawn out delivery. I was left by the nurses in a waiting area as Erick's mother was taken back in a wheelchair. I was told that they would come get me after she was settled into her room.

After no more than a half hour, someone came to show me to her room. As I arrived at the room I looked up at the sign above the door, it read: Delivery Room.

"What? You mean it's over?" I exclaimed to the nurse who had escorted me.

Yes, it was all over. The baby boy had arrived at 3:42 in the morning. Then I saw my son Erick for the first time. He was wrapped in what looked like aluminum foil. Erick was this little bundle that looked just like a baked potato with a face.

For those who have never experienced the whole pregnancy journey, one challenge during those nine months is "What are we going to name . . ."

This was a time before the doctors were able to tell parents ahead of time if they were having a boy or girl. I don't recall if we had a girl's name chosen. I think we believed strongly all along we were having a boy.

We decided finally on the name Mikhail Erick Lovain, Mikhail was the Russian equivalent of Michael, Erick was from the last half of my name Frederick, and Lovain was from my father's name. It was agreed from the start that my son would be called and known by all as simply Erick.

In Erick's newborn pictures you can see the sense of wonder and thoughtfulness in his eyes. He carried that same sense of wonder with him always.

When Erick was small, his family moved to Florida. Unfortunately, his parents' marriage didn't last long, so Erick went to live with his father in Indiana at the age of five.

Erick often joked around that he had to repeat kindergarten because he couldn't color inside the lines. In actuality, he had to repeat due to his age and different state requirements. Nonetheless, Erick excelled throughout his school days. He moved back and forth between his parents during his early years, but he was raised primarily by his father and step-mother.

Erick's father is a hardworking man full of laughter and love for his children. He's a master carpenter, and he instilled those skills into his oldest son.

When Erick was eight years old, his parents welcomed a baby boy they named Kyle into the world. He was thrilled to have a little brother. Erick told many stories of teasing, play fights, playing Army, and of Christmas mornings that included his little brother. There was an undeniable bond there.

When Erick was seventeen, he moved to Florida to be with his mother. In Florida, he completed his senior year of high school with honors. He also completed several college credit hours via the dual enrollment program. He loved learning, and it came easy to him.

In 1994 on graduation night, I visited friends that were having a party. Just past the bonfire light I saw a tall, awkward, chubby guy that I had never seen before. He had glasses and this amazing smile that lit up the night sky. There was an air of mystery around him.

I remember thinking that he looked incredibly familiar. I was just sixteen years old. I sat next to him around the dying firelight. We exchanged names in the standard introduction way. I asked if we had met before because he looked familiar. He said he was sure we hadn't. I asked if he had a brother who perhaps I had met. He chuckled and said, "Yeah I have two brothers. One lives in Michigan and the other in Indiana."

As the conversation continued, I asked him what his middle name was. "Erick," he replied with a smirk. I said with a chuckle, "Okay, smartass, what's your first name then?"

He replied with a name that made him sound as if he were of royal blood. He said his name with such pride, "Mikhail Erick Lovain Plunkett." I was in awe of this long and noble sounding name. We chatted for a while longer before I had to leave for the evening.

A while later, I went back to the place where the party had been. There was Erick again. This time a bass guitar was strapped to him. As he played I could feel the energy and the love of music. He felt the music; he didn't just play it.

Years later, Erick and I would travel all over the country to go to concerts. We'd sit for hours and play songs to each other, discussing what they meant to us. Music was a part of both of us and a part of our relationship.

I left that night and returned days later to find that Erick wasn't there. It had become obvious that I had developed a crush on the curly-headed mullet man. Another friend teased me relentlessly about my attraction to him and went as far as to call Erick at home to tell him I was there waiting for him.

I didn't expect Erick to show up, but within twenty minutes, he was there. Now that he knew about my feelings, our exchanges were awkward. We both fumbled with our words as we tried to piece together a conversation.

We ended up walking away from the crowd and sitting in my small blue Ford LTD. As we talked, the ease returned. We laughed together while we recounted our favorite scenes from the movie Monty Python and The Holy Grail. We talked about our families and how we both came to be living in Florida.

Then there was a pause in the conversation. I looked at him, and through the moonlight I could still see his perfectly thought-filled blue eyes begging to ask me a question. "What?" I said in a voice just above a whisper.

"Can I kiss you?" He asked in the sweetest, most innocent tone my ears had ever heard.

I wanted to kiss him so badly. It was one of those moments where the entire Earth's gravitational pull is between you and this one person. I remember looking at his lips, so perfect. He had the sharpest point to his top lip with all the other curvatures being soft. When he smiled, my heart sang for joy.

"No," I replied, "but you can hold my hand."

Erick reached out and took my hand in his. They were strong, large, rough, manly. His hands said, "I'm capable of anything you ask of me." Those hands wiped tears away, held babies, cut stone, laid brick, and made me feel as if nothing else in this world existed.

"Now doesn't that give you a warm fuzzy," I said jokingly trying to cut the sexual tension that had been building between two teenagers after sitting talking in a car for four hours.

"Yes, actually it does," he said while flashing me that dazzling smile again.

I drove away that night in July 1994 looking up, seeing a moon that was full and bright. I knew without a doubt that I had just met the man I was going to marry.

Our first date was on July 31, 1994. I baked homemade brownies and drove to his house to pick him up. During our last conversation, we'd discovered that we both loved to fish, so we made plans to go fishing together off a little pier on the Gulf of Mexico.

When I arrived at Erick's home, I saw his face pressed against the glass in the front door making a silly face. I was nervous. I liked him so much but wasn't sure what to think of this goofiness. Part of me wanted to run, but the larger part of me was eager to be alone with him to talk more.

Erick answered the door and handed me a bouquet of flowers from his mother's flower bed. I stepped inside, and he briefly introduced me to his mother and his sister, Laurie. I'd never met a boy's mother before.

We then walked down a narrow hallway to his bedroom. He had knives, swords, and his prized garden weasel hanging on the walls. He showed me the tool that was used to remove the staples he had in his belly years prior after having his appendix removed.

I remember laughing hard and loud as we talked. Erick never failed to make people laugh. It was truly a God-given gift. His ability to tell a story and to make absurd exaggerations was a skill that he had down to a science.

His laugh was infectious as well. It would start out hearty, but the more tickled he got, the softer his laughter became until he was silent with his mouth open, face red, and this Y-shaped vein bulging from his forehead.

We left his mother's house and headed to our fishing spot. We talked without pause all the way there. When we arrived, we realized that we'd forgotten to stop to get bait for our fishing trip, so we got back in my car and headed to the marina.

I don't think either of us was that concerned about fishing as much as we were about just being together. We cast our lines out, and the time passed. The tide receded, yet we still sat there not catching anything but the budding feelings of new love.

The day turned into dusk. We decided to retire our fishing expedition and head to the beach to watch the sunset. Before we got to the beach, we pulled off on a road next to the canal. You could just see miles of palm grass swaying in the gulf breeze.

Just beyond, we could see the sun setting on the gulf water. The reflection of the colors made for a romantic view. We sat in complete silence together. Soon, just a few words I'll keep in my heart were exchanged. The kiss Erick had asked me for just days ago finally happened. We found ourselves throwing open car doors and throwing tackle boxes, fishing poles, and bait buckets out of the backseat.

We kissed and held onto each other there on Bayou Drive as the sun said its farewell. We made love for the first time. Afterward I looked up at him and tears filled my eyes. I started to say the words echoing in my mind, "Promise you'll never hurt me."

Before I could utter those words, his voice, so gentle and loving said, "I promise I'll never hurt you." I wrapped my arms around his neck and kissed his cheek. We were in love.

Two days before Erick's death, we talked of this night as we held hands driving home from a concert we'd just attended in Birmingham, Alabama. Erick told me that he knew he was in love with me then.

After that date, we were nearly inseparable. Time flew by; we grew closer. Eventually after Erick when he got his own home, I moved in with him. We built a little nest out of what we had. It wasn't much, but it was ours.

One night he looked at me and said, "I want to tell you something, but you can't tell anyone else."

"Okay," I said hesitantly.

"When you get out of high school, I want to marry you."

That's what we did. The day after I turned eighteen, I became Mrs. Mikhail Erick Lovain Plunkett. Erick wore a black tuxedo with tails, and I wore off-white lace. We loved each other.

We drove to Orlando to a hotel, and we honeymooned at Disney World. Our hotel room had a jacuzzi tub. We mistakenly put in too much bubble bath and turned the jets on. We were covered in bubbles, as was the floor. All we could do was laugh at our innocent mistake.

Years went by. We moved here and there. Erick began working for a brick mason and learned the trade. As with everything Erick did, he excelled at it. Erick loved his work and made a friend in his new boss.

We eventually got a cute little apartment and began talking about having children. Alas, it wasn't meant to be for us. We tried to conceive for seven years with no success.

In 1999, we moved to Erick's home state of Indiana. He had missed his father and little brother and wanted to be closer to them. I'd heard many stories of his friends and extended family, and I'd met many of them during vacations and during a brief period after our marriage when we tried lived in Indiana.

Erick found our first house in Indianapolis and moved there to set it up. I stayed in Florida to finish my last days at my job. Erick had found work doing masonry restoration. Erick truly loved the work. He learned that he enjoyed working at great heights.

It was also at this time that he attended Indiana University - Purdue University. I remember Erick reading his Greek mythology books to me. Erick had a way of talking and teaching someone that was so easy and natural. One could walk away from a conversation with Erick with so much knowledge.

Erick loved history, especially history about the great wars. When we would lie in bed at night, he'd tell me stories that his father had told him about World War One and World War Two fighter pilots. While the subjects weren't of particular interest to me, hearing Erick's passion about them made me long to learn more.

In 2001, we bought our first home. Erick was a skilled painter; he gained this skill from his work and his father. He made our house a home. He patiently stood behind me, holding my hand and the paint roller, to show me the proper pressure and movement. I'd roll and he'd trim paint. He was always eager to teach me how to do something.

In 2005 we welcomed our first child, a little girl, by adoption. At first, Erick was nervous about becoming a father. I was always the one to dive in to a new adventure while Erick maintained his composure and sensibilities.

I often misunderstood his apprehension, thinking he didn't want to do something. At times this caused friction between us. We always worked through our differences though and came out stronger and more in love with each other.

When it came time to name our daughter, we discussed her name at length. There were lots of names I liked, but nothing struck Erick. Then one day while driving down the road, he said to me, "There's a name I like. I like it because I came up with a nickname that only her daddy could call her."

I was overjoyed as most new mothers are when their husbands want to give naming input.

Erick announced: "Katy, so I can call her my little Katy Pa-Taaty"

I loved it. We decided that the name Katherine was more fitting for a young woman, but we'd call her Katy. Erick wanted to honor his paternal grandmother by naming her Katherine.

Erick loved his family and was very close to them. They were warm and welcoming to me and had become my family as well. He especially enjoyed sitting around his aunt's dining room table, swapping stories, seeing who could come up with the most elaborate exaggerations, and laughing until some liquid shot out of some orifice. It was dangerous to take a drink when Erick and his cousins were together. You were sure to choke, which just caused more roars of laughter.

On October 8, 2005, we received a call that our daughter's birth mother's water broke. We rushed with our uneaten Applebee's meal to Saint Vincent Hospital, the same hospital chain Erick was born in thirty years previously. We suited up to go into the delivery room.

As Erick and I stood outside the delivery room doors, we held hands and recited the Lord's Prayer together. Erick hadn't been brought up in any faith but had recently come to know Christ and His love during our adoption journey.

We entered the delivery room and took seats next to each other. Soon we heard the cries of our newborn daughter. I couldn't see Erick's smile due to the mask over his mouth, but his eyes were filled with pure delight. He rushed to the warmer to get the first look at his daughter. Erick had seen her on ultrasound monitors several times prior, but now here she was with her little fingers wrapped around Erick's index finger.

The nurses wrapped our new little daughter tightly and placed her in the strongest and safest arms she'd ever know, her father's. Words cannot describe that moment. Erick never said a word. He didn't need to; his blue eyes danced with joy. He was a father. Erick was in love with this little girl. He was hers and she was his.

Days went by as we settled into new parenthood. Erick eagerly came home every evening to scoop up his baby and lay her on his chest. He'd nap in a chair with little Katy balled up on top of his heart after a long day at work.

He never shied away from diaper changes, feedings, or any other parental duties. We delighted in our roles as parents. Erick painted murals of cartoon fish on her nursery room walls. He had an amazing drawing style all his own. Being a father allowed him to let out his inner child in a beautiful way.

As our daughter grew, Erick was always there for birthday parties and in the spring, he dressed up as the Easter bunny. He helped sell Girl Scout cookies and attended daddy-daughter dances. He was there for just about all our daughter's activities. He worked hard so that Katy and I could have the life he believed we should have.

We were active in our local Catholic Church. Erick had been baptized on Easter, and he developed a deep faith and love for the gospel. It was a major part of our lives. Erick taught Sunday school and was a lecturer at the church.

In 2008 we embarked on a new journey. We became foster parents. We had longed for more children and believed fostering would provide us that opportunity to grow our family.

After a heartbreaking loss of two children we had fostered, we agreed that we'd abandon our idea of more children. We bought a house in the country closer to Erick's parents and extended family.

In 2010 I was surprised to be approached by a woman I knew who was pregnant. She wanted to place her unborn baby with us for adoption. Without consulting Erick, I told her yes.

I called Erick to discuss it. He was working and couldn't talk long, but he said, "We have to put our faith in God. He gave us this chance, so we must take it. Even if it doesn't work out, we've saved a life."

Erick and I were both active in the right to life cause. We volunteered together, and we both spoke at rallies. My husband had a powerful testimony from a father's perspective, and he readily shared it with others.

In April 2011, I stood in the delivery room while Erick stood in the adjoining room as our son Finnian entered the world. When Erick first walked into the room, he said, "I heard his first cry. It choked me up." The look of pure bliss on his face has been captured in pictures from the day of our son's birth.

Erick said he never knew he wanted a son until he had a son. Finn grew to be Erick's buddy. That's what he always called him, Buddy. Finn helped his daddy with car repairs and household repairs. Erick even took Finn to work with him at times and taught him how to do tuckpoint masonry.

Erick gave his son his own hard hat and patiently. He taught him not to give up when Finn would cry if he couldn't do something his daddy was teaching him. He attended Boy Scout meetings with Finn, took him camping and canoeing, and took pride in teaching his son about the world.

Erick's job at the time of our son's birth was demanding; he worked sixteen to twenty hours a day. Our family life was very stressful with two children now, and my father had moved in with us. Erick began to feel the pressure; he wanted to change jobs so that he could be with his family more, so we took a leap of faith, and Erick changed jobs during the early days of Finn's life.

In 2013 things began to take a dramatic change for Erick. I don't know what the catalyst was. We stopped going to church regularly. We stopped socializing as much. Erick became sick in December 2013 with diverticulosis. He was in the hospital twice for dehydration before being properly diagnosed and treated.

The day after Christmas in 2013, Erick and I had a life-changing conversation that led to revelations of things that Erick had been hiding and felt shame about. He agreed that he needed help. I agreed to stay with him if the behaviors stopped. I didn't realize at that time that the cycle of addiction had already begun.

Our marriage became a shell of what it once was. Infidelity crept in. Fights fueled by anger and bitterness left us both empty and alone. Erick and I were desperate for help but unaware of what to do. We sought counsel within the church as well as with therapists, retreats, friends, family, and everything else we could think of. I pulled away from Erick, and he pulled into himself.

In 2014 Erick was sent out of town for work. He came home only on weekends, spent and exhausted. I too was exhausted from being with the children by myself all week. We just couldn't seem to find common ground to come together.

For two years we floated past each other like ships in the night. We no longer laughed and played with our children. Erick and I were consumed by the wrong things, and we soon fell into alcoholism.

Friends and family we once held dear walked away due to our poor choices. We lost each other; we lost ourselves. Drugs entered the picture. We both longed for each other and for closeness, but we couldn't connect. We were in self-destruct mode and had no idea where we were headed or how to stop it.

In September 2016, I had had enough and demanded that the lies, drinking, and everything else we were both engaging in should stop. Erick, my once bright-eyed husband, so full of life and love, walked out on his family.

We tried to reconcile. Erick and I both believed that with time, we could make it back to where we'd been. We agreed to date each other, to start fresh. Neither of us wanted to lose our history.

In late October, Erick relapsed into old behaviors. He thought he couldn't face what he had done, so he attempted to overdose on his prescription antidepressants and antianxiety medications. He survived this attempt and was hospitalized for a week.

He came home for a few weeks, but our fighting continued; we both played the blame game. Erick hurt me so I would hurt him. I hurt him so he would hurt me. We oozed bitterness. We shouted hateful words at each other. We struck each other. We lied to each other. The two teenagers that had been so in love and so full of life and promise were long forgotten.

In November, Erick admitted to having delusional thoughts including homicidal and suicidal thoughts. I removed the children from our home for their protection. Erick was again hospitalized. At this point, law enforcement and other agencies became involved in our marriage and our children's lives.

I believed that I had no other option than to move forward with the divorce. Erick was court ordered to get counseling, attend twelve-step meetings, and take his prescribed medication as directed. A protective order was put into place barring Erick from contacting me or our children.

Erick later told me that that was his lowest point. He followed the court's orders and sought therapy. He was turned away multiple times due to his diagnosis of mixed personality disorders and severe depression. His medication helped, but he often would forget to take it.

In February of 2017, after sixteen years in Indiana, I moved to Tennessee with the children to start a new life. Erick and I agreed to change our last names and start over fresh. He had already been working for a company in Nashville for a couple of months.

Erick would come for supervised visits with the children on the weekends. Eventually, the protective order was dropped, so he moved in with the children and me. The hurt from the past was too great for both of us. We tried many times to get past it.

In July Erick stopped taking his medication and stopped attending his meetings. He soon relapsed again. This led to a four-day hospitalization for suicidal ideation. He was trying to fight. His past mistakes were eating at him, as was the sexual abuse he endured as a child. He wanted so badly to be better. We both wanted to be back where we had been, but neither of us had a map to get there.

Erick poured himself into his work and into being the amazing father he'd always been. He coached our son's soccer team. We searched for a new church. We started to make new friends in our community.

In September 2017, Erick stopped taking his medication again. He lost his job, quit coaching, and withdrew from the children again. One day after a fight, I found him getting ready to jump from a bridge. He came home, but we just fought more and harder.

Some days later, I woke up next to Erick and realized that he was different. We'd had an amazing family weekend full of fun and laughter, just like it used to be. We had stayed up talking like we used to. We had buried some of the old hurts and offered forgiveness to each other.

We sat with our daughter while Erick counseled her on boys and the changes coming to her life. He took our young son on a trip to Alabama to see hot air balloon races. We attended a concert and danced together to the songs "Fire Away" and "Broken Halos."

That Monday, Erick was calm. He woke me up gently after putting the children on the bus for school. He did the dishes and folded laundry. He brought a cup of coffee to me, and we talked.

I felt something wasn't right; things were too perfect. I felt an unbelievable, strangling sadness. We were sitting on the porch talking when Erick stepped off the porch. The light was gone from his eyes; he looked weak and defeated but maintained that he was okay.

I asked him what he was doing, as he was searching for something in our yard. He told me he was looking for cigarette butts.

I got out of the chair and walked into the house. I never saw my husband, my best friend, my love, my children's father, my heart, my Erick again.

Thirty minutes or so later, I discovered that he'd left our home and had taken both guns with him. I started to drive after him, hoping that I could find him, but I had no idea where he'd gone. I screamed and banged on the steering wheel, my tears making it impossible to see.

A mile down the road, I turned around and came home to call the police. I called Erick's phone and left eleven voice mail messages. I texted him forty or more times.

The police came and took a description of his truck and of Erick. They set out to find him. They returned an hour later to ask for a better physical description.

As they started to leave, I said through my tears, "I know he's gone because I don't feel him here anymore," and pointed to my heart. I was right.

Since Erick's death, I've learned that mental illness is progressive. I've learned about trauma. I've learned about addiction.

Erick was a good man. He fought as hard as he could. In the last days, Erick lost a huge amount of physical weight but took on a tremendous amount of emotional weight. He felt alone and unloved. The boy that had asked "Can I kiss you?" was buried deep inside of him.

Erick's memory and story will live on. He is, was, and always shall be known for those beautiful gifts he left each of us. Erick taught me strength. Erick taught me love. Erick taught me how to give until it hurts. His story is beautiful but full of pain. We each can learn something from this amazing, talented, kind, and loving man and his story. Erick, even though he left us, also left us many gifts. His strength, hope, and love will live on forever.

About the Author

Rachel Anne Brennan, wife of Erick Plunkett for twenty years, lives in Lincoln County, Tennessee with their two children, Katy and Finn. She wrote this story with help from Frederick Lovain Plunkett, Erick's father. Rachel enjoys volunteering and advocacy work for the causes that are near and dear to her heart. She remains active in her church and surrounding community.

Shawn Preston Rego

29 May 1990 - 22 March 2006
New York

Shawn Preston Rego
by Debra Rego (Mother)

I was blessed to be Shawn's mother. After the birth of my first child, my husband did not want me to have any more children. My daughter was my entire world. I was so happy.

I wanted to share more of my love with more children, though. Amazingly, I knew exactly the moment Shawn was conceived.

This pregnancy was very different, everything from how I carried him to how energetic he was. Three days before my due date, on May 28, 1990, I was having sharp pain in my legs, so I called the doctor and explained my symptoms. He told me to just relax, it was nothing. In the early morning of May 29, 1990, I called the doctor again. The pains were five minutes apart. The doctor said, "Fine, go in and get checked."

I called my older sister to watch my daughter. She was at my house lickitty split. I arrived at the hospital at 1:00 a.m. They could not believe I was having the baby now; the doctor was not even there yet. They laid me on my side to wait for the doctor.

As soon as the doctor arrived, the nurses turned me over and there was Shawn. The doctor did not have any time to wash up, shouting "Wait for me."

Shawn Preston Rego was born at 1:30 a.m. He came out so fast that he was blue. I was screaming,"My baby, my baby, why is he blue? Give me my baby".

The doctor helped Shawn start breathing. Before they could even clean him up, they gave him to me. Oh, Shawn was so beautiful. He had gorgeous blue eyes. My unconditional love started for him at that moment.

My daughter was like a sponge. Donaway soaked up all the love and kept it all to herself. Shawn shared his love with everyone. He was just full of so much love. I did not mind.

My husband wanted to make sure I did not have any more kids. He said, "We have a girl and a boy, we do not need any more". He convinced me to have surgery. No more babies, but I was okay with that because Shawn gave me so much love. Yes, I would have liked more; who would not?

Hold this thought: When Shawn was born, I did know something was wrong.

When Shawn was twenty-one months old, he got very sick and fell into a deep sleep. I took him to the doctor and then ran him to the hospital. For days, they did tests on him. They did a spinal tap and said, "I am sorry, but this will hurt him real bad and he will wake up", but he did not.

I slept in the hospital every night. I thought, "I cannot lose my baby". Before they flew him to Boston, they diagnosed him with spinal meningitis. They told me they would try some medication, but people do die with this disease. It turned out well. I got my baby back.

Okay, remember I said I thought something was wrong? Three months later, when Shawn turned two, the doctor said Shawn was born with a hernia and had to go for surgery. I thought "No, do not put my baby to sleep".

I cried the whole time; I was hysterical. I thought, "What if my baby does not wake up? I just got Shawn's life back three months ago". The surgery was successful.

Shawn was a typical boy. He was very adventurous. I spent much time in the emergency room, mostly for stitches.

As Shawn got older, he had a hard time breathing. One night when I got home from work, my baby's chest was caving in. He said, "Mommy, it hurts to breathe". I was at the hospital very quickly. If the police were around, I do not think they could have caught up.

Shawn was diagnosed with bronchitis. With every season's change, we would be in the hospital, just Shawn and me. We would have great talks then.

Years later, when we were on vacation in Pennsylvania, Shawn had another attack. We went to the hospital; he was diagnosed with asthma, which meant easier treatments. Still, if Shawn had another attack, it would be just Shawn and me for three hours in the emergency room.

We moved to the Finger Lakes in June 2004. Shawn's asthma stopped; no further attacks. Shawn would use his inhaler if he needed it.

When we lived in Massachusetts, I waited until both of my children were in school to start working again, at first part-time, then it slowly increased to full time. Before I knew it, I was working sixty hours a week; but now, no more.

While I was working, Shawn used to jump really high ramps (that even adults were afraid to jump) with his bicycle. When I heard about it I scolded the adults that were there. (Yes, his father and friends.)

Shawn also used to do trick riding on his four-wheeler with Donaway. Yes, they scared me when they had to show off and show me the crazy stuff they learned.

Another thing Shawn used to master all video games he played within 24 to 48 hours to conquer the game, so playing multiple players made everyone else feel dumb.

When my daughter was 15 and Shawn was 13, we bought a house in the Finger Lakes in New York.

Wait, I am getting ahead of myself again. Because of what I went through with suicidal thoughts and attempts, I watched my daughter extra close. Like a sponge, Donaway would keep her feelings to herself. I was aware that age thirteen was my first attempt, so I worried a lot.

My little sister also tried at age thirteen. (She survived, but one month later, she passed away while saving my daughter in a car accident.)

My daughter was only eight months old. My little sister never got the chance to know Shawn. Thirteen is the scary number.

I thought it was only female genetics, but I was stupid. My daughter did try to get attention by drinking a whole bottle of Nyquil; she got sick and threw it up. I did get her psychiatric treatment.

When we planned to move to New York, my daughter was in high school. She said, "I will die before I move to New York". I got her into a hospital in Boston to help her adjust to the change. Mind you, I was working sixty hours and running to the hospital every day, a drive of an hour and a half if there was no traffic.

Shawn could not wait to move; he was excited because Mommy was going to be home all the time (semi-retired). My daughter did adjust in New York. Donaway had more friends than she had ever had. Everything was great. They were typical teenagers; little arguments about who is right. Shawn and I still had some good talks.

Once, my daughter told some friends she was thinking about suicide again; boom, I went and got her a psychiatrist. My husband said to Shawn, "You would never do this to us, would you?" Shawn said, laughingly, "Nah, I would just kill myself, not threaten to do it."

My heart dropped to my stomach. "What? What do you mean?" I asked. Shawn said, "I would hang myself or something; I would not stress you out". I asked, "Are you serious? Do you want to talk with someone about your feelings?"

Shawn answered, "No, I am just saying." He looked me in the eyes as he said that. What an ass I was for not doing something about it; fifteen months later that is what he did.

We would talk often within that time. I asked, "Shawn, if you had a chance to move to Rhode Island or Massachusetts or even New York City for a better job offer, would you go?"

He thought about it for a moment. Shawn answered, "No, I would give up a lot of money to stay here where we live and be happy". I felt all warm inside; I did the right thing by moving my kids out of the city and moving here.

Awww, Mommy has to share Shawn's love again. Shawn had a girlfriend, and how he loved her. He loved her so deeply. She was scared that nobody had ever loved her like Shawn did, so she broke up with him. He was so hurt. Shawn did date other girls, but when Shawn heard the girl wanted him back, he was ecstatic.

The girlfriend had a little brother who was slow and had no friends, but Shawn was his friend. Whenever the brother tried to be friends with other boys she liked, they would just tolerate him.

After they broke up, Shawn was still her little brother's friend. She saw Shawn was true and wanted him back. They talked about marriage, family, having kids, jobs and the kind of house they would have. I found that out after Shawn's death.

One day, Shawn and she went to the library. He did not take the bus or call. I was worried, so dad punished Shawn by restricting him. For one week, Shawn could not go anywhere with her. They could talk on the phone and see one another in school, but no dates; no movies or going over one another's homes. That was on a Friday.

On Saturday, my husband and I went out with a couple of friends. Shawn called us and asked if he could go over to her older sister's house. Of course we said no; he had only been on restriction for one day.

Shawn was very upset. He was talking to her on the phone and said, "I should just take off and go over. They aren't home. I'll lock my door and they'll never know."

Shawn did not know my daughter was eavesdropping. At that point, something was in the pit of my stomach. Shawn was there when we got home. We did not say anything; the pit stayed.

On Wednesday, Shawn skipped a class to be with her at the library and got caught by his sister again. I had to go to the school on Thursday.

I asked Shawn if he skipped and told him,
"Tell me the truth because I have to go to the school tomorrow. I will find out".

Shawn shook his head to reply, "Nope."

Let me remind you, his punishment was going to be over by Friday. Thursday was the last day.

Shawn asked me if he could go to the school Wednesday night to see her sing in chorus. I told him to ask his father since he was the one who punished him. At supper, Shawn did not say a word. I hate myself for not bringing it up.

After supper, my husband and I had to go to the store real quick. I asked him if Shawn could go. I said, "He will really not be just with her. There are going to be a lot of other people around". He said, "Yeah, Shawn can go, but he has to ask me himself. Do not tell him". I think it was some type of pride thing. I kick myself for not saying anything then either.

We had gone five miles away to my mother-in-law's house; we were only a phone call away. Before we left, Shawn did not get permission. He asked his sister to take him, but she said she did not want to be punished if it was a test from dad.

The whole time I was at my mother-in-law's house, I wanted to call Shawn and let him know he could go, but I just did not. We left the house around 6:00 p.m., and Shawn's sister left at 6:30 p.m. I had my car in the garage; I was driving the van.

On the way home, at about 8:00 p.m., my husband said, very smugly, "I cannot wait to tell Shawn he could have gone if he had asked me."

As I drove up the driveway, I noticed the lights on in the garage. Shawn was standing next to my car and was looking down at the floor by the driver's seat. I beeped and got no response. I beeped again. I asked my husband, "What the hell is he doing?"

He said, "How am I supposed to know?"

I told my husband to find out; I was going into the house.

As soon as he went into the garage, he shouted, "Call 911!"

"What", I asked.

"Just call 911!" he shouted again.

I did not call. I went into the garage to see what was going on. There was my 6 foot 2 inch baby hanging by a stupid cheap dog leash that had only cost a dollar.

We tried to take Shawn down. His toes and the balls of his feet were touching the ground. He was so heavy and cold. It was March in New York, so the temperature outside was cold that night. I then called 911. It seemed like forever until they got there. I was so hysterical that the operator told me to leave the garage so my husband could try CPR.

When the police, then the paramedics arrived, they were coming to me. I was screaming, "Get the hell away from me and save my baby!"

It took so long to drive out of the driveway. They did not drive the way I would have. They did not have sirens on or I did not hear them. They stopped at the railroad tracks. At the beginning of the ride, I was still freaking out. They told me if I did not calm down, they were going to sedate me. I did not think so.

Instead, I prayed to any and every god; I thought, "Yes, you did let your son die, but that was only for a minute. You have your beloved son with you right now sitting on your right hand side. Please don't let my beloved son die. I want a second chance". I continued pleading with God. "Please don't let my son die". As I said those words louder and louder.

I had gone to the doctor in December 2005, and my cholesterol was nearly 500; it is supposed to be in the high 200s. I had a liver problem, so they could not give me medications.

I wanted to live for my kids. I changed everything about my eating. In six weeks, I got it down to approximately 260. They were amazed because they said they had patients that could not bring it down in six months, let alone six weeks.

I told my kids I planned on living a long time for them. I told Shawn I was going to lose weight so that we could go skydiving when he was 18. I had gone when he was younger, and he always wanted to go, but the law said he had to be at least 18. I told him we would definitely go.

The doctors tried to bring some light to my baby's death. They told me, "Good thing you got your cholesterol down, otherwise you probably would have had a heart attack". I wish I did. We all died that night.

The service was beautiful. People drove for hours; some flew from Florida and California to be here at the funeral home. The director said he never saw so much love there. People I never knew were there. There were so many that there were no more seats. Some stood and others sat on the ground.

Because my son was an atheist, Shawn believed in science, not God, and the people that were coming had many different religions. I said, "Respect Shawn and do not bring any religion here."

Anyway, I hated God. I wanted it to be a memorial for Shawn. Anyone could go to the podium and say something they remembered about Shawn; a lot of them did. At the end of the service, kids sang "You Raise Me Up" and "Will You Remember Me".

About the Author
Debra Rego is Shawn's mother; she's also mother to Donaway Rego, whose story is also in this book. She and her husband live in New York.

Donaway Shylow Rego

23 May 1988 - 24 October 2009
New York

Donaway Shylow Rego
by Debra Rego (Mother)

When Donaway was a baby, my little sister Angel loved her so much. Angel loved spending a lot of time with us.

My mother was in a hospital over an hour away. On January 16, 1989, we were returning from visiting her when we got into a tragic accident. The pickup truck I was driving flipped and rolled over many times. Angel had Donaway in her arms. They both went through the windshield.

Angel saved Donaway by cradling her in her arms. My sister died instantly, which I did not know at the time. The truck crushed me upside down. The police and doctors did not tell me until hours later. Angel was only 13 years old. Donaway was only eight months old.

Donaway had tried to take her life a couple of times, but I think it was more of a cry for help. I did try to help her any way I could.

Donaway and Shawn's birthdays were only two years and six days apart. We always had their birthday parties together, usually on Memorial Day, but I still did something small on each of their birthdays.

In the year 2006, Donaway would be 18 and Shawn would be 16. In January, or maybe February, I asked them if they wanted their birthdays together and we could rent a hall like the Veterans of Foreign Wars or something. They could invite everyone they knew from the school. Or, if they wanted to have their own birthday party because each was so special, they could. They both wanted to think about it.

We had just moved to the area June 2004. Shawn died two months before their birthday. Donaway, who does not like to show her feelings, had a tear in her eye when she said, "I guess Shawn made the decision. He decided he did not want to share another birthday with me".

That hurt so bad. I wish I could have taken away her pain. She felt some guilt for not taking him to chorus that night.

Donaway and Shawn always looked out for each other. Donaway was short for her age and Shawn was tall for his, so a lot of people thought they were twins. They were my Gemini twins.

What was funny, when we moved to New York, Donaway stayed her height 4'11" but Shawn sprouted up to 6'2"

Because I worked so much Donaway learned a lot from her father. She used to do trick riding on her four-wheeler with her brother Shawn. She wasn't afraid to get dirty. She knew how to change a tire, change the oil in her car, and she even installed her whole sound system in her car which sounded really loud.

Whenever Donaway wanted to try a new instrument, we would get it for her. When we wanted to get her lessons, she refused and said she would teach herself, but I signed her up for the classes in school anyway.

One time, for Shawn and Donaway's birthdays, I had their party at a comedy club I managed. Their friends and a couple of comics did some clean jokes for them.

All of a sudden, Donaway took the microphone and started singing. She had such a beautiful voice. Apparently, Donaway was singing and working as a disc jockey at the Boys and Girls club after school. I cried when I heard how awesome Donaway was.

Donaway asked me one time if she could try out for a talent show. I took her and some of her friends for the auditions. This was many years before America's Got Talent and American Idol. The judges didn't pick her.

Oh, I almost forgot; when Donaway was a baby, she was a baby model. We went to many of the shows, but they wanted us to sign her up so they could make decisions for her. My husband and I wouldn't allow that. We didn't have tons of money for the outfits they expected us to buy, so that ended.

Donaway had a lot of talent. She was disc jockeying for school dances in New York, and for weddings. In school, Donaway was in chorus and drama. She was in plays and even sang solo while someone played guitar. Whenever I hear that song on the radio, I can remember Donaway singing it.

When Shawn died, Donaway was crushed. They were each other's best friend, even though they did not like to admit it.

We still had a small party for Donaway's birthday. I found out after she died that she had told people she never wanted any more birthdays without Shawn.

Donaway turned eighteen that year. Soon after, she met a wild boy. We didn't like him much. He was a dropout of school and did not seem like he was going to do anything with his life.

Donaway loved him though, so we put up with him. Donaway moved out and moved in with her best friend's family so she could party and be with the boyfriend more. Then, Donaway ended up moving in with him. As he started to grow on us, all of a sudden she broke up with him. Donaway wouldn's tell us the real reason.

He said he did not want to live without Donaway. He signed up for the Army and told us he asked to be on the front line. He's still here on Earth. He has married twice and has children.

Donaway moved in with two girls. After some time, she said she wanted to date one of them. That was a surprise. I told Donaway, "I do not care who you're with as long as they love you as much as you love them. If you're happy, then I'm happy."

My daughter thought that maybe she and her girlfriend could make a brand new start in California where my older sister lived. They went for a visit for a month in August. They made some money working for my sister and came back.

They stayed in New York for two weeks. Donaway didn't want to return to California but her girlfriend did, so they went back to California in September.

A week after they returned to California, my best friend passed away. He was always like a second father to Shawn and Donaway. He believed in them. When Donaway said she wanted to disc jockey, he gave her a lot of his old equipment. He used to get them great gifts. He treated them great.

Donaway was devastated when she heard that he had died. She would have needed to borrow the money to return for the funeral, so she decided against going to it.

That's when everything went really bad for Donaway out in California. I found out after the fact that she ran away twice out there. The first time, she went only a few miles away from my sister's house to my sister's office. The second time, she was ten miles away. Donaway was scared and upset, so she called my sister.

The day before Donaway died, we talked for hours. She said stuff that I didn't understand; I was too blind to realize what she truly meant.

She also said that she would be home for Christmas, and she would never leave New York again. Now I understand what she really meant, but at the time, I was so excited that she was going to be home I didn't think about what she really meant.

While Donaway was in California she got a gig at a very popular club where she was going to work as a disc jockey. She had no idea, but when Donaway told me the date, I wanted to go out there to show her how proud I was of her and how I was going to support her with any decisions, but obviously, not her dying.

When Donaway didn't want to talk, she would only answer questions with very short words. Usually, either hours later or the next day, she would be back to being talkative. I usually let her have some space and did not bother her when she wanted her quiet time.

When I called Donaway on Saturday, October 24, 2009, she wouldn't say too much. I thought she needed her quiet time. I never thought Donaway was going through so much pain that day that it would be her last.

Whenever Donaway would ever mention suicide, all her friends knew to let me know. No matter what, I was always there for Donaway.

My sister's fiance's daughter and her boyfriend came by to see Donaway. Her girlfriend said, "I do not know where she is." No one knew where she was.

They searched for hours and finally found her in the attached garage. Donaway was hanging from a skinny little cheap dog leash like Shawn, but this leash was even thinner. Since Donaway was short, it was not quick.

Donaway died on Saturday, October 24, 2009, around 6:00 p.m. pacific time, 9:00 p.m. eastern time. My sister never called me. The New York State Police showed up at my door the next day, Sunday morning.

I tried to call my sister, but she didn't answer my call. My husband and I jumped in my car and drove from upstate New York to California in about a day and a half through snow and ice storms.

We saw Donaway before she was cremated and as soon as we could, we brought her back home. We buried Donaway's ashes next to Shawn in our family plot.

About the Author
Debra Rego is Donaway's mother; she's also mother to Shawn Rego, whose story is also in this book. She and her husband live in New York.

Dannielle Elaine Rogtke

29 September 1987 - 8 September 2016
Missouri

Dannielle Elaine Rogtke
by Marian Spring (Mother)

Dannielle was born September 29, 1987, the youngest of four children. There was an eleven-year gap between Dannielle and her oldest sibling. Danni was born in San Bernardino, California. My labor with her was induced. I thought she was such a beautiful baby. Just as she was being delivered, her father hit something on the table that made it drop. The doctor told him he wouldn't want to go home with me after that.

Even as a child, Danni was a free spirit and caring person, but her childhood was not an easy one. My marriage to her father ended in divorce when Danni was nine. Her father terminated his parental rights.

Danni loved to ice skate, starting when she was about ten. The skating rink was in Davenport, Iowa. I bought skates for both of us and skated with her and helped her. I made her the most beautiful emerald green skating outfit for her first and only competition. She won second place in her competition. She took weekly lessons, and we always skated for a while afterward. Her skates are still in my closet.

When I met my current husband, Danni seemed to like and get along with him. My husband had a daughter who was five years younger than Danni; they appeared to get along great. What I didn't know is that her kind heart did not allow her to tell me that it wasn't always the case.

As Danni became a teenager, she became even more free-spirited. She verged on the edge of difficult, sometimes even crossing that line. Danni was on the dance team in high school, where she got along with both the popular crowd and the not-so-popular crowd.

Danni told me one December day when she was about seventeen that she was going Christmas shopping with friends. I told her not to be out too late. I went to bed as usual. I awoke the next morning and discovered that she wasn't at home.

In a complete panic, I started searching for her. I finally learned that she had boarded an airplane and had gone to visit someone in Pennsylvania. Her father, who had not really been part of her life for years, picked her up from there. He was an over-the-road truck driver. Danni stayed with him for quite a while.

Danni married when she was eighteen years old. After she got pregnant, she discovered that there was a problem with her baby shortly before her due date, so labor was induced, The most beautiful baby boy was born. Danni named him Shawn Matthew Rutherford. He was born at Barnes Jewish Hospital in Saint Louis, Missouri. He was born with hypoplastic right heart syndrome, so he was immediately transferred to Children's Hospital nearby.

Everything looked good. The baby was first on the list for a new heart until suddenly he turned septic and his intestines started dying. The doctors did surgery to try to repair his intestines, but the surgery was not successful. We had to make the decision to remove him from life support, something no mother, especially a first-time mother, should ever have to do.

When Danni's beautiful baby boy died, something inside of her broke. She was holding him at the time they removed life support. Afterward, she bathed and dressed him. She was lost without him and felt crushed and heartbroken. She had nightmares. She was just plain not functioning.

Danni later had four more children, two girls and two boys. But as hard as Danni tried, she always seemed too afraid to make the complete bond with them for fear of losing them too.

She started making worse and worse decisions despite knowing that they were the wrong decisions to make. She started drinking, did some drugs, got in some trouble with the law, and just couldn't seem to make her life work.

No matter how hard I tried to make Danni see just how beautiful and kind she was, she never saw that in herself. My beautiful daughter didn't like herself, even though she had the kindest heart and would give anyone the shirt off of her back. No matter how little she had, Danni was always willing to give it someone who she believed needed it more. Danni somehow couldn't feel the incredible amount of love that everyone had for her.

Danni left her husband when her second son was young, a decision she regretted for the rest of her short life. She then had two children who ended up living with their dad. Danni desperately wanted to be the mother they needed, one they could be proud of, but as hard as she tried, she couldn't make it work.

Danni went on to marry again and have another son. Once again, she had another failed marriage. She had yet to forgive herself for losing her first son and letting her life spiral out of control. Danni placed this son with me for a while to get her life back in line, all the while keeping a very close relationship with him.

Danni made the decision to marry again to a man she barely knew when her younger son was three years old. Then she had another daughter. She was determined to make this marriage work and fix her life. She hoped that her older son would want to come back to live with her. She was always willing to give him the choice and do what was best for him.

Unfortunately, there were problems in the marriage, something Dannielle's sensitive soul could simply not deal with. She lost all faith in herself. She was consumed with guilt and self-hatred for not being the mother and person she wanted so badly to be. She had made poor choices, so she lost her driver's license and was at the mercy of her husband. Her youngest daughter was removed from her home by the Department of Family Services and placed with me.

Danni tried hard to get her daughter back, but conflicts in her home and her alcohol consumption increased as she tried to deal with an unbearable situation. She began to send photos to me to document some of the things that were going on in her marriage. She had many ways out of the situation, but she couldn't see them. Her world had become dark. She had lost all her children. She couldn't take care of her needs in a rural area with no transportation. She hated depending on other people; it made her feel like she was a burden.

Dannielle lost her father just a little over a month before her daughter was taken from her. The weight of the world and the challenges in her unhappy marriage became too much for her fragile shoulders to bear.

The last conversation I had with Dannielle was early on that fateful night. She told me that she was the only one trying to work to get her child back. She understood that she could not stop her husband from doing the things that he did.

In that conversation, Dannielle seemed fearful that something may happen to her. She asked that if something bad did happen, would I please use the pictures she had sent me and fight for her daughter. I suggested many ways out to her, but Dannielle didn't see them as solutions. I assured her that we all needed her and that I would always take care of her children, but that they needed her more than they needed me.

I thought that since her husband had left, the situation would cool down. I also thought that I had time to persuade her that there were many options available to her. I didn't realize that her fragile, broken soul could take no more.

The next morning, I took Dannielle's son to school. I went to a meeting and then picked him up after school. We came home to find out that my beautiful sweet daughter had chosen to leave, that my love was not enough to save her broken soul. My baby girl was gone. I never knew what it was truly like to walk in darkness until her beautiful light went out.

When we got home, my mother was there. I remember asking rather rudely, "Why are you here?"

My husband approached me with tears in his eyes while my mom took my grandson into the other room. He told me that they had found Danni that morning, and that she was dead. I hit him and called him a liar. For whatever reason, I asked him for my gun. I remember feeling like I couldn't breathe.

The next thing I remember, I woke up on the floor with an emergency medical technician (EMT) standing over me. I asked him why he was there and said that I didn't need help because I have a pacemaker. He said they were just making sure I was okay. He asked if I had any anti-anxiety medication and told me that I should take some.

My husband handed a card to me shortly after they left and said that I needed to call the coroner as soon as possible. The coroner informed me that Danni's husband had relinquished his rights to make her final arrangements to me, so I went into auto-pilot mode and did what needed to be done.

Danni is buried in a very small cemetery about two miles from my house in the country. Her brothers and sisters helped as I styled her hair, put makeup on her and painted her nails. We bought a new outfit for her to wear. Danni's service was a graveside service with a local minister. We played the song "Jealous of the Angels." We had a small family viewing for just our side of the family. We put roses in Danni's grave with her after they lowered her down. (They were probably white roses.)

Afterward, everyone met at the church for a gathering, but instead, I had my son and husband take me to the lake to the place where Danni and I had spent much of our time.

About the Author
Marian Spring is Danni's mother. She lives in Bethel, Missouri, with her husband and son. She enjoys spending time in the pond area that Danni helped her build.

Joe Dennis Scott

7 January 1960 - 11 February 1979
Tennessee

Joe Dennis Scott
by Harold Ray Scott (Brother)

In this life, we as mankind know,
  people come and people go.
The time they spend while passing through,
  is often short it seems,
And we think they will always be here,
  to share our hopes and dreams
But as we learn each passing day,
  Special people go away.
Yet, still with us they will always be,
  kept alive in a memory.
- Harold R Scott, written in memory of Joe D Scott. 1979

Born the fourth child of six, the third son of five, Joe joined our family on a cold day in January of 1960.

Our parents, both born in rural, middle Tennessee during the Great Depression years, welcomed him two years prior to my arrival. My siblings and I were all born within an eight-year period, from 1954 to 1962. Making us what I have called "stair-step-siblings", because we came along about every eighteen months apart. Growing up as children of the sixties and seventies, we were a very close-knit team and anything that affected one, affected all.

Joe, like most of the rest of us, bore the dark features of our mother. He had black hair, brown eyes, and an olive skin tone. A somewhat shy child, he grew into a tall, quiet natured and well mannered young man. Joe enjoyed nature and loved riding his horse, Sparky. He loved hunting, fishing and living life as a farm boy. Life was simple, unassuming and carefree.

Summer days were spent playing in the nearby creek, riding our bikes up and down the dusty, country roads. Our young lives could have easily been depicted in a Norman Rockwell painting.

Rural life was all we knew as a farming family living in one of the poorer counties of Tennessee. This, however, did not mean we lacked for love from our parents. It just called for an imagination that would allow myself, Joe, and our other siblings to escape into our own created space; these were the days before video games, cell phones, and social media.

Joe was two years older than I, and while the relationship between myself and all my siblings was good, due to our age order, Joe and I naturally had a close relationship.

Growing up on a working farm, we spent many hours together as youngsters and as teenagers tending to the crops and other chores that farm life entailed. School days also provided a lot of together-time for us as siblings. We shared many things, whether it was toys, clothes, or funny stories.

There would be, however, one thing in particular that Joe would not share with me, as this story will reveal.

Joe reached the age of eighteen in 1978. He had gotten his first job away from the farm and bought his first car: a green, Dodge Charger. This gave me, at sixteen, the opportunity to enjoy rides with my older brother without a care in the world. Joe seemed happy. He was beginning to live his life, having obtained his driver's license the day after his eighteenth birthday on January 7, 1978.

The summer of that year brought many happy times for us as siblings. We enjoyed drives in the country and into the little town, five miles or so from the family farm. It allowed us the opportunity to spend time on the river near our home, enjoying the cool water and having time together as brothers.

Little did I know, that it would be our last year together and that the memories we were making would come to sustain me in the coming years.

It was a cold but sunny Saturday morning. February 10, 1979. By this point in our young lives, I, at age seventeen, and Joe, having celebrated his nineteenth birthday a month prior. He had begun dating and continued to work. He had what appeared to me to be a good life.

There was not much to do in the area where we lived, so sometimes it called for some creativity to pass the time. Otherwise, we would be bored teenagers.

Joe still lived at home with myself, our parents, and some of my other siblings, but had on occasion not come home at night. I assumed he was spending time with either friends or the person he was seeing at the time.

On this particular morning, I was visiting with cousins who lived near our home. Joe dropped in and I was happy to see him. He proceeded to share with me about his previous night's outing to a local movie theater and about how much he had enjoyed the movie.

We laughed, talked, and shared a good visit as we stood in the snow that was beginning to melt on the bright, sunny morning. It was a perfect day and all was right with the world.

We said our goodbyes after Joe had shared his plans for the day. There'd been no indication of the earth shattering news that would come to me only hours later. It would be the last time that I saw my brother Joe alive.

As darkness fell that night, I was still at my cousin's home. At about eight o'clock the phone rang. I could tell by the conversation that something was obviously wrong. It was another brother of mine who called to tell me that I needed to come home. Something very serious had just happened and I was to get there immediately.

Upon arriving home, I was told that my brother Joe had been shot and was being taken to a local hospital. The extent of his injury was unclear, as were the circumstances of the shooting. I assumed it was likely an accidental shooting of some sort. Never did it enter my mind that Joe had intentionally meant to shoot himself.

My parents would be making the nearly one hundred mile drive to be with my brother. What they must be feeling, I could only imagine. Things like this only happen to other people, right? It would prove to be a long night.

The plan was for my parents to make their way to be with Joe and then provide updates to the rest of our family as they became available. I was instructed, along with two other siblings, to go spend the rest of the night with our grandparents (our mother's parents). By this time, it was near midnight.

While the details of the situation were still sketchy, we had learned that Joe's condition was extremely critical and that he would be transported from the small, rural hospital to Vanderbilt University Medical Center in Nashville.

Within a short time, I learned that the shooting, which was originally thought to have been done by an unknown source, or an accident, was in fact at the hands of my brother. He had tried to take his life.

My mind raced wildly as I tried to make sense of what I was hearing. It had to be untrue. After all, I had just been with Joe only hours earlier and he was making plans for the next week. What had happened in the short time since he and I had been together?

I trudged through the snow from the car upon arriving at my grandparent's home, unsure of how to tell them the news I knew. I banged on their door to wake them, as they were already in bed and unaware of what was happening to our family. Once inside, I broke the news and total chaos ensued.

With the breaking of a new day, life as we knew it would never be the same.

As Sunday morning daylight broke after a sleepless night, my parents arrived unannounced.

Both my mom and dad looked frazzled, to say the least. My mother seemingly in a shock-like state. My dad began to inform those of us gathered at my grandparents that Joe was very critical and being kept alive by mostly artificial means.

My parents were of strong faith and attended church regularly. They had made the decision to come home so we could all attend church together then return to Nashville to be with Joe.

As a seventeen-year-old kid, I did not understand why this decision was made, yet, I did not question it. I attended church and all the while wondering if my brother was scared or knew anything about his condition.

By this time, word of my brother's condition and suicide attempt had begun to spread throughout the little country church and community in which my family lived. The church service was cut short to allow my family time to make our way back to the hospital which was over an hour away. All I could think of was that Joe was all alone.

Upon arriving back home from church, we were hit with the devastating news... Joe had died at 10:10 a.m.

My world was shattered. At seventeen, this was the first person I had ever lost. My nineteen-year-old brother was gone . . . by his own hands, nonetheless.

How could he have done this to me, to us as a family? What was so bad that he felt this was his only option? He had been so happy only hours before as he shared his stories with me.

Suicide? How could this be happening? It wasn't fair. Joe had so much to live for. His whole life was ahead of him.

My family was lost in the whirlwind of the ringing phone, the endless line of family, friends, and neighbors, who were coming by to offer whatever they could to help us get through this.

This was the first time I ever remember seeing my dad cry. He was one who rarely showed any kind of emotion. My mom seemed to go into her own world of shock, sadness, and denial.

My dad made the phone call to the local funeral home to set a time to make arrangements for Joe to be brought home from Nashville. He would be laid to rest in the small, country cemetery within sight of the home that we as siblings had grown up in together.

Once arrangements for the visitation and funeral were made later that evening, it was decided by my parents that it would be an around the clock, two day visitation time. Joe would be laid to rest on the thirteenth day of February. I am still unsure how we were functioning after having been on this rollercoaster ride for nearly four days. The grieving process was only beginning. None of us had ever experienced such a loss, so, it would be a minute by minute journey.

In the days that followed Joe's death and burial, it seemed as if I would suffocate. Everywhere I turned there were reminders of life with my brother. We were still just children, so my parents tried their best to maintain some sort of normal routine.

In the midst of all the sadness, my mom decided she wanted to go through Joe's things to put them away. She did not want to get rid of anything. It seemed that she needed to keep every piece of her baby boy close. I offered to help her. We began the hard job of carefully placing Joe's clothes and personal belongings into a chest.

I found during this process that we did not talk about Joe. It was as if we feared that if his name were mentioned, or if questions about his death were asked, we would totally crumble. So, we kept everything inside. A part of the grieving process called denial, I would come to learn.

It was during this putting away of Joe's things, that I discovered a small notebook. Without letting my mother know, I took it and placed it where she could not find it.

In the notebook, I had found Joe's handwritten suicide note that had been written two weeks prior to the actual event. I was torn whether or not to share it with my family, especially my mother. She had somehow concluded that the shooting was an accident and not an intended act. I suppose it was denial and her way of coping with the loss of one of her children. I made the decision to keep the suicide note a secret.

Although, with the passing of a few years, I shared with some of my siblings that I had found it, but had read and burned it to spare my mother any more pain. It has now been almost forty years, and I have never told my mother of my discovery of Joe's words that he had decided to end his life.

It was a heavy burden for a seventeen-year-old child to carry, but as I have thought back on it all these years later, I feel I made the best decision. Although perhaps it would have opened up a dialogue and discussion about suicide and how we learn to deal with the aftermath.

It would be a number of months before my parents erected a headstone to mark Joe's grave. I assume it was just too painful for them, and once done, would make it all so very final and real; they had indeed buried a child of their own.

I visited Joe's gravesite almost every day for a long time after his death. I worked through the process of grieving in my own way, as did the rest of my family, I suppose.

We never really discussed my brother. It was as if he had been forgotten. I did not want to forget Joe or be ashamed of how he had died. I wanted to try to understand why he had chosen to end his life. Could I have done more? Did I miss the signs? Was he reaching out for help in the last conversation he and I shared and I just did not see? All of this, I have learned, is normal for those of us left behind.

Over the years since Joe's passing, I have known several other people who opted for suicide, and as with my brother, there continues to be blame placed, judgments passed, speculation, and all sorts of comments that lack understanding made.

It is often seen as a selfish, weak, and an easy way out option. In reality, I feel it takes strength, courage and is likely a hard act to follow through with.

I often wonder what my brother would have accomplished. He would have likely gone on to be a good husband, father and a citizen who would have contributed much to society. Unfortunately, he could not see beyond what he struggled with at the time and felt the world would be better off without him.

I cannot truly say exactly what my brother felt, even after reading the suicide note left behind. It did, however, reveal his pain and the uncertainty of a future. He did a good job of hiding the intention to take his life, which caused me to question my role in all of it for a number of years.

With the passing of years, in fact on the tenth anniversary of Joe's death, after I had posted a notice in the local hometown newspaper in memory of my brother, my mother spoke her son's name for the first time since his death. The grieving process for her had taken ten years. I felt that perhaps she had finally reached the acceptance phase.

After all the years of not talking about Joe, we seemed to have broken through the wall that had kept some of us silent for far too long. It would not bring back my brother, but it did seem to bring back a part of my mother who had been missing for so many years. Even my dad, who rarely visited the gravesite began to do so, even though he stated it was still very painful for him. Today, he rests alongside my brother, as he too has since passed away.

My brother is one of thousands of people who left this world far too soon and in a manner that is still all too often a taboo, touchy and painful subject.

It is my hope that by sharing Joe's story, his short life of nineteen years will have had a positive impact far beyond the farm where he, myself and our siblings enjoyed life together. If only for a brief time. Joe, you are remembered and loved still. You will be forever nineteen.

About the Author
Harold R "Scottie" Scott, is a brother, two years younger to Joe Dennis Scott. Harold currently lives in Lebanon/Wilson County, Tennessee. His hobbies include genealogy, photography, travel, and gardening. Harold currently serves as President of the Tennova Lebanon Health Care Volunteer Auxiliary and is a former floral designer. He is a community volunteer/educator/public speaker for HIV/AIDS awareness and education. He is an author and has published two books.

Scott Wilson Simpson

1 April 1993 - 14 July 2017
Ohio

Scott Wilson Simpson
by Ann L. Simpson (Mother)

Snow was falling in Ohio on April 1, 1993. I had a baby that day. Scott was a healthy, beautiful baby boy, my firstborn. He had white-blonde hair and a darling dimple on one cheek. I never knew such joy.

His first years at home included a new puppy, lots and lots of visits from grandparents, and surgery to remove a benign cyst on the top of his head. The puppy was a sweet challenge, visits from grandparents were so special, and the head surgery was traumatic.

He was a thumb sucker and had a special piece of black fur he called Fuzzy to give him comfort, especially after his surgery. Fuzzy even went in the operating room with Scott. Overall, Scott's life was filled with so much love and happiness.

Scott had a wonderful imagination. He loved playing with toys, especially small dinosaurs and other animals. He enjoyed Barney on TV, especially when his sister was born. Later, he and his sister watched The Land Before Time movies; even later, it was Jurassic Park. He loved dinosaurs.

Scott took a bus to and from school. He wore cowboy boots to kindergarten every day, and every day he climbed on the bus with his boots on. The bus driver adored him. One time, while in first grade he left his backpack on the bus. He went to the school secretary to let her know. She asked him to describe it; he described the bus, not the backpack.

Another time he never got off the bus. He was found sleeping, still in his seat on the bus while parked in the bus garage. I was terrified that day, so then I was relieved once my sweet Scott was found.

When Scott was seven years old, he was a big fan of Pokemon. By then, he had two younger sisters. He and his sisters played with small Pokemon toys, played Pokemon games, played with Pokemon cards and sang the Pokemon rap song. On Scott's seventh birthday, he was allowed to invite friends over for a party, so he had a Pokemon themed party. When his Pokemon cake was served, the boys enjoyed a Pokemon burping contest. The boys were hilarious. I started referring to myself as Pokemom.

Being outdoors was always one of Scott's favorite things to do. He enjoyed a lot of outdoor activities with his dad, like camping, fishing, hiking, and geocaching. He also enjoyed Cub Scout camp and swimming for the Rising Tide youth team.

Scott played on a youth soccer team as well. One time, he was running down the field dribbling the soccer ball while kindly saying "Excuse me" every time he pushed past his opponents. The referee told us he never saw a soccer player with manners like Scott's.

Every summer, my husband and I took our family to a quiet island in northern Michigan that is filled with nature and the beauty of the surrounding lake. Scott loved being outside and free to roam, bike and swim. He, his sisters and cousins enjoyed playing games and creating funny dance competitions.

Scott was also quite a mischief-maker. A few examples are when he started a jet-ski on dry land, crawled through a stream tunnel and came out covered with leeches, took a jet-ski out on the lake without a life jacket and without my permission, flipped our golf cart by going too fast around a corner, and dragged one of his sisters into a beehive.

He could be mean to his sisters, but he could also be very kind. He and his sisters played well together and enjoyed each other's company – even while fighting. Yes, Scott was definitely ornery, but we loved him and looked forward to watching him grow up.

In addition to being ornery, Scott was a night owl his entire life. He stayed awake late at night and slept all morning whenever he had the chance. And no matter how urgent things were, he only had one speed. We called it Scott Speed, which was not speedy at all.

He was consistently slow at things like getting ready, being prepared and meeting time commitments. Scott had several other character traits worth mentioning. He was a bit immature and became frustrated easily. He was smart but lacked common-sense. I thought he would either outgrow these traits or learn to live with them. It breaks my heart he never had the chance to grow up and become the person God intended him to be.

Scott was a good student. Physics and German were his two favorite subjects. He was involved in many activities while in junior high and high school. He marched in the high school band when he was in junior high playing the clarinet. He continued marching in the band during his first two years of high school, playing the saxophone.

He played on the soccer team one year, but he competed on the swim team and tennis team all four years of high school. He enjoyed weight lifting and keeping fit as well. Scott was fun-loving and had a wonderful smile.

Scott had a lot of friends and liked his teachers and his activities. In fact, he never had to ask a girl to homecoming or prom before his senior year because a girl would always ask him first. Though he never had a serious girlfriend, he maintained close friendships with all his high school friends while in college. He drank alcohol and smoked some marijuana also, but I never thought they would become issues for him.

Scott was accepted to the University of Wisconsin, Madison and began as a freshman in the fall of 2011. Issues followed, and then he began to decline. Looking back, I never realized these incidences became so frequent; I only saw one at a time and didn't think to look at them as a whole.

To begin with, Scott was kicked out of his dormitory for a late night drunken brawl and for writing homophobic remarks on another student's door. But his grade point average (GPA) was over 3.0, so I believed he was doing well in school. He even went to the wrong math class for half a semester before realizing, but still maintained his GPA.

For these reasons, we moved him into an apartment to finish out his freshman year. In subsequent years, I asked him about his grades, but I could not see them for myself, because parents aren't allowed to see student grades without permission from the student. I never forced him to show me either. He said his grades were fine and I believed him; that was a big mistake on my part.

The first summer home from college, Scott was hired to work for the family business. It was a small manufacturing company whose employees were submitted to random drug testing. Scott tested positive for marijuana and lost his job - yet another incident.

During his third year of college, Scott joined a fraternity. He was a founding father of the University of Wisconsin chapter as he helped establish the group on campus. He was very proud to be a leading brother in this effort. A big dinner was held with family, friends and nearby chapters to celebrate and officially establish the chapter. Scott was part of the program and did a nice job speaking in front of the large crowd. We were so proud. Unfortunately, he was drinking too much while dropping and failing his classes at this time, which we were unaware of.

After four years in college, Scott admitted he needed another year in order to graduate. His father and I both took five years to graduate, so we were not worried or surprised.

At the end of the fifth year, I asked him if he was graduating, and he told me he was one class shy, but allowed to participate in the spring graduation ceremony. He asked me to bring his high school graduation gown saying he didn't want to purchase another one for college; after all, they were both black.

We attended Scott's graduation weekend that included several dinners, plus the big event held in Badger Stadium. It was a large crowd and a large graduating class, so I could not see Scott on the field. His name was in the directory listed as graduating in Physics. What was not to believe?

But, in fact, he was never on the field that day and had failed every course that semester. When Scott died, he needed thirty more credits to graduate. He either failed or requested to drop many of his courses.

I remember talking to him about possibly joining the Coast Guard. He liked the idea; I suspect it was because he was not being entirely truthful with me about his college situation. Of course, he never took steps to join up; instead, he told us he graduated. I asked to see his diploma, and he said he needed to pick it up. I asked if the diploma could be mailed, but he insisted on picking it up. I never saw his diploma.

In spring of 2017, Scott told me he had several job offers, one in Minneapolis and two in Nashville. Since he preferred to live in Nashville, he chose one of those companies. He told me the company's name, the job description, and the August start date. That worked well because he was renting an apartment in Madison with a lease ending in August. He refused to talk any more about his upcoming job.

Scott stayed in Madison last summer. The last photo of him was on his Instagram with a group of friends at Milwaukee's Summerfest.

We were at our summer home in northern Michigan. Scott planned to come up in July to see the family and take a fishing trip to Canada with some of the guys. I texted him asking what day we would see him, and he texted back saying he would come north on Saturday or Monday. We didn't hear from him after that.

We called our nephew who was working in Madison at the time and asked him to run by Scott's apartment to see if he was at home. He called saying Scott's car was there, but he didn't answer the door. We asked him to look in a window, as we thought maybe Scott was sleeping, but we were also worried.

Scott was seen dead in his apartment with a gunshot wound to the head.

The toxicology report came back months later. He had no drugs in his system, but there was an extremely high level of alcohol. He didn't leave a suicide note.

As far as we know, he never talked to any of his friends about ending his life. He mentioned to me several times he wished he had an older sister, but does that make him suicidal?

What was causing his pain? I can't bear to think of his pain while deciding to end his life. I wish I could have taken away his pain. Why did he not call me? It never goes away – the constant "woulda, coulda, shoulda". Suicide is a dark place. This is so hard.

As a parent I often wonder about signals I should have noticed and questions I should have asked…
Why would he write a homophobic remark – he was never brought up that way?
Why did he want his high school graduation gown for college graduation?
Why did he tell me he graduated?
Why did he want to keep his old beat up car rather than owning a new one?
Why did he tell me he had a job in Nashville, but not want to talk about it?
Why did he never discuss current events?
Why did he watch so many movies?
Was he an alcoholic?
Was he gay?
Why did he lie to me when all I wanted was to help him? Did he know that?

All I know is that I hope everyone remembers Scott as the lively, friendly, happy, hilarious guy he was. For everyone who knew him, I know he made an impact and you cherish every memory of him you have. Hold your loved ones close and never take anything for granted.

My son, Scott W. Simpson lived. He was loved and he mattered - and he died by suicide. I never knew such sadness.

About the Author
Ann Simpson is Scott's mother; she lives in Coshocton, Ohio. She's also the mother of two daughters plus a beautiful dog who has been very therapeutic over this past year. Ann is a stay at home mom, community advocate and volunteer. Ann thanks the Parents of Suicide (POS) group for their continued emotional support during this incredibly sad and difficult experience.

John Clayton Sims

3 March 1994 - 2 September 2017
Texas

John Clayton Sims
by Karen Grace Sims (Mother)

Cadillac cowboy is defined as the backwoods cowboy stuck in the big city, Bubba J (a nickname we had for Clay) was an old Texas soul in a young body. As a young boy, it wasn't unusual to find him in boots and shorts. His sweet, kind personality was evident as a child and throughout his young adult life. He was a fisherman. He was a hunter. He was the most patriotic 23-year-old anyone had ever met. He was our son. "He had a tender heart with a tortured mind" (quote by Rick Warren).

September 2, 2017, at 12:51 a.m., my oldest son Clay, made the decision to take his own life. Everything has changed.

Clay was born on March 3, 1994. He was our first child. We didn't want to know his sex until he was born. My gut feeling was correct. I knew all along we'd have a boy. He was a good baby and slept through most of the night by six weeks old.

My husband was so proud that Clay looked just like him. Clay was a big baby. He had beautiful blue eyes that later settled as a hazel grey color. He had light brown hair with a hint of red and later dark brown. He was very talkative and friendly and rarely threw fits. He was a pleaser and followed the rules. He didn't challenge us. We laugh and say the other two younger siblings introduced him to breaking the rules.

Clay was the oldest of three children; he was older than Ruben by 23 months and older than his sister Malee by 4 1/2 yrs. He was sweet, protective, and aware of them. He would constantly remind them of the rules.

Clay enjoyed the outside, playing video games, being in Boy Scouts and Weblos, Tae Kwon Do, playing the double bass. He enjoyed the Royal Ambassadors, animals, and hanging by the bonfires with friends.

In high school, our son was a late bloomer, but he had two good friends and was good with everyone. He developed a social life probably around his junior year. He had dysgraphia, so school was not his favorite place be.

However, Clay loved animals, hunting, and outdoors, so he blossomed in the Future Farmers of American (FFA). He raised chickens and a goat and helped with any animals at the barn. He really developed a liking for an abandoned wild goat that he named Paschal.

The teachers really helped him stay focused to finish out high school. It wasn't unusual for Clay to hunt squirrels in the schoolyard. The school principal even stored one squirrel in his office refrigerator to preserve it for Clay to take home later and cook.

Clay could be obnoxious at times. Often, he said things he should have kept to himself. He loved to joke about inappropriate topics. He had a lot to say about how Obama was running our country into the ground.

His favorite activity on weekends was to hunt with my husband, his grandfather and his uncle. Even if the hunt was unsuccessful, being at the land in the middle of nowhere was healing therapy to him. He loved to fish.

In high school where Clay was known as JC, he frequently went to the lake with his spit can and baited hook. There were many days he fished during lunch at the nearby neighborhood lake just blocks away from the high school. He would also spend four or five hours at the school barn with his goat, Levi Garret (chewing tobacco) and all the other animals in the FFA facility. There was a small group of cowgirls and cowboys who hung out at the barns. They enjoyed telling me that Clay smelled like the goats.

After Clay graduated from high school, he enlisted in the US Army; he was proud of following his childhood dream of serving in the military. We visited him in Georgia for his boot camp graduation. Shortly after we left Georgia, we learned that he had injured his knee in the 26-mile ruck run, part of Advanced Infantry Training.

Within a few months, Clay was dismissed from the Army and his dream was shattered. Later after his death, we found paperwork that said the dismissal was because when he injured his knee and was informed of the dismissal, he attempted suicide twice. He was detained for a few months without any contact in a hospital to help him decompress and adapt to civilian life.

Clay arrived home in November of 2014. He was happy to be home, but we had no idea of his crushed heart. He had a rough few months trying to get a job and got a Driving While Intoxicated (DWI) ticket, so he decided to check himself into a treatment center for the first time in his life. Clay was falling apart and we couldn't figure out how to help him.

Clay's heart was big. Anyone could call upon him if they were in need of help or needed a listening ear. One morning at 4 o'clock, Clay got up because a friend called. His friend had a flat tire and needed help. Anytime anyone needed help, they knew they could count on him.

Although he possessed all these great qualities, Clay's mind was constantly racing with thoughts of, "You're not good enough," or "What the hell is wrong with you?" He was tortured.

Time after time, we took him to get tested to see where the sadness and brokenness he tried to hide came from. He was diagnosed with bipolar 2 and schizoaffective disorder in the spring of 2015. There were several medications that these disorders required, however, he refused to take them. He insisted he was fine, even though we believed deep down he wasn't

On September 1, 2017, Clay went partying with some friends. From what his peers have told us, he seemed happy that night, but everything changed when he was driving to a party in Aledo, Texas. He lost control of his car.

Clay swerved off the road in a countryside subdivision, crashing through metal pipe fencing and ending up in a dried out ravine covered with brush and small trees. The wrecked car was hidden fifty feet from the roadside.

First, he called his friend for help. Having totaled his beloved, 2006 champagne-colored, rag-top Cadillac, my son realized that there would be severe consequences for a second DWI.

While he searched the trunk for straps and chains to extract the car he found his 22 rifle, which he kept on hand for spontaneous varmint hunting. Devastated by the damage he caused, he decided to send his last group-text to me, my husband, my mother and my father (his grandparents) at 12:51 a.m.

"My last known tracking location is where I'm at." No one knew the meaning of a text like that until 10:00 in the morning when detectives knocked on our door. They told us that our son, Clay, had chosen to take his own life.

My stomach dropped. My eyes filled with tears. Our lives had become a complete, unimaginable, nightmare. As the detectives gave us more information, I could envision Clay freaking out. I could only imagine the devastation in his face. He believed there was no turning -around from this.

I sat in quiet. Speechless. There was no way Clay could be gone. I had seen him the night before. We had just arrived home from our weekly family Bible study at Grandma's house, and he was there too. He had sat on the sofa with me as we unwound for the night getting ready for bed; I had stroked his head like a five-year-old child. He had propped his head on my legs while we passed his cell phone back and forth playing a word game. He seemed fine. He seemed happy. My mind could not wrap itself around the fact that I would never see him again.

Clay loved us all, so I know he couldn't have considered the pain his death would cause. Otherwise, he never would have made that snap decision. Old adages such as, "He's in a better place" or "We'll see him again someday" are well-intended attempts to comfort me, however, the only peace I can rest on is that he was saved as a young man and is now resting in the arms of Jesus.

Clay's funeral was very masculine. He was buried in a pine box as he wanted to be. He had watched westerns on television and always told us to bury him in a pine box when the time came. Well, he got his wish. It was much prettier than what he might have chosen. It was a beautiful big pine box. The flowers we chose were reminiscent of the creek where he hung out as a young kid and there were sunflowers that grew taller than our six-foot tall fence. All of the flowers had a weedy Texas look. Clay's buried in Fort Worth, Texas at Greenwood Cemetery.

Clay had a big heart, I am confident he didn't do this to destroy us. He always wanted everyone around him to be happy. He had so many friends I couldn't have known them all. He never met a stranger. We have met so many people and friends that he touched. We've heard many stories of him encouraging their faith in God to get them through tough times. Friends have told us that he convinced them not to take their own lives. They've also said that he was their only friend.

It's been a bittersweet thought to know while he was a bit untamed by his mental illness, he was very tamed in his loving kindness. That's a legacy a mother and father can be proud of.

About the Author
Karen Sims is Clay's mother. She lives in Benbrook, Texas with her husband of 25 years. She's also the mother of three wonderful kids. She's worked off and on throughout their lives. She's a believer in Christ. Her faith drives her understanding of circumstances over which she has no control.

Stephen Kenneth Sokolowski

21 March 1987 - 11 July 2017
Florida

Stephen Kenneth Sokolowski
by Janis Sokolowski (Mother)

The year is 1987. Downstairs in my parents' home in Deer Park, New York, I have a craving for a cheese calzone. My husband Joe and I live in North Babylon, the next town over. We have a three-year-old son, Joey. It's only Joey and me in the downstairs of the house. My parents are upstairs in the kitchen, and Joe is sleeping in our home.

I visit my parents' house often because Joe works as a delivery driver for a bread company, so he puts in many hours and his sleep schedule can be "vampiric."

I get off the chair and go to the black phone hanging on the wall and dial the Italian restaurant to order. Then it happens.

My water breaks. My dad drives me back to my house where I wake up Joe to get started with the next part of our story: having our beautiful son Stephen. All is well, so we celebrate the birth of our second son at the hospital with champagne and a steak dinner.

Fast forward three years and we are now living in paradise, or so we think. My side of the family moves to Florida where my parents now fit the cliché role of Florida retirees. We follow soon afterward, though Joe and I are only in our late twenties. We build a beautiful home to provide our sons with a beautiful life. At least that is our wish.

Things never turn out as planned.

Stephen is three years old. Joey is part of a soccer team and we all enjoy attending his games. Afterward, there is a nightly ritual of bathing and story time. I am fortunate because I am able to be a stay-at-home mom. Joe and I decided early that is what we would do. I love this period of my life because I spend quality time with my boys. I want them to grow up knowing how loved they are.

During the first part of our nightly routine, I lift Stephen from the tub and mess his hair as I dry it with a towel. Then, after I wrap the towel around him, I run my fingers along his scalp to fix the wild strands. After Stephen dresses, he runs to the living room and collapses. He cannot walk. Panic sets in and we take him to a hospital that is twenty minutes away.

Despite countless tests including a spinal tap to rule out encephalitis, the doctors have no answers. Stephen is monitored in the hospital and eventually, he is able to walk again. We can get him an MRI, with the warning they are extremely expensive (it is 1990). Joe and I are far from wealthy people but there is no question we will risk debt if there is a test that could help our son.

I feel like we are walking on pins and needles. I just want to protect Stephen and keep him safe. We are able to get an MRI scheduled in Orlando pretty quickly.

I am young and do not know what lies ahead for my family. I have no clue that in 27 years this unknown will be the cause of me losing my precious son.

I am in my happy place, my home, watching Stephen and Joey play together. They always play together. They use their imagination to play with Sesame Street toys and Little People figures. The phone rings. I move swiftly to the landline because I am waiting for the results of the MRI.

Recognizing that the call is from the doctor is enough to raise my anticipation so much I feel unsteady.

It's a phone call that I will never forget.

The doctor tells me it is urgent that I get my son to the hospital immediately. If not, he could become a paraplegic at any time.

Stephen has a tumor within his spinal cord. I find it unbelievable that the doctor tells me such devastating news on the phone. For a moment, I make a slow retreat away from my sons. I don't want them to see me panic. The coils of the phone cord straighten as I respond to the doctor. Then I am back, putting the phone on the receiver and looking at my sons before picking up the phone again to dial my parents. I can always rely on them.

We all drive to the hospital, Joe, our boys, my mom and dad. We are met by the doctor and he shows us the MRI. We are told there are three doctors in the United States that can perform this type of surgery: one in Florida, one in New York and one in Texas. The decision needs to be made quickly, so we choose the doctor that practices at the University of Florida in Gainesville.

For weeks we are terrorized by the words of the first doctor, who without an ounce of bedside manner insists that the tumor might explode. Joe and I are so fearful of the unknown that we question even touching Stephen. We are afraid of moving him in a way that would lead to him rupturing in our arms.

Dr. Mickle, the neurosurgeon in Gainesville, is extraordinary and makes up for how terrible the first doctor was. Dr. Mickle is who we need. He makes us feel as though Stephen will be fine and that he will not break.

While in Dr. Mickle's office for an examination, Stephen sits on the check-up table with his legs swinging back and forth. With a West Virginian drawl, Dr. Mickle says to us, "He's fine. Let him run. Let him play." He lifts Stephen down from the table and tells him, "Go run down the hall and come back." Stephen follows the doctor's direction.

Under the supervision of this amazing doctor, Stephen darts down the hall. Joe and I watch our son and feel a degree of comfort we have not had in a very long time. We no longer handle Stephen with kid gloves as though he was made of crystal. Just this amount of reassurance is enough to fortify us to endure this trauma. Joe and I feel comfortable giving our child to Dr. Mickle to fix.

The morning of the surgery, Dr. Mickle greets us after his bike ride from his home to the hospital. Unsure of how far he rides, I am surprised at the sight of him nonchalantly walking in with a smile on his face to perform a task that seems beyond comprehension. Dr. Mickle is a very special doctor.

After a very long surgery, we learn that the tumor is an astrocytoma, usually found in the brain. Dr. Mickle tells us it came out in a nice long strip.

It is July 1991, almost a year since the surgery. After experiencing Stephen's health issues, I no longer want a big family as we'd planned. I want no more children. The pain and heartache are unbearable. I do not want to ever witness the suffering of someone I love so much again. I already feel pulled apart into a million pieces.

Joe and I stay at the Ronald McDonald House while Stephen undergoes procedures. It is wonderful to have a place to stay through this terrible time. It is there that something positive comes out of our stay in Gainesville. I become pregnant. Despite our initial desire to stop growing our family, with the birth of my third son, Thomas, I realize I really do.

It is six years since the removal of the tumor and Stephen has severe scoliosis. He wears a body brace that fruitlessly attempts to keep him straight. The turtle shell encompasses him day and night. I can tell that he is uncomfortable, but he wears it. He is a good son and does what he is told.

Because of scoliosis, Stephen is scheduled for a second surgery for a spinal fusion. This time, the surgery is in Orlando. A new doctor, Dr. Price, will lead the surgery to fuse Stephen's spine from the seventh to the eleventh thoracic vertebra. Our special doctor, Dr. Mickle, is going to make sure he is present to check if there is a recurrence of that nasty tumor.

On his drive to the hospital, the police due to a hostage situation in the area, stop Dr. Mickle. He tells the police to let him through because he is a brain surgeon and needs to get to the hospital immediately. He makes it to the hospital and is able to assist with Stephen's surgery. Unfortunately, the tumor is found growing in Stephen's spinal cord. Again, what can be removed is removed.

Stephen says to me, "You should get a better job, Mom, something that pays you more than just helping at school."

I work as a paraprofessional at his elementary school. His aunt is a registered nurse, and I consider a job like that, but I don't think I could handle working in a hospital or with sick children. It would break my heart to see the families face turmoil on a daily basis. Instead, I choose to become a teacher for students with disabilities, and I enroll to earn my bachelor's degree. This journey begins in 1997.

Stephen stands on the pitcher's mound during a Little League game. He wears an Atlanta Braves baseball uniform with clay staining the side of his white pants. His skinny and adorable frame hurls balls at the opposing batters. He even manages a few curve balls.

One after another, the batters strike out. Then a chubby boy on the opposing team goes to bat. In the bleachers, I can hear the boy's parents shouting, "The pitcher has nothing!" Stephen throws nice and slow; they are perfect strikes. The kid is struck out quickly.

After the game, Stephen is given the game ball. He lights up with a smile that shows his two large front teeth.

Baseball practice, baseball games, piano lessons, piano recitals, playing around with magic tricks and a magic hat I make. Making up scientific concoctions that only dad drinks (unknowingly, ha). Skateboarding and zipping around on a gas powered stand-up scooter. These are the things that amuse Stephen while he is a young boy.

The year is 2003. Stephen is 16 years old. He is scheduled for three more surgeries within a month. One is to remove hardware from his spine, the second is to put him in traction to stretch and straighten him, and the third is to put the hardware back in. He is courageous, determined, and wants to be free from all of this nonsense.

I keep a journal. In the pages I document his strength, writing about how he never complains or asks, "Why me?" My Stephen is an amazing person.

During this ordeal, he is in a crazy bed that resembles medieval torture rather than medical procedures of 2003. He lies in bed with pins through his knees and the metal framework of a halo around his head, both of which are attached to weighted pulleys meant to stretch and straighten him. This is called traction.

It is an awful thing to see him go through, but he makes it and moves on. When Stephen is back home, Joe and I buy him his first vehicle: a white Ford Ranger.

As Stephen ages, he enjoys video gaming and building computers. He loves his music and enjoys his beer. Slowly, being able to walk on his own becomes too difficult and he needs the aid of a cane. Stephen is asked to be the best man at his cousin's wedding. We get him a camouflage cane with a swirling green and brown pattern that he uses to support himself as he stands at his cousin's side during the ceremony.

Because of all the metal, MRI's do not help monitor Stephen's health. The doctors say that he is the best one to know his body. He certainly is, often recognizing a decline in his health that signals when a medical procedure will be needed.

Another surgery at 18 years old finds more tumor; another surgery at 20 in Miami with doctors who are renowned for spinal tumors; again at 22. More metal is implanted into his body: a shunt that drains fluid building in a cyst on his spine to his stomach.

These surgeries seem to do as much damage as help. At one point, Stephen loses the mobility of his hand. Thankfully, with therapy and determination, he regains the use of his hand.

He also loses strength in his legs; being able to drive to school becomes more difficult. We install hand controls in his truck. He earns an associate's degree, but getting around on a large campus becomes too difficult and he stops pursuing his education to focus on his health.

Eventually, even a cane is not enough and a walker with tennis balls on the bottom is used to guide him. He also gets a large blue walker that he can use outside the house.

Stephen is 22 years old. He and I stay in a Jacksonville apartment together for over a month as he goes back and forth for daily radiation treatment at the University of Florida Proton Therapy Center. I enjoy this time with him. He is my rock.

Stephen's legs shake as he supports himself on his walker. I learn this is called clonus, an uncontrollable shaking of legs and feet. It's been three years since his radiation and it is clear the treatment will not be his final medical procedure.

The aid of a wheelchair becomes necessary. We remove the wheels on his wheelchair so that it can fit in the bed of his truck. When going out, Stephen parks and swaps between the walker and the chair. He contends with this maneuver for a while, but eventually, the routine becomes too strenuous and he no longer drives. He uses the wheelchair to get around outside the home.

Stephen is 24 years old. I ask him to come work with me at the school. I head a program called AVID, Advancement Via Individual Determination, for students who want to go to college. These students are usually the first ones in their families to attain that status.

Stephen becomes a tutor for my class. Working with Stephen are the best years of my teaching career. Stephen is fantastic with all the students. They love him and he helps them in many areas of their lives. He is a good listener. He is a good teacher. He is a good friend. He is a good worker. He is a good brother. He is a good son. He is good.

It is May 2012. Stephen is 25 years old. His clonus is severe. He takes oral medication, Baclofen, to combat the spasms, however, the medication causes constipation. To help with the side effects that assault his bowels, an intrathecal Baclofen pump is implanted into Stephen's abdomen.

It is the size of a hockey puck and it is slipped into the pocket of an incision on his side. It slowly and continuously secretes medicine directly into his body while avoiding his digestive system. He is thin, so the device protrudes. They tell us the battery should last for five years and that he will have surgery in July 2017 to change the battery.

Stephen will never make it to that last surgery.

He is starting to see further decline of his body. He cannot urinate without catheterizing himself. His clonus is increased and he can only get around the house by dragging himself using the walker.

There are also other problems. Stephen only has one working lung. I wonder if it is from the radiation treatment or the curvature of his spine smashing his insides. He sees a pulmonologist and a urologist; another MRI is done. There are no answers.

It is June 29, 2017. Stephen is 30 years old. He sees a new neurosurgeon in Miami with his brother. I do not go with them.

I will never know what was said. Later, I will wish I went with them. I will wish I knew what was said to him. I will wish, I will wish, I will wish, but it won't matter because it will be too late. I will only be able to guess what was in Stephen's thoughts that day.

What I know is there is nothing I, or anyone else, can do to help him at this point. Often, I want to ask, "What can I do for you, Stephen?" This question will only aggravate him and the answer will surely be, "Let me be."

I make Stephen a bowl of cereal as he sits at the kitchen table with his leg and foot shaking uncontrollably. I want to do more for him, but I know that to ask will just make him feel more dependent. I give him space and try not to annoy him; remember he is a 30-year-old man.

Stephen compliments my new, large eyeglasses. The trend now is large frames and of course, my husband jokes with me, even going so far as to call me Harry Caray. Stephen says, "Mom, you look good in your glasses."

Stephen struggles to his room and I occupy myself with cleaning the porch, washing the outdoor carpet and moving the table. We plan for a family night out to celebrate Thomas's upcoming birthday. It is Taco Tuesday. We think this is a good choice since Stephen enjoys Mexican food.

Getting ready for our night, I check on Stephen and he tells me he is not feeling up to it. I accept that. On top of everything, he has problems moving his bowels and I don't want to push him. I ask, "Do you want me to bring home tacos?"

"Sure."

We leave to pick up my dad. On the way, my oldest son Joey, now living in Arizona, calls and asks after Stephen. Joey says he gave Stephen a call but there was no answer. I reply Stephen is probably in the bathroom.

Thomas and his girlfriend, Jenna, meet my husband, my dad and me at the restaurant. We eat without Stephen.

After our meal, Thomas and Jenna leave to go out and Joe and I drive my dad home. There is an ambulance next door to my dad's house. His neighbor is being taken away. I say to Joe, "Let's not sweat the small stuff."

We arrive home. Joe walks in with Stephen's tacos and tells me to get him a drink. Stephen is not in his room, and there is no sign of Stephen in his bathroom. The back porch door is opened.

Joe goes out and then yells, "Stephen killed himself." He jumps in the pool and retrieves Stephen from the bottom. I run out.

It is a sight that will never leave me.

Weights and tape are attached to him. I think of my water breaking and giving birth to Stephen. That image morphs so that I see water all around my son and he is no longer alive.

My son. My brave, strong, smart, determined son decided that this is what he needed to do for himself. I accept this. Throughout his life, he did not complain or pity himself. He was a strong, determined individual and he had so much fighting spirit.

I love you my son, and I will never be the same. Until we meet again…

Stephen's last written words:

Dear Mom, Dad, Joey, and Tom,
I love you all so much but I have been on a steep decline for a while and I am getting worse each month. You have been the best and most supportive family one could ask for but my life and where it is headed is not the one I want to live. I am physically broken and there is nothing anyone can do to change that so I ask that you forgive me and Embrace my decision to end it on my terms.
Love Always,
Stephen

About the Author
Janis J. Sokolowski lives in DeBary, Florida, USA. She and Joe, her husband of 36 years, have three sons" Joey, Stephen, and Thomas. They have two grandchildren, Darian and Aubrie.

Megan Kristine Vogt

16 June 1991 - 6 June 2017
Pennsylvania

Megan Kristine Vogt
by Kristine Lynn Vogt (Mother)

Megan was my first child. I was so excited to be a mother. We did not know if we were having a boy or a girl so we had chosen a name for each prior to delivery. We had chosen Megan for her first name because, at the time, it wasn't popular and we really liked it. With boys' births, you often hear of them being named after their fathers or at least in part, but with girls, that does not normally happen.

My husband suggested, if our baby were a girl, she be named after me. I thought that was a great idea so "Megan Kristine" it would be. I loved the name very much. I love her so very much.

Of course, I didn't know what having a baby would feel like, so when my contractions were five minutes apart that Friday night, I asked her daddy, my husband Steve, to take me to the hospital. I wasn't even close to giving birth, so they sent me home after telling me to walk as much as possible and come back when labor was stronger.

It was a hot Saturday in June, so my husband suggested we go to Muddy Creek to swim. We took our dogs and our nephews. I sat on a rock in the middle of the river having stronger and stronger contractions. By late afternoon on Sunday, I couldn't stand it any longer,so we went back to the hospital for the third or fourth time.

On Fathers Day June 16, 1991, at approximately 11:30 p.m., Megan Kristine Vogt was born. She made the most wonderful Father's Day gift. Megan grew to love Muddy Creek and my husband says it'ss because she was almost born there.

I was so excited and scared at the same time about having and taking care of a baby who needed me so desperately. She made it easy. She was a wonderful, joyful, sweet, loving baby. What pure joy to me. I always wanted to be a mother and she made all my dreams come true.

Megan was so snuggly. She loved being held. Even when she was in her 20's she would sit on my lap, hold my hand or lay with me. We said, "I love you" to one another often. She gave the best hugs. She was the most loving, kind, compassionate, warm, caring, empathetic, smart, funny, daring and adventurous girl I knew.

Megan grew to be so loving and compassionate with all creatures, human and otherwise. She was a joyful baby, toddler, child and young adult. I loved watching her grow into the young woman she was. Megan had spirit. She was so wise and yet naïve at the same time. She made everyone happy and she made people laugh. She was my best friend.

She was wonderful with her sister, Jordan, who arrived 18 months after Megan's birth. Megan was the best little mommy's helper and was great with Jordan, whom we call Jordi. They had occasional arguments but they were always each other's best friend. Megan was faithful, understanding and loving. Everyone loved Megan. She made that so easy to do.

Jordi has been devastated with the loss of her only sibling and best friend.

My husband and Megan were buddies. Steve taught her a little about many outdoor activities. Megan loved the outdoors. She loved to hike and swim and mountain climb. She also snow skied very well and eventually taught at our local ski area. She loved to camp and did so often, whether in winter, spring, summer or fall, rain, snow, sleet or shine.

As she grew older, she took Steve's teachings and expounded on them tenfold. Steve taught her to kayak but she became a tremendous white water, trick, play boat kayaker. Her most favorite experience of her life was an 18-day adventure down the Colorado River through the Grand Canyon on her kayak.

Steve taught Megan how to go spelunking or caving, and she loved it. In time, she began leading her own groups of novices through the most adventurous caves. Steve taught her to climb when she was older. She soon bought her own equipment and mountain-climbed with the experts.

Steve initiated her in these activities, and Megan would grow them into adventures that she loved. I was there too, although I was the overly cautious mother watching out for her child. Without Steve, I don't think I would have done all of it.

Steve has been devastated; he also says that he lost his best friend.

Megan was like Switzerland; she was neutral and we could all go to her. She loved her family like crazy, warts and all. She didn't take sides and was always there for us whenever we needed her. Family was so important to her. She loved us with all her heart. Our little family, myself, Steve and Jordi, have all lost their best friend. The pain has been unbearable to us all.

Megan was a very natural girl. She was more comfortable outside with messy hair, dirty clothes and playing than she ever was all cleaned up with pretty clothes on. She had a natural beauty, a glow, inside and out.

Megan was a vegetarian of sorts. She wouldn't eat commercial foods. As a family, we eat a lot of venison but not much else. Megan would eat venison, all vegetables, and some seafood, but no other meats. She believed in a natural life and natural healing. If doctors could be avoided she avoided them.

When Megan graduated from high school, she wasn't ready to go to college right away. Instead, she took a full-time job for nearly two years, saving all her money. She knew she wanted to work outside with and for the environment.

She took classes at our local community college and earned her associates degree. She couldn't quite decide what to get her bachelor's degree in so she put that off a little longer.

At age 20, Megan bought a camper, outfitting it so she could travel, work, and have her own place to stay while on the road. With her boyfriend at the time, she drove across this vast country of ours for months, exploring and experiencing all that our great land has to offer. Oh my, she was hooked after that. You couldn't keep her contained. Megan's enthusiasm and joy for this land were contagious when you heard her speak of it.

Megan joined AmeriCorps and traveled to California with her boyfriend to explore the country again before AmeriCorps started. She sold her camper and bought a four wheel drive truck with a cap and outfitted it for their travels. They lived out of the truck while traveling and had everything they needed for their outdoor adventures.

She loved the idea of helping others in need and couldn't wait for her assignments. When Megan ended with AmeriCorps, she stayed in California for months longer and worked on an organic farm. She fell in love with the people and the work there, and they loved her.

When Megan returned home again, she told us she wanted to go on a meditation retreat as an uplifting and learning experience that would help her to stay calm and focused in a natural way. All of Megan's adventures were uplifting to her and to all of us whom she shared them with. So this was another adventure for her and her friends and family were happy for her.

Meditation, in my mind, isn't scary or worrisome. It is supposed to be uplifting and gentle. We had no worries when she left for her ten-day retreat.

After the ten-day retreat was over, we received a phone call to come pick Megan up. We were told that she was confused and couldn't drive herself home.

My husband, Jordi and I drove out to get Megan. She was far more than confused. She had come out of the retreat in a meditation induced psychosis state. We had never heard of such a thing. All we knew was that Megan needed help. We rushed her to the nearest psychiatric hospital. This had to be the worst time of our lives.

Our child, who had been joyous her entire life, was no longer. Megan was completely out of her mind and suicidal. It was so very scary. She stayed in the hospital for ten days and then sent home with some medications. We were told she should continue therapy. Megan talked about death a lot and couldn't seem to focus on much of anything.

I took a leave of absence from work in order to stay home and take care of Megan during this most difficult time. She couldn't drive; she couldn't focus. Half the time she made no sense. She was afraid of people yet wanted help so badly at the same time. She didn't want doctors. She wanted natural help. She saw Gurus and holistic doctors.

Nothing seemed to help including medical doctors. Megan told us time after time that she was supposed to die at the retreat but because she hadn't she had damned the entire universe. She was especially very frightened for us, her family. She thought she had damned us to death.

After eight weeks of this struggle, Megan left us. She climbed onto the nearest, highest bridge's catwalk and jumped to her death 130 feet through the trees to the rocks below.

Total devastation. My world stopped. To this day, I still cannot believe this really happened. When she was so sick, I'd thought that that was hard on us. But her death; there are hardly words to describe it. Pain. Total pain. My baby, my beautiful, beautiful baby, inside and out, is gone. It only took eight weeks after the retreat and now she is gone. I cannot believe it. I will forever be broken.

I love her so much. I miss her so much. She died for me, for her family, for the universe. It may make no sense to anyone, but that was her reality. That's how much Megan loved.

Postscript: Megan's many, many dangerous adventures of climbing mountains, skiing, caving, kayaking, white-water rapids, etc., were so worrisome to me, but not this meditation retreat. Isn't that ironic?

About the Author

Kristine Vogt is Megan's mother. She lives in Delta, Pennsylvania, with her husband, Steve and lots of pets. Occasionally, they are visited by Jordan, their surviving daughter who is also an environmental wanderer. Kristine worked full time for the Department of Defense but has not returned to work since she lost Megan. Being outside brings her peace for the time being. Outside makes her feel close to Megan.

Michael Gene Watson

25 January 1990 - 27 August 2017
Mississippi

Michael Gene Watson
by Susan Chapman (Mother)

When I found out I was pregnant with Michael, I was ecstatically happy, as I had been trying to conceive for some time. The entire family was happy. I was working for the State of Mississippi at that time. I had a very easy pregnancy; however, the birth was not so easy.

I was at home about to lie down on the couch. As I bent over, I felt my water break. Even though it was my first pregnancy, I knew it was time to go to the hospital. Michael's paternal grandmother was a nurse and worked at the local hospital. We called her to let her know what happened. She insisted that before we traveled forty-five minutes in a storm to the hospital where I would give birth, we should come by and let her check me.

She got to confirm I was in labor, so that made her happy. After we got to the hospital, I was given an epidural that eventually numbed me to the point that I was not able to push when it came time. I was also loopy from the pain meds. I had to labor on my back because every time I turned over, it cut his oxygen off, and we kept losing his heartbeat.

Ten hours later, with the help of nurses and forceps, we delivered a seven-pound eleven ounce healthy baby boy. He was twenty-one inches long. He was born on January 25, 1990.

Because he was delivered with forceps, one of the nerves in his right eye was damaged; he had Marcus Gunn Syndrome. This means that with the movement of his jaw, his eyelid would move as well. The University Medical Hospital in Jackson, Mississippi, met us at the local hospital and filmed him because they were studying this syndrome at that time in class.

Three months after Michael was born, and we had many trials and tribulations, we discovered he was lactose intolerant. When he was two, we discovered he was allergic to many things, so that meant starting a series of allergy shots; he took the shots until he was seven. Later Michael would have to have his tonsils removed along with his adenoids and later had tubes in his ears. Yes, he was a little sickly in the early years.

As he grew, he grew out of these things and became as healthy as a horse. He loved to eat and loved family gatherings. Tomatoes were one of his favorites. He could eat a pot of greens (mustard and turnip) by himself. Yes, he was a country boy. I took him to a fish house when he was about two, and all he wanted were the greens that were brought out before the meal.

When he graduated from grade school, the class performed "Rub-a-dub-dub. three men in a tub," and Michael was the baker man. I got him the baker's hat and the apron; he was adorable.

I always went overboard with gifts for birthday and Christmas. We were in the dollar store once, and I heard him tell the clerk "My mommy loves me. She will get me whatever I want." He was right; I would do whatever I could to make sure he never went without. One Christmas I bought close to five hundred dollars or more in gifts, and he played with a two-dollar set of cowboys and Indians.

Michael wasn't much of a sports person, although he did play T-Ball for a couple of years. However, he did love the New Orleans Saints and University of Southern Mississippi Eagles, thanks to his Aunt Carr and Uncle James.

When Michael was seven, I gave birth to his sister Kayla. He called her Bug. He got that from his step-dad, Kayla's father (Billy), who called her Kayla-Bug.

I remember once looking out the window; Billy was planting a garden and Michael was stepping in his footprints behind him. Kayla and Michael were inseparable when they were together. Some of my fondest memories were watching them play together. I also loved it when they would crawl up in a recliner to sit and watch a movie while eating popcorn. Michael shared everything with her; she was his everything.

As Michael grew up, his interest in hunting grew; he was an avid turkey hunter. He was so proud of the only turkey that he ever shot. He loved music. He hated talking on the phone and preferred to text.

Michael was the type of person who loved life, his friends, and his family; he loved deeply. Michael was so much fun to be around. He absolutely loved to make people laugh. He loved watching movies, but he hated scarey movies. One friend reports that he would sit in his camoflauge recliner, wrapped up on a fire department blanket I had given him for Christmas one year and watch television. My son had a very kind heart.

Michael got his general equivalency diploma and went on to graduate from Copiah-Lincoln Community College with a degree in Heat and Air Conditioning. He wasn't going to walk for graduation. I talked him into doing so and was right there to watch him in one of his proudest accomplishments. I celebrated with lunch with Michael, his sister (Bug/Kayla) and his best friend Bo. This accomplishment led him to travel with one of the companies he worked for.

Michael eventually got involved with the fire department (another influence of Uncle James), and he was so proud. That led to his being employed at his last job as a security officer at the Nissan Plant in Canton, Mississippi. This is where he was when he ended the pain that he felt he could not bear any longer. He never left the parking lot of his job.

He did have a dark side; if he lost his temper he would black out and not remember what he did during that time. This is what I feel like happened the morning of August 27, 2017.

Michael had lost a very dear friend to suicide two years previously; he carried that burden because he did not answer the friend's phone call. The day we lost Michael, he and his girlfriend had argued very intensely the entire night before.

Michael had made arrangements to move out of their home the next day, but something made him snap during that argument. That plan was never to be carried out. When it came time for shift change, Michael did not show up or answer the calls. Coworkers went to look for him; his friend was the one who discovered him inside his truck.

His sister, Kayla, and I live in Tennessee, but Michael was in Mississippi then. I got a call that morning from my mom wanting to know if I had tried to call her; I said, "No." My mom said that she had heard the nurses in the nursing home say my name; I told her that it was not me. We talked a few minutes and hung up.

A few moments later, Kayla called my husband's phone and told him she was on the way over. She said that she had something to tell me and asked him to have me sitting down.
My first thought was that she was pregnant.

Little did I know the devastation that was about to happen. She had my brother on the phone, and he was the one that told me my first born, my only son, was gone.

I felt like my heart had been ripped from my chest. That day our world, mine and Kayla-Bug's world as we knew it was forever changed. The six-hour trip to Mississippi was the longest one I had ever made.

I remembered the last time I saw my son. When I left him, I had told him that I loved him. For the first time in years, he told me he loved me too. I forever will treasure those last words.

I did get to see Michael before we granted his wish of being cremated. I will never forget the touch of his hair, the black eye he had from the gunshot wound, the feel of his skin, and the final look of peace on his face.

We were going back to my sister's; just before we got to her house, a baby deer stood on the side of the road and just looked at me. Michael loved to deer hunt as well turkey hunt. There is no doubt in my mind that he sent me that sign to let me know he was with me.

Even still, Michael will mess with my phone to let me know he is still around. The day of his memorial service, it rained all day. It was just like the day he was born. Just before the service, the rain dried up. We were blessed with a rainbow; there is no doubt in my mind that Michael sent it to us.

Not long after he gained his angel wings, he did come to me in a dream and assured me that he was okay. He asked me not to leave him. Sometimes he will surprise me with signs such as a rainbow over my house. That had never happened before in the previous two years that I had lived here. My precious gift from God is now gone for now. His Kayla-Bug and I are now learning to live our new normal. We will never forget him and are always thinking of him. My sweet angel, we will see you again someday.

About the Author
Susan Chapman is Michael's mother. She lives in Lawrenceburg, Tennessee.

Billy Lee Williams

3 October 1964 - 19 July 2012
Tennessee

Billy Lee Williams
by Brenda G. Williams Denbo (Wife)

935 Miles… and Six Years Later

The day Billy and I arrived in Nashville in May 1986, we'd driven 935 miles in two days. Married just nine months, we were two Texans who wanted to chase our big dreams – like a million other people – in Music City, USA.

Billy's drum set and the rest of our worldly goods were jammed into the back seat and bed of his red Chevy pickup, packed into a U-Haul trailer, and stuffed into every nook of my silver Chevy Monza.

It was a two-day trip to Nashville. Actually, we turned a 16-hour drive into two-and-a-half days. We left Amarillo so late the first day we didn't even make it out of Oklahoma before we had to stop. We had dinner at Godfather's Pizza – I think we were in Weatherford, Oklahoma – and spent the night in a cheap motel. The next day we only made it through Arkansas, stopping again in Memphis for the night.

When we hit the city limits of Nashville on day three, neither of us knew how to get to our destination. Both of us had visited the city separately: Billy during a week-long jaunt to explore the music scene, and me for a weekend job interview and a quick look for housing.

I actually found and signed a contract on an apartment in the Antioch/Hickory Hollow neighborhood, and that was where we were headed. My future boss was the one who took me apartment hunting; I had not been driving so I had no idea where the place was. Billy obviously didn't know either, but he had the map. We plotted our route at a gas station on the outskirts and got back in our vehicles.

As we headed into town on I-40 East, Billy led the way. At the split where the Interstate headed right into downtown and left onto I-265 North, I changed lanes so Billy could do the same. Traffic had other ideas.

I recall watching Billy as we veered in opposite directions, seeing his loaded truck with its wildly-flapping blue tarp and trailer for a few moments before it disappeared. Cars were all around me but, in a split second, I was alone.

Where was that road taking him? Should I get off the highway at the first opportunity and stay put, hoping he'll come back around and find me? Or keep going to the apartment complex? Wait, Billy has the map; I'm the one who has no idea how to get to Antioch.

I fought some measure of panic and took the first exit and found a gas station. The two attendants worked up a mild interest in my plight and sold me a map. They allowed me to use their phone to call the apartment complex to alert them about a missing husband with household in tow. I got specific directions and hit the road, hoping I had done the sensible thing.

Those were some scary moments. Would I ever see my husband again? Were we doomed to wander the highways, hoping to catch a glimpse of each other in the opposite lane? Maybe I'd see him on stage someday, living his dream. "Hi, Billy! Yeah, I'm the girl in the silver… yep, the Monza. From Amarillo. Your wife!"

Pulling into the entrance of the apartments in Antioch, I was able to breathe normally again. The red pickup with its trailer and tarp was there, sitting outside the office. Whew! Billy had to be inside.

I parked and went in, thanking God that calling the Highway Patrol or the Find-a-Missing-Musician hotline wasn't necessary. He was talking to the apartment manager and turned to look at me with that cocky, dimpled smile. He'd beaten me there, dang it.

It took all weekend to empty the truck, trailer, and Monza. We moved drums and furniture up two flights of stairs in between rain showers; just the two of us. It rained a lot in Nashville, we decided.

I started work that Monday and Billy hit the road two weeks later with a gospel band led by two Russian brothers. He was on the road 280 days that first year; I got pregnant that fall and we had our son Aaron the next June. Our Nashville adventure had begun.

We moved three more times over the years but they were never as full of sheer nerve as our first. Billy lived out his music dream, touring for about 11 years, making two albums, even enjoying a few hit singles with his band, Legend Seven.

When he came off the road and turned his creative talents to other endeavors, he still played drums as often as he could, mainly at church. There was always a chunk of his heart that belonged to music and he mourned its loss. I heard it in his voice when he talked about his glory days and in his sigh when he listened to someone else's new project.

As with so many creative people, Billy struggled with depression for most of his life. He wrestled with his own feelings of inadequacy, self-worth, and his ability to love and feel loved in return. He took his failures to heart and felt his successes weren't enough.

He was officially diagnosed with Major Depressive Disorder thirteen years into our marriage. It was a complex, serious, insidious illness that we fought together. We had countless successes and failures, ups and downs, doctors, therapists, and medications.

In October 2009, Billy wrote a personal essay about his struggle with depression. I thought it would be appropriate to share it here.

The Fall

I can still smell the sweet aroma of burning hay. It permeated the air and announced the start of the fall.

Each year growing up in a small town in Texas, the farmers would burn the hay stubble and prepare the fields for the winter's rest. I loved the fall. It was a time of year that held a certain soft sadness.

The days of summer were gone, now the days grew shorter and colder. Schoolwork began to hit its stride and I would feel myself becoming more and more withdrawn from the world around me. Hours I would sit in my bedroom thinking, thinking, thinking. I could feel myself start to slip deeper and deeper into the fall.

It was the fall of 1973 when my dad died. Late fall. I remember eating Thanksgiving dinner at The Big Texan steakhouse with my mother, great grandmother, and older sisters. I was nine, dinner was quiet, we all felt the sadness, but deep in my young soul I also felt the weight of the fall. The crisp wind of the Texas panhandle, the smell in the air and my own slide into the season. It was the beginning of my love-hate relationship with myself, my deepening emotions, and the fall. I was at my creative best this time of year. There was something about the sense of melancholy that made me want to write, read, paint, do something. The more my mood darkened, the more I created.

A few short years later my mother bought me a set of drums. Money doesn't come easy for a widow with three children to raise. I remember she took a loan from a local bank and spent the next couple of years working extra to pay for them. I got them in the fall. They became my refuge. As the summer slipped away and my own demons began to appear, I could keep them at bay with my drums. Here was a creative outlet. I poured myself into them; hour upon hour I would play to my favorite music. The lights would dim and the band would be announced... Ladies and Gentlemen, put your hands together and welcome the hottest band in the land, KISS! It was me, not Peter Criss, at the drums. I poured my soul into learning every crash, crack, and stomp of the music. It was okay to be overcome with emotion, to feel my heart and mind burn, to sweat, grit my teeth... to cry. I struggled with it as much as it struggled with me; we had become wrestling partners, but for now I had the upper hand.

The summer of my seventh grade year, my mother began to date Jim. He was a true gentleman. Salt-and-pepper hair, a picture of fashion in his lime green western cut leisure suit and cowboy boots. He loved to hear me play my drums. Later that summer, my older cousin came over and asked my mother if I could play for his bar band. My mother, thinking he would say no, left the decision up to Jim. We started playing that fall. That is how things went with Jim. Though he wasn't married to my mother and didn't live with us the whole nine years they dated, she trusted him and he loved us. He never missed a show. He and my mother would dance until she couldn't take anymore and then he would dance with my sisters. He married my mother in the fall of 1985, two months after I married Brenda.

The thing I remember the most about moving to Nashville was that the fall came and went without much fanfare. I felt the coolness in the air and the shortening of the days. But I had busied myself with my music. There was touring to be done, songs to be written, news of a baby in our future; I was too busy for the fall. It would try to push in and I would ignore it or push it back. We no longer wrestled; I had found who I was in music and would no longer look to it for my identity. It's funny how we take for granted the now and never consider that time is not our friend. Season after season came and went and I had forgotten about the fall.

October of 1993 found our band in the midst of a record label change. Our manager met us all for dinner at Shoney's and asked where we planned to go from here. We stood at a crossroads of our collective lives and all chose different directions. It seemed to me to be the dreariest October I could remember; there was a familiar heaviness in the air... I could almost smell the fields of West Texas. I spent the next few years trying to catch up with my wife and son, trying to make up for all the time I had spent on the road away from them. Each fall seemed to come with more and more fervor. I could feel my old nemesis stalking me and now I no longer felt I had music to keep him back.

Jim died in the summer of 1998. Going home to the funeral was excruciating. The flood of memories almost drowned me. I remembered everything that he had taught me, I remembered the countless weekends at the lake with nothing to do but fish and laugh. He, like my music, had always been there for me. Now another part of my refuge was gone.

I went back home that fall to do some much-needed repair on my mother's house. It was the house I grew up in. It was the first time that I had been home for any length of time since Brenda and I moved to Nashville. I thought about my mother, widowed for a second time in 25 years – it didn't seem fair. This time the fall came with a vengeance. I was sideswiped, caught unaware by my thoughts, my emotions...my fall. By the time I finished and headed back to Nashville, I had been wrestled into submission. The fall became winter and all I saw was the bleak gray skies and cold reality of my captor. I remember thinking that there was no hope – for me, for my family, or for my life. I felt hopeless at the feet of grace. My earliest weapon had been music and I had left it behind some years ago.

The fall of 1998 sent me to the bottom. I tried to write, to play music, to paint...I tried everything I could to beat back my feelings. Creatively, it was my most prolific time. Words and images filled my head but were left impotent by the fall. I had to take control, I had to come to grips with it, I had to put a name to this season.

Depression is an angry muse. It tears at the very heart of our being. My wife and a good friend had convinced me to see a counselor. I thought it would be useless but I went anyway. I remember well sitting on the leather couch in his office, surrounded by books and an unusual number of clocks, wishing I were anywhere else. He asked questions and I spouted answers and as time went along I came to understand. No one had ever named the fall for me before; now I could put my hands and my mind around it. I could let it be what it was and it would no longer define who I am.

I was home a couple of years ago for a friend's wedding and while I was there I visited my dad's grave; it had been years since I had done that. Here I was back at the beginning of my journey. In the cemetery among the spinning leaves, I thought about the years past and the seasons of my life. I could still feel that nine-year-old boy from some thirty years earlier but now only as a shadow. They no longer burn the fields there in the Texas Panhandle, but as I stood beside the grave, there was a familiar soft sadness... I knew it well and it knew me, but we were no longer at odds. The wind had just

the slightest memory of burning hay. It was the fall.
Billy L. Williams
October 2009

In July 2012, my funny, talented, smart, wonderful, beautiful husband lost his battle with depression. My heart breaks that I was ill-equipped and unable to save him. I've spent my own countless hours in prayer, therapy, support groups, and education, trying to figure out a way to live with this loss and keep it from happening to someone else. I've become a volunteer and visible suicide prevention advocate in my community. For me, this work gives Billy's loss some meaning.

Five years and three months after his death, in October 2017, I remarried. It's funny how life turns out. The man I married was a good friend of Billy's and, I firmly believe, is a gift from God. When I am struggling, missing Billy and mourning his loss, my husband Tim reminds me that he loved and misses him, too. He tells me I can always talk to him about my feelings for and about Billy. I am blessed a second time with a man who loves me and I am overwhelmed.

As we enter the sixth year without Billy Lee Williams on Earth and I get these thoughts down on paper, it occurs to me that, once again, he and I were headed to a destination we'd never been to before. And he beat me there.

Billy, you are with your Maker. And now you know just how amazing, how worthy, and how loved you were and are. I hope you're making that long-awaited music, and I look forward to seeing that cocky, dimpled smile.

About the Author
Brenda Williams-Denbo had been married to Billy Lee Williams for nearly 27 years when he took his life in July 2012. She lives in Tennessee. She is a board member for the Middle Tennessee chapter of the American Foundation for Suicide Prevention (AFSP) and a peer support volunteer for the AFSP's Survivor Outreach Program. Brenda is now remarried to Tim Denbo, a friend of her late husband's, and works as a fundraising and development coordinator for a non-profit recovery program in Brentwood, Tennessee. She is a grandmother to three beautiful boys, Lennox, Jace, and Kai. Her son Aaron, his wife Audrey, and their boys live in Indiana..

Sean Adam Wiseman

4 January 1995 - 6 December 2015
North Carolina

Sean Adam Wiseman
by Susan Blumberg (Mother)

I missed my own baby shower. And I was told I would never get pregnant. My son Sean Adam Wiseman had other ideas and was anxious to enter this world. January 4, 1995, he decided to show up on the night my shower was scheduled. My friends carried on without me. I still laugh about that to this day.

When I was a young woman, I decided that my child would be born as I listened to the Schubert Cello Quintet. This is a gorgeous piece of chamber music for five players, two violins, viola and two cellos. It is my favorite piece of music.

I mistakenly felt certain that my son coming into the world surrounded by the otherworldly beauty of this music would shield him from anything and everything that is bad. I was determined to have it playing while he was born but I left the CD of the Budapest Quartet in the jewel box in our CD player at home.

Sean's dad said "We have Mozart. How about that"?

I said, "No way.". I planned to use that for breastfeeding. So I called one of my best friends, Nancy, who was hosting the shower and asked her to go to our house, retrieve the CD from the player and bring it to me.

Then I pushed through the entire piece. It was worth it because Sean was not only born to that piece but during the beautiful B theme in the first movement. I was so thrilled. I tell many of my younger colleagues that they will have a crush on their own children. At the beginning, that is how it felt for me.

In many ways, Sean was a normal child, but for his story, I will focus on the unusual. He was quick-witted and people often commented they never heard anyone talk so fast. He told me he talked fast because his mouth couldn't keep up with his mind. Younger kids always loved him. He was often compared to John Stewart and Robin Williams.

While I was tucking Sean into bed one night, as I always did, I told him how much I loved him. He was already in that sleepy alpha state, then said "I always knew you would love me"
I asked "Always? You're four."

He then said, "I mean before I came here."

I asked him if he really remembered that and he told me yes.

Then Sean asked if I would like to hear about it. So he proceeded to explain to me his time in my tummy; he didn't like it. It was dark, uncomfortable and he especially disliked having to wait until after I ate to eat. He went on, "But I loved when you ate candy because it made the water sweet. And when I slept, your heart was my pillow."

Sean then said something that was disturbing. "But I always knew I was here to help you."

I told him, "No, Sean, you're supposed to be here for your own life."

He said, "Well sort of, but I'm really here to help you." Most of what he said was beautiful, even poetic, but that comment felt ominous.

As Sean grew up, he became more and more curious. All through elementary school, he would receive the most creative writing award, even though his handwriting was awful.

He was in first grade during 9/11. When the teachers had the kids draw houses, Sean drew his with locks on the windows and an alarm system. He also wrote a letter to the soldiers thanking them and telling them he hoped they came home in one piece. His teacher found that comment amusing. He always had friends, was very active, loved to talk and state his opinions.

Sean said so many abstract and hilarious things. At age five when he finally learned to whistle, he said whistling was air with songs in it. He had a unique way of seeing the world.

When he was seven, he asked me about nuns. I have a dear friend who is a devoted Catholic so he was interested. He wanted to know why nuns wore wedding rings. "Are they married to Jesus?"

I answered the best I could. I said "I guess you could say that. Yes, they are."

The question Sean asked next was truly in earnest but left me laughing and speechless. "Well, wouldn't that make Jesus a polygamist"? He was seven. It did have a particular logic. I couldn't think of what to say other than "Where did you get the word polygamist at age seven?"

While in middle school Sean loved to gel his hair in different colors. I allowed it because I loved that he expressed his creativity. One day he had his hair done in bright red, blue and yellow. He came home and said that during math class, one of his friends raised his hand during the teacher's talk and said: "I can't hear you; Sean's hair is too loud." Everyone was hysterical.

Sean had many friends and could get along with anyone from every type of social group and background. As an only child, he was used to talking easily to adults. He held my feet to the fire many times when he felt I wasn't being honest with him or myself. He was very direct. It was never boring. I admired and even envied the fact that he wasn't a people pleaser.

At age eight, Sean became interested in Tae Kwon Do, so I gave him lessons for his eighth birthday. He had begged for that. He was gifted and won many of the tournament trophies. He was a black belt by the age of eleven.

Sean's father did all of the outdoor athletic activities with him. They took long bike trips. He was a natural at skiing; he was on the intermediate slope by his second ski trip.

He loved playing guitar and loved all the classic greats: Hendrix, Jimmy Page and of course the Beatles. While in tenth grade Sean and his guitar teacher played a brunch together at a restaurant.

For a while, Sean thought he wanted to be a trial lawyer. At age eleven and twelve, he volunteered for something called Teen Court. It is a program for first-time juvenile offenders that hopefully keeps them from going into the juvenile legal system. Based on the level of offense, their peers assign them various types of community service. It is facilitated by practicing attorneys. Had he not gotten sick, Sean would have eventually been a brilliant lawyer.

Sean was on his track team in middle school and on his cross country team in high school. He won the audition to sing the solo at his elementary school graduation and won other awards for the entire school including the reading award and the Padeia award. Padeia is a Socratic method of learning at which he excelled.

One of his most notable discussions in second grade was about the fairytale Cinderella. It was a round robin discussion and the question of the day was "Should Cinderella forgive the stepsisters"?

Everyone took a turn. Forgive because it's divine. Don't forgive, they were terrible to her. Then came Sean's turn.

His answer: "Doesn't matter if she forgives them or not. She learned how to do everything because of how they treated her. She could be independent. It didn't matter if the prince was on her doorstep; she didn't need him."

His teacher shot a glance at me, and we smiled.

Sean's bipolar disorder was likely showing up around middle school before I really understood what was going on. He began a slow decline in his interests and ambitions. He was a teaching assistant in Tae Kwon Do and was about to get his third-degree black belt.

Then he was diagnosed. He was 17. As with many bipolar kids, Sean self-medicated with drugs, illegal and whatever prescription drugs he could find.

It was during his first hospitalization when he was in eleventh grade that Sean began to talk to me about suicide. When he was on his way up in his mania, he confessed a lot. He told me one evening after I picked him up from a friend's house that he had planned to kill himself that day but had decided against it. "I didn't do it because I'm not sure where I would wake up."

Yes, those were his exact words. There were a few other times he talked to me about suicide. We were close. I encouraged him to be open because I did not want him to feel shame about his disease. His dad and I did all we could to get the proper help. He hated his medications. To protect him, we had him do his senior year online at home.

Sean decided to be a computer science major, but he dropped out of his second semester of college. He was having psychotic episodes and was in total panic.

We got more help for him. He went to our community college and for a while was doing well. He had good grades, friends and got on the Dean's list. He was re-accepted to college and was a few weeks away from going back. Sean had even found a nice roommate and moved into his house. He had a good job with Chipotle and felt good earning some of his own money.

By the time Sean was 19 he had been to a 50-day wilderness treatment program, was hospitalized twice for bipolar disorder, and had gone through three other drug treatment programs. And of course, he attended many AA meetings, as well as met with therapists, counselors, and doctors.

During his last few years, I constantly tried to stay a step ahead of Sean. I called and texted him and his friends. I drove around looking for him at night, chased him, showed up places, yelled at his drug dealers, tried to reason with him. When I would return from work, I would run to his room to make sure he hadn't hanged himself or that I did not find anything suspicious.

I would literally crawl on Sean's messy bedroom floor looking for whatever I could find, a clue, a way to save him from himself. He nicknamed me Nancy Drew.

Alas, at age 20, one month before his 21st birthday, Sean talked his friends out of the house, went to his room, sat on his bed. He then put a gun to his head and pulled the trigger.

It was a Sunday, December 6, 2015. His roommate found him that night. Two policemen rang my doorbell at 2:30 the next morning.

The world lost a beautiful, intelligent, funny and sensitive soul.

Did the music Sean was born to affect his life in a positive way? I would like to think that perhaps it enriched or even elongated his life. I really don't know. He did have an appreciation for not just the classic rock guitar greats, but also Bach, Ravel, and many other classical composers. Plus, his insights were truly profound.

So how did he help me? What was he referring to that night before he slept, and what wisdom was he trying to impart at his ripe age of 4? These are questions that in my quiet trauma I will ponder forever.

This is my journey. Our journey. Sean's choice affected more of us than he knew. Sean helped by being here, by existing. He helped me see that anything can happen to anyone, that the love I thought I understood before he came here was only scratching the surface.

Now I understand unconditional love and that a broken heart is also an open heart. That it is so easy to be bitter and that it takes some moxie to choose love. That I now look up to people I did not even know I had looked down on.

Most of all, Sean helped with letting go of the external and looking to the internal. To the silence. This is where I find him. Where I feel him. Where I hear him. The sudden messages that pop into my head. Some of them make me laugh. "Will you stop telling people I'm dead? I haven't gone anywhere."

About the Author
Susan Blumberg is Sean's mother. She is a professional violinist for the Charlotte Symphony in North Carolina. She feels closest to Sean when she is playing.

Benjamin E. Joslin Yoshikawa

8 June 1994 - 26 November 2017
Montana

Benjamin E. Joslin Yoshikawa
by Sandra Joslin (Mother)

In the summer of 1993, I became pregnant with my first and only child. I would soon have a new life with a ready-made family of five. Within twenty short months, I would assume responsibilities as a stepmother to twin boys, age eight, from my spouse's previous marriage, a wife, and new mother to an infant son who would enter this world on June 8, 1994. On August 8, 1994, Ben's dad and I were married. I was very much in love and thrilled to be having a child and fulfilling a long-awaited dream of becoming a parent.

Ben was welcomed as the youngest of three boys and loved by all, hence his name which, in Hebrew, means beloved youngest. After initial difficulty with colic and pneumonia, Ben emerged as a happy, healthy boy.

He was a beautiful mix of his mother and father, reflecting his Japanese-American ancestry with dark hair and a beautiful complexion. We teasingly joked he looked a bit like Kojack when he was born. He was long and lean at seven pounds eleven ounces, hence his nickname, The Bean. Ben's father was a practicing dentist and I was a dental hygienist.

Ben's infancy was anything but idyllic because there were serious conflicts in the family. When Ben was in the third grade, his father and I separated for the third and final time. Despite the chaos, Ben greeted his surroundings with an even and mild disposition.

Ben was pure boy, always looking up to his bigger brothers, physically active, very coordinated, intellectually bright, and artistically inclined.

As a toddler, Ben had a plastic motorcycle he powered with his feet, like Fred Flintstone. From the time he was on his feet, he was like an escapee barreling around the neighborhood with his police helmet on, exploring our quiet neighborhood.

Twice, I remember Ben's curiosity took me to the brink of despair. The first was when he disappeared while I was at a rummage sale. At the point I'd noticed he was missing, I began a desperate search in and out of the building, up and down the streets, frantically running in every direction several times until I discovered he'd never left the building at all, but had wandered only as far as the building's elevator where he was busy mastering how it worked.

He had been riding up and down and was totally oblivious to everything else except his fascination with the magic buttons that gave him the thrill of being carried up and down over and over. He must have done this a dozen times before I found him.

Another instance was in an open-air market. While selecting my vegetables, Ben lost sight of me and thought I had left without him. Out of the corner of my eye, I saw panic on his face as he ran out of the market, crying for his mommy as though he believed he would be lost forever, desperately searching the road for me or my car, which he was sure were gone for good.

Ben had to repeat the third grade, which was the same year the towers fell in New York City. Ben experienced this as punishment and/or rejection, no matter how I tried to smooth this transition. To Ben, this was a setback, an indication he had failed somehow, that he was not good enough or smart enough. He had to leave his friends behind and make new ones. His other friends would "see" he was not able to move ahead with them.

His teachers recommended he gain an extra year to help him mature and cope with the changes he was experiencing and to address his wandering attention. I now believe Ben became hyperactive and his attention and focus appeared to wander because of the anxiety of family instability.

At the school's recommendation, Ben was tested by a school psychologist, who suggested he had Attention Deficit Hyperactivity Disorder (ADHD). A few modifications were put into place for him in the classroom and medications were not recommended. At no time did his grades change.

Ben absorbed the material he heard, but he didn't always seem to be listening; perhaps he was bored. In any case, his grades never indicated any sign of suffering, although he may have had some other childhood condition we were never aware of.

In his new grade, Ben made friends easily and formed tight bonds with Owen, Ben, Ian, Willy, Max and a few others. He was loved by friends and teachers alike. Ben had a flair for drawing caricatures and doodling all manner of humorous mishaps, often depicting him and his friends engaged in wild, very aggressive, often violent interactions with one another.

Ben seemed to have an amazing aptitude for math that he demonstrated consistently. In high school and college, Ben tutored other students who were having difficulty. I was always very proud of Ben and praised and encouraged him often.

He played soccer for many years, then discovered the thrill of skating and took off into the world of hockey sticks, diving, sliding and checking to defend that little black puck. When he first discovered that others valued him as an important member of a team, he blossomed before our eyes as a skilled defenseman.

One day when Ben was around the age of ten, he exclaimed to me, "Finally, I'm no longer a nobody, I'm a somebody!" When he was playing a game with his friends on the Hanover Wild Team, he experienced something that was missing in his family life; it was like he became part of a big family he never had.

In one of the early years, Ben was voted the player who made the most improvement that year. He skated gracefully and learned to push back in aggressive play, skating fast, with accuracy. He took to heart the motto 'You miss 100% of the shots you never take.' He never complained or thought much about an injury when it happened to him. He learned that the cost was all joy if it helped the team.

Ben succeeded similarly in the classroom, absorbing more and more levels of advanced math, and writing thoughtful creative essays and papers. He was an honor student all the way.

On the ice and into his music, he escaped from the pressures and conflicts of his family life. On the ice, he was a winner.

Though Ben had an outlet for his emerging testosterone, he also felt deeply sad that his father and I divorced, a feeling I think was one of the hardest for him to reconcile.

Ben enjoyed the love and affection he gave to and received from the many family pets whose care he participated in, especially his beloved Roxie, a black Labrador. He would harness his razor scooter to Roxie's collar for free "rides" around the neighborhood, Roxie always in the lead. One day just before a final court hearing, Roxie was hit by a truck in an unfortunate accident while Ben was away at his dad's house. When Ben came back and learned his Roxie was gone, he was crushed.

Similarly, the family dog at his dad's house, Augie, was hit by a truck as he raced after it leaving the driveway. Together, we buried Roxie and Augie and talked about heaven.

He watched, with wonder, as his pet cat DC (Darned Cat) gave birth to her five tiny kittens. He learned to treat animals with respect and tenderness, but tragedy struck again.

One year while Ben and I were visiting my sister out of state in Long Island, New York, Ben's cat DC mysteriously disappeared from his fathers' house. The cat had recently made the transition from my home to the construction site just as we all had moved in that fall. DC was having trouble using her litter box in its new location.

Before we arrived home, we got the news from Ben's dad that DC had gotten out and never came back. Later, we had a memorial service for DC.

Again, Ben experienced a devastating loss of yet another pet. He did not get over this sadness for a long time.

When Ben was in grade school, we got a dozen baby chicks and raised them for eggs to sell at nearby markets so Ben could learn about operating a small business. There was an aggressive rooster that would periodically lunge at Ben, which intimidated him. Eventually, he learned he could handle himself if he lunged back and looked tall.

Soon enough, our small flock was picked off by nocturnal animals and what remained would eventually be given to a local farmer when we had to move back to my house after a separation that followed a domestic dispute.

Ben and I would often take long walks in the woods after school. It was a time Ben enjoyed and a time when he shared the days' challenges. No matter if had been a good or a bad day, I tried to end it with cuddling, reading a story and saying prayers.

Ben enjoyed paintball with his brothers, his two-wheeler and hanging out in his tree house, and building elaborate buildings and moving objects with his Legos. He made forts with blankets and slept in his tent. He collected bottle tops from soda for the chance of winning the prizes on the inside.

As he grew, he became conscious of his body, trying to bulk up like his brothers, from drinking protein shakes to running. He enjoyed target practice in the woods with his dad and shooting arrows into the deer target stuck in the driveway.

We had bonfires in the summer, made snow forts and igloos in the winter, gathered maple sap for maple syrup one spring, and always had a house project he could tag along and help with in the summers. There were plenty of trips to Montpelier to visit his grandparents, and they would visit too.

Because Ben's brothers were significantly older than he, Ben often was alone, and I had to work hard to see he had enough time to be with his best friends, who did not live close by. This got easier when he was able to drive himself. He was an eager participant in most everything he did.

On one occasion, Ben diagnosed a problem I encountered with my lawnmower, went and bought the part it needed and fixed it one afternoon, good as new after taking it apart to get to the broken part. It was the best Mother's Day present I ever had.

Like his twin brothers, Ben too would have to adapt to a life shuttling between two houses until, at the age of 15, he left home to board at Valley Forge Military (High School) Academy in Wayne, Pennsylvania. Ben chose this school himself as it was his father's alma mater. He wanted to make his father proud. In the spring of 2009, Ben had an admissions interview at the Academy in Pennsylvania. Ben was accepted on the spot.

After Ben's death, I learned that his father did not want him to go to Valley Forge and told Ben not to go to his same school because of problems he had had when he attended. In the end, it was Ben's final choice for this to be his home away from home for the next four years until he graduated in 2013.

Ben excelled in every aspect of the military environment. He was an exemplary cadet and proud of his choices. He was a fine leader and respected by his fellow cadets in the chain of command in E battery, also his father's company. He made many friends and earned academic distinction every quarter. He also continued earning merit badges with the Cradle of Liberty Scout Troop 971.

Ben was baptized and raised a Christian. He was carefully and lovingly mentored throughout his life, and eventually made his own public declaration of faith on July 30, 2017, four months before he took his life.

I believe that at Valley Forge. Ben's values came under regular attack in ways he was unprepared for, despite his involvement with Focus, a campus ministry. Ben was schooled in a traditional church, with clear boundaries and clear biblical teachings. While in high school and college, Ben continued to pursue the reading and study of scripture on his own, attending weekly bible study with fellow Valley Forge cadets and local students from Wayne, Pennsylvania.

At Valley Forge, Ben continued his love of hockey and became the captain of his school's team, The Trojans. He loved the game and played hard in a group with few players against complete teams. That first year was exhausting for the players.

Ben learned to drive during his first two summer breaks at home. When he graduated, he bought a black 2001 Mustang. He learned a lot about how to fix his car by reading the repair manual. He was so proud of his car.

When Ben's brothers went off to college, Ben was only eight or nine. By the time he went to college, his brothers were married and beginning their families. The boys loved each other and always stayed in touch right up to the end of Ben's life.

Ben got to be an uncle, but sadly he never got to meet his other brother's unborn baby, only two months in utero at the time he died. Ben lived with his brothers for a brief time after high school and before going to live in Montana.

Ben found several jobs during his high school summers. He worked at Gypsy Meadows Farm, a produce farm, learned about irrigation, organic farming and harvesting. He was often reprimanded for being distracted with his headphones, a sign Ben may have been having trouble coping with his emotions.

Ben was a security guard for a company on the waterfront in Burlington, Vermont and alternated between this job and Dicks Sporting Goods Department where he was a customer representative and got to help people wanting to purchase weapons for hunting. He learned about the background check system, and the mechanisms and parts sold for many guns.

Ben also drove a truck for the United Postal Service, UPS, during one busy holiday season. I began seeing less of Ben during his summers off from high school as he devoted more of his time to leadership trainings and time with his roommate and friends back in Pennsylvania. He had truly left home at 15 when he began finding his way.

Ben entered college in the fall of 2013 and earned a near full Air Force Reserve Officer Training Corps scholarship to be used in the field of engineering. Of the several acceptances he received, he chose to enroll in the engineering program at Clarkson University in Potsdam, New York.

Ben did well the first semester, but not the second. He left Clarkson at the end of his first year, in the spring/summer of 2014, and he never wanted to go back.

At this same time, Ben's roommate from Valley Forge was preparing to ship out to Paris Island. Ben said he, too, wanted to enlist but was unable to get the military occupational specialty code (MOS) he wanted.

Five months later, in the spring of 2015, Ben drove his car across the country to where he had taken a job at Dome Mountain Ranch in Emigrant, Montana, an elk and fishing ranch where he served as a ranch hand. He rolled the dice and drove to Montana, a few states away from where his friend was now stationed. He bought a motorcycle in the hope, perhaps, of visiting.

He also met a lovely young lady who came to Dome for her high school graduation present. They became very good friends, nothing more.

Ben's thoughts turned frequently to the Marines. He missed the esprit de corps of his Academy days. He missed his roommate. He missed being a leader of men, part of a team with a high purpose. Four years at Clarkson would have been too long a wait to be commissioned as a second lieutenant in the Air Force. Four years of Valley Forge and four years of Reserve Officer Training Corps (ROTC) may not have been a smart plan for Ben.

By the time Ben was 21, he had earned his Eagle Scout merit award. He had traveled to several European countries and been part of a mission trip to Mississippi after Hurricane Katrina. He had summited a couple of 4,000-foot peaks in the Rocky Mountains of Colorado with his uncle Randy, and he had been to the states of Washington and California to visit his Yoshikawa grandparents.

Ben had also gone fishing in Alaska with his dad, seen the seat of our government in Washington, D. C. and attended his cousin's graduation; Missy was graduating from Georgetown University. He spent a February vacation with me touring New York City, including the Empire State Building, the Statue of Liberty and the site of the former World Trade Center.

He had seen both coastal waters, pitched a tent in the wilderness while on a scouting survival exercise, and set foot in Roanoke, Virginia, where settlers established the first home in colonial times.

Ben hiked dozens of miles in the Green and White mountains of Vermont and New Hampshire, watched the sunrise in the beautiful Diamond Peak mountains of Cimarron, New Mexico, and listened to music concerts with friends in New York City and the Jersey shore. He visited the Left Bank in New Orleans, Louisiana, and helped a family who lost their house in the floods.

He loved his friends and was loved by them in return. He spent countless hours at his roommate's house in New Jersey, his home away from home during leave time. He learned about the importance of wildlife conservation at Rocky Mountain Elk Foundation fundraising dinners in our area.

Ben learned to ski and to snowboard, even though he broke his leg on skis his first time out. He bought a Yamaha motorcycle and drove it to Colorado to visit his girlfriend. He saw beautiful vistas of the Sawtooth Mountains, as well as mountain lions, grizzly bear cubs jumping in tall grass and pristine wild places of the bighorn sheep.

He learned to play the keyboard and how to lead guided tours into Yellowstone. Ben rose to the rank of Commander of his high school company, received many math, leadership and other scholarly awards and stood vigil over the Tomb of the Unknown Warrior in Dover, England.

As Ben wrote in the note he left behind, "I have seen incredible things, I am so grateful for the life I've had."

Sometime around 2015 or 2016, Ben's roommate met and became engaged to marry a young woman. Ben was to have been the best man at their wedding on December 8, 2017, but he would never live the next twelve days to take the flight to Las Vegas he had purchased.

Ben wanted to enlist in the Marines. I told him that if being a Marine was what he needed to do he had my blessing. I also told him that he would have many friends who would follow their own dreams and best he decide to stick to his own path, whatever it be.

We all encouraged Ben to go back to school and we would help pay and that it was not the end of the line. He would hear none of it, or my advice to seek medical/spiritual counseling. He was not into that, he said.

On November 26, 2017, his manager told him he had to leave the ranch and find work elsewhere for the winter. She was concerned for his mental health if he stayed alone. Ben's focus had slipped away as his depression increased.

On that same day, after the final hunt was finished, he made a permanent decision and ended his life that had a temporary problem he did not get help for in time.

The other ranch hands had already scattered to the four winds and Ben was alone. He was not found until two days later.

The last time I saw my son alive were the days between August 14-23, 2017 when I arrived in Emigrant to spend some time and check on him. Ben was reluctant to have me present. He kept me at a safe distance. He was lost and not seeking a mother's solution.

He was reluctant to discuss his life, careful not to let me see just how much pain he was in. I believe he felt ashamed of his pain and felt it was evidence of his badness. I think nothing mattered to him except finding a way to end that overwhelming pain and sadness he had slipped into.

At that time, I had not learned that Ben had been cutting himself; how long he hid this I do not know exactly. Only after I left the ranch and met his girlfriend in Maryland did I learn from her that he had been cutting himself and that at least two people knew about this in Montana, but kept silent when I went to him. The long sleeves Ben wore carefully concealed the scars and wounds from the razor blades.

We rode through Yellowstone together, drank coffee in the early mornings, drove to the Grand Tetons and saw the unbelievable breathtaking sights of the Grand Canyon waterfall in Yellowstone and the Prismatic on our way back, something he had really wanted to see. We saw elk and bison.

Ben was relaxed and had a few days off work. He wanted me to listen to a podcast from The Liberation Project. I later would speak to the Chief Executive Officer of this organization to see that the mission was meant to empower men who felt emasculated.

I saw the place where he worked, the fences and the irrigation equipment he mended, the elk that were so prized in the region. We ate pizza and shared a beer and talked about life. We ate elk cut up in thin little strips for our sandwiches on our car ride, we went to the store where he got all his groceries, met the manager and saw his hangouts in the bluffs.

I bought a cowboy hat in West Yellowstone and wanted to give it to him, but he refused, saying he wouldn't wear it. We marveled at the wonders in our first National Park, chuckled at the little Picas we saw on the Bear Tooth Pass in the Sawtooth Mountains on our way to the Battle of Little Bighorn State Park.

We listened to the history of Custer and the slaughter he and the United States Army faced when they declared war on the Native American way of life. I saw something had died in Ben, but I did not know what and I could do nothing to fix it.

I talked frankly about anything I could to draw him out, encouraged him to go back to school in Bozeman, and said he could talk to his manager about getting time off if he could see to taking a class.

We went to the 3D screen in West Yellowstone and watched a movie of the same name; we were the only ones in the gigantic theatre; it was the middle of the week.

Ben spoke of things I had done that hurt him, forgave me for the times he sometimes felt lost in the blended family, but not deeply enough; he would not let me in, would not forgive or talk about his pain. He told me I did not know the half of what was on his mind.

I told him I was concerned about the number of beers he was drinking; he blamed me some more for things he would not elaborate and that I did not understand. I was paralyzed by the flatness of his speech.

I told his manager I was worried. I told the family close to him I was concerned; they had seen trouble in their family, they seemed to understand. If they knew things, they did not say. I was deeply worried when I left and wrote the longest letter I ever wrote to Ben all the while on the Amtrak train ride back to New Hampshire.

I kept in touch with his manager from time to time, but this only angered Ben more; it made things worse and nothing I did made it better. I called Ben's dad and told him I was worried he was sleeping way too much or was not getting enough sleep. I told him I was worried that he was drinking way too much, smoking - chewing gum in hopes it would help him quit, not eating right, depressed, flat.

Ben's father said he would talk to him. I was afraid of losing what little ground I felt I had, so I said not to tell him I informed him. He wasn't concerned, he said. When I called him again, he told me not to worry, to lighten up, that our son only wanted for me to be happy.

Ben seemed fine up until November 2013. This was the same month I asked my second husband to leave.

I called Ben at Clarkson University in November. Out of concern for his well-being, I asked him questions life and about how much he knew about the reasons both of my marriages had failed. I told him that my second husband and I were no longer together. This was the most difficult, but honest, conversation Ben and I ever had about the realities of life and our family.

I believe that Ben reached for God, and perhaps He saw Him – I hope it is true. The other side beckoned him to let go. He reached for the alcohol, he reached for the razor blades and then he reached for his gun. He felt defeated, he was confused. When he had a choice, he would not take it.

Ben passed the point where he had a choice and entered that narrow place where the choice had been made for him. He wrestled with his pain. He set himself free.

About the Author
Sandra is Ben's mother and lives in Hanover, New Hampshire. She is a certified public health dental hygienist. She has enjoyed working in her garden, being in nature, loving her pets and spending time with close friends or family members. Sandy is part of the student ministry at Riverbank Church in Vermont where she meets and fellowships with high school students who are searching. On Wednesday evenings, she and many other adults have joined a rapidly growing rescue mission for Christ doing the same work Ben had begun at Paradise Valley Community Church in Montana.

Section Two

Photo Remembrance Gallery

Remembering
Jeffrey Alan Amati

25 December 1962 - 26 July 2012
California
Submitted by: Karen Amati Stewart (Mother)

Remembering
Tyler Alan Barton

29 October 1990 - 17 February 2017
Washington
Submitted by: Marda Barton (Mother)

Remembering
Jason David Brandt

17 February 1977 - 24 June 1999
Minnesota
Submitted by: Shirly Joppru (Mother)

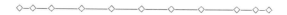

Remembering
Christian Victoria Carrigan

14 November 1986 - 6 December 2001
Maryland
Submitted by: Kathie Carrigan (Mother)

Remembering
Courtney Cherese Coin

28 July 1988 - 8 November 2011
Arkansas
Submitted by: Robin Coin (Mother)

◇—◇—◇———◇———◇———◇———◇———◇———◇—◇—◇

Remembering
Vincent Gamboa

17 May 1991 - 14 July 2017
California
Submitted by: Catherine Gamboa (Mother)

Remembering
Joshua David Goddard

25 May 1978 - 25 November 2005
Missouri
Submitted by: Lynn Zarda (Mother)

Remembering
Jessica Kassandra Haffer

2 October 1989 - 23 November 2003
South Dakota
Submitted by: Keith and Jeri Haffer (Parents)

Remembering
Jeffrey Michael Hoffelder

9 January 1988 - 24 October 2006
Connecticut
Submitted by: Lynn Hoffelder (Mother)

Remembering
Kenneth Thomas Hohman

16 October 1994 - 28 August 2015
Colorado
Submitted by: Christina Pearson (Mother)

Remembering
Jeffrey Austin Kinder

12 April 1975 - 22 August 2012
Utah
Submitted by: Sherry Stirling (Cousin)

Remembering
Christine Marie Klein

30 January 1975 - 26 February 2002
New York
Submitted by: Brigid Ross (Mother)

Remembering
Anthony Scott Martin

11 July 1963 - 7 September 2014
Kansas
Submitted by: Amanda Groves (Daughter)

Remembering
Jacob Leroy Masker

10 November 1987 - 20 September 2009
Pennsylvania
Submitted by: Gladys Masker (Mother)

Remembering
Dennis M. McCloskey

20 August 1991 - 14 March 2015
Pennsylvania
Submitted by: Evelyn McCloskey (Mother)

Remembering
Matthew T. Laidlaw McIntosh

22 August 1990 - 2 October 2011
New Jersey
Submitted by: Mary F. McIntosh (Mother)

Remembering
Sean A. Christopher McKitrick

28 November 1984 - 28 April 2004
Tennessee
Submitted by: Diana McKitrick Kulas (Mother)

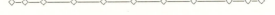

Remembering
Michael Joseph Melotto

15 September 1971 - 18 June 2000
Connecticut
Submitted by: Barbara Melotto (Mother)

Remembering
Kathleen Ann Murray

4 March 1983 - 2 November 2015
New York
Submitted by: Susan Kross (Mother)

Remembering
Nicholas Tristan Novak

3 June 1996 - 13 August 2016
California
Submitted by: Boris Novak (Father)

Remembering

John Michael Pittman

16 July 1962 - 30 May 2009
Kansas
Submitted by: Jeri Haffer (Mother)

Remembering

Kyle Holden Rigby

1 April 1984 - 19 June 2014
New Jersey
Submitted by: Jacqueline Branch (Mother)

Remembering
Evan Andrew Ritter

27 December 1991 - 20 October 2014
Pennsylvania
Submitted by: Robin Goudy (Mother)

Remembering
Michael Anthony Rivas

19 December 1989 - 4 May 2017
California
Submitted by: Mary Rivas (Mother)

Remembering

Sgt. Ryan Patrick Schetter

20 March 1986 - 15 February 2018
Missouri
Submitted by: Barb Gleason (Mother)

Remembering

Jason Brian Seek

25 May 1971 - 30 November 2017
Tennessee
Submitted by: Jamie Seek (Wife)

Remembering
David William Shelton

11 November 1992 - 25 August 2016
Texas
Submitted by: Lynette Shelton (Mother)

Remembering
Jesse Anders Short-Gershman

22 July 1992 - 29 October 2014
British Columbia, Canada
Submitted by: Erin Short (Mother)

Remembering
Anthony James Shott

13 December 1982 - 25 December 2013
California
Submitted by: Kathy Shott (Mother)

Remembering
Andy Wayne Stirling

10 October 1975 - 18 October 2017
Utah
Submitted by: Sherry Stirling (Sister)

Remembering
Lawrence Paul Ulrich

30 June 1961 - 22 November 2016
North Carolina
Submitted by: Jill VanZandt (Fiancée)

◇—◇—◇——◇——◇——◇——◇——◇——◇—◇

Remembering
Marcus Tyler Walker

30 July 1999 - 10 November 2016
Washington
Submitted by: Carey Walker (Mother)

Remembering
Jay Kelley Wall

17 April 1962 - 3 July 2007
Oregon
Submitted by: Karen Wall (Wife)

◇—◇—◇———◇———◇———◇———◇———◇———◇—◇—◇

Remembering
Ciara Jolie Whitney

18 September 2000 - 28 March 2016
Pennsylvania
Submitted by: Karen and Steve Whitney (Parents)

Remembering
Martha Elizabeth Williamson

9 January 1989 - 17 April 2018
Hampshire, England
Submitted by: Nicola Black (Sister)

Reaching Out: Resources

The Parents of Suicides - Friends and Families of Suicides Internet Community reaches out to the world remembering those who took their lives.

Members of the POS - FFOS Internet Community maintain several websites and a FaceBook groups volunteering their time and talents to do so. We invite you to visit our sites and to pass information about them on to others.

To Join the POS or FFOS E-Mail group

Go to the link below and follow the directions or send an e-mail to **arlynsmom@cs.com** and ask for an application, specifying the group.

Parents of Suicides
https://groups.yahoo.com/neo/groups/parentsofsuicides/info

Friends and Families of Suicides
https://groups.yahoo.com/neo/groups/ffofsuicides/info

Our Websites:

Faces of Suicides Memorial:
www.facesofsuicide.com

Suicide Memorial Wall:
www.suicidememorialwall.com

Parents of Suicides (POS) - Friends and Families of Suicides (FFOS) Resources:
www.pos-ffos.com

We Remember Them Memorial
www.we-remember-them.com

Sibling Survivors
www.siblingsurvivors.com

On Facebook: POS - FFOS Suicide Grief Support Group
On FaceBook: Art Beyond Loss

Made in United States
North Haven, CT
14 February 2022